Making Links Across Specialisms

Understanding Modern Social Work Practice

Jan Horwath and Steven M. Shardlow

RHP

Russell House Publishing

First published in 2003 by:
Russell House Publishing Ltd.
4 St. George's House
Uplyme Road
Lyme Regis
Dorset DT7 3LS

Tel: 01297-443948
Fax: 01297-442722
e-mail: help@russellhouse.co.uk
www.russellhouse.co.uk

British Library Cataloguing-in-publication Data:
A catalogue record for this book is available from the British Library.

ISBN: 1-898924-42-2

Typeset by Sheaf Graphics Ltd, Sheffield

Printed by Antony Rowe, Chippenham

About Russell House Publishing

RHP is a group of social work, probation, education and youth and
community work practitioners and academics working in collaboration
with a professional publishing team. Our aim is to work closely with the
field to produce innovative and valuable materials to help managers,
trainers, practitioners and students. We are keen to receive feedback on
publications and new ideas for future projects. For details of our other
publications please visit our website or ask us for a catalogue. Contact
details are on this page.

Contents

List of Tables and Figures   iv

Acknowledgements   v

Preface   vi

About the Authors   vii

Introduction

Chapter 1   **Specialism: A Force for Change**   1
Jan Horwath and Steven M. Shardlow

Part One: Common Issues Across Specialisms

Chapter 2   **Disabling Chains and Enabling Links**   22
Sally French, Maureen Gillman and John Swain

Chapter 3   **Evidence-Based Social Work with People Who Have Substance Problems**   33
Philip Guy and Larry Harrison

Chapter 4   **A Holistic Approach to Working with HIV and AIDS**   41
Di Hart

Chapter 5   **Working with Carers: A Specialism that Crosses Boundaries**   53
Christine Heron

Chapter 6   **Assessment and Role Across Social Work Specialisms in Working with Domestic Violence**   63
Catherine Humphreys and Audrey Mullender

Chapter 7   **The Protection of Vulnerable Adults: The Role of Social Work**   77
Bridget Penhale and Jonathan Parker

Part Two: Making Links: Working Together with Service Users

Chapter 8   **Meeting the Needs of Children and Families Through Working Together**   90
Jan Horwath

Chapter 9   **The Assessment Process in Work with Offenders**   103
Charlotte Knight

Chapter 10 **Mental Health: New World, New Order, New Partnerships?** 118
Sam Mello-Baron, with Aileen Moore and Ian Moore

Chapter 11 **Learning Disabilities: Overcoming a Social Handicap** 132
Roy McConkey and Theresa Nixon

Chapter 12 **Working with Older People to Challenge Ageism** 147
Stephen Pugh

Chapter 13 **Making Links Across Specialisms: Education, the Panacea for Good Practice?** 157
Jan Horwath and Steven M. Shardlow

Bibliography 176
Index 192

List of Tables and Figures

Tables

Table 1.1	Types of Specialism	2
Table 7.1	Levels of Prevention: The Tripartite Prevention Typology (Created by Browne and Herbert)	81
Table 9.1	Kemshall's Format for an Initial Record of Risk Assessment	105
Table 9.2	Other Risk Factors	106
Table 9.3	Millner and Rollnick's 'Wheel of Change'	114
Table 13.1	The Organisational Relationship Between the Management of Operations and of Training and the Impact on the Delivery of Training Across Specialisms	160
Table 13.2	Types of Specialist Training and the Implications for Participants and Facilitators	161

Figures

Figure 1.1	The Social Work Process: Types of Social Work Specialism for a Child in Need under Section 17 of the Children Act 1989	11
Figure 8.1	The Assessment Framework	94
Figure 10.1	A Partnership Approach	129
Figure 13.1	The Relationship Between Training and Operational Management. (Adapted from Stickland)	158

Acknowledgements

This book has its origins in a PHARE project located in the Czech Republic. As part of this project, it was agreed that a book should be produced that drew together aspects of good practice from a variety of areas of social work practice as found within the UK. This collection would then be translated for use within the Czech Republic. Hence, a specifically Czech version of this publication will be produced, based upon this current version.

Many people have contributed to this book in a variety of different ways. We would like to offer our thanks to all of them. In particular, we would like to acknowledge the help of the following by name, from the Czech Republic: Jaroslav Sekot, Pavel Vozabal; Mary Scalley and John Richards for their help with the preparation of Chapter 11.

As always in acknowledging the help of others, any mistakes are those of the editors and authors alone.

Preface

In the UK, specialist practice has become the dominant paradigm for practice. We believe that there is a fundamental need to help specialist practitioners understand other forms of specialist practice in order to improve their abilities to work with specialist practitioners from other aspects of social work. We are aware that some specialist practitioners will on seeing the table of contents take the view that their particular specialism has not been included. We have been forced to make selections in the hope that the reader will take these as being reasoned judgements.

About the Authors

Sally French is Senior Lecturer in the School of Social Sciences at King Alfred's College of Higher Education, Winchester. She has a background in physiotherapy but for many years has taught psychology and sociology as it relates to health, illness and disability. She has written and researched extensively in the field of Disability Studies and has recently completed her PhD thesis which examines the working lives of visually impaired physiotherapists.

Maureen Gillman's research interests include adult learning, family psychotherapy and disability. She has been a Principal Researcher with Professor Swain and Professor Heyman in a number of research projects where the focus has been upon the experience of young adults with learning difficulties in relation to primary health care and social services provision. Recent publications include Gillman M., Heyman B., Swain J. (2000) 'What's in a Name? The Implications of Diagnosis for People With Learning Difficulties and Their Family Carers.' *Disability and Society*, 15: pp 389-409.

Philip Guy MA, PhD, CQSW, is a Lecturer in Social Work (Addictions) in the School of Community and Health Studies at the University of Hull. He is Chair of the Hull and East Yorkshire Council for Drug Problems. He was formerly a specialist social work practice teacher in the addictions field. He gained his social work qualification at the University of Hull in 1992. His research interests include the cultural representation of drug use, issues of policy and prevention in relation to illicit drugs and other substances, and the effectiveness of drug treatment programmes. Recent papers have appeared in *The British Journal of Social Work* and *Practice*.

Larry Harrison MA, CQSW, is Reader in Social Work (Addictions) in the School of Community and Health Studies at the University of Hull. He is co-director of a World Health Organisation Collaborating Centre on Substance Problems, based at the Universities of York and Hull. He gained a professional social work qualification at the West London Institute in 1979, and a post-graduate degree at the University of Essex in 1983. His research interests include issues of policy and prevention in relation to alcohol and other drugs, and furthering the social scientific understanding of the way that risks associated with substance use are taken, communicated, assessed and managed. He is Reviews Editor and member of the Editorial Board of the journal, *Health, Risk and Society*, and member of the International Board of the *Journal of Social Work Practice in the Addictions*. He is co-editor, with A. Alaszewski and J. Manthorpe, of the book, *Risk, Health and Welfare: Policies, Strategies and Practice* (1998). As a member of the UK Economic and Social Research Council's Addiction Research Centre 1983-88, he contributed to their series on Preventing Alcohol and Tobacco Problems (1990). He is editor of *Substance Misuse: Designing Social Work Training, and Alcohol Problems in the Community* and recent papers have appeared in *Addiction, Alcohol and Alcoholism* and *Substance Use and Misuse*.

Di Hart has worked as a social work practitioner and manager in a range of social work settings. She is currently employed by the National Children's Bureau in a development role, looking at the needs of children in public care. She has also undertaken research on pre-birth assessment and has an interest in the needs of children living with drug using parents.

Christine Heron has worked as a social work practitioner, manager and lecturer for a number of years. She is currently Planning and Policy Development Manager in Wirral Social Services, where her responsibilities include user/carer involvement and health partnerships. Christine is chair of Wirral's multi-agency carer's strategy group.

Previous publications include *The Relaxation Therapy Manual* (1996) and *Working with Carers* (1998). She is currently undertaking an MA in

Writing at Liverpool John Moores University. For further information visit her website at www.christineheron.com

Jan Horwath is Senior Lecturer in Social Work Studies at the University of Sheffield. Her professional and research interests focus on professional development, multidisciplinary child care practice and the management of child welfare services. Her recent publications include: *Effective Training in Social Care. From Theory to Practice* (1999) written with Tony Morrison, *Working Together for Children on the Child Protection Register* (1999) edited with Martin Calder and *The Child's World Assessing Children in Need* (2001). She has been responsible, in partnership with the NSPCC and the Department of Health, for the production of the training pack, *The Child's World Assessing Children in Need* (2001) that accompanied the introduction of *The Framework for the Assessment of Children in Need and their Families*.

Catherine Humphreys PhD is Senior Lecturer in the School of Health and Social Studies at the University of Warwick. Her research, writing and practice interests have been in the areas of domestic violence and child abuse. Recent research projects and writing have included: outreach projects and the experiences of women and children leaving violent men; statutory social workers' responses to domestic violence; the use of third party applications for protection orders, issues in child contact where domestic violence is an issue; as well as mapping domestic violence support services in the UK and developing a framework of indicators for good practice. She has been an active member of her local Women's Aid group for the past six years.

Charlotte Knight is Principal Lecturer and Head of the Division of Community and Criminal Justice at De Montfort University. The Division is responsible for the delivery of the BA (Hons) Community and Criminal Justice/Diploma in Probation Studies programme. This is an employment based programme for trainee probation officers run in partnership with the East of England Probation Training and Development Consortium. She has previously worked as Senior Lecturer in Social Work responsible for running the probation option of the Diploma in

Social Work programme at De Montfort University. Before this she worked for the Leicestershire Probation Service (now the Leicestershire and Rutland Probation Service) for sixteen years, as a main grade officer and as a senior probation officer in the Home Office Training Unit and in the Family Court Welfare Service.

Roy McConkey is Professor of Learning Disability at the University of Ulster; a joint post with the Eastern Health and Social Services Board. Previous to this he held posts in England, the Irish Republic and Scotland. He has acted as consultant for various UN agencies and international NGOs.

Sam Mello-Baron is Senior Lecturer in Social Work at the University of Salford. She is Director of the Diploma in Social Work, the largest taught DipSW in the UK. In addition, she is course leader for a post-graduate programme in community care. Previously she worked as a service manager within mental health services for a metropolitan borough council.

Aileen Moore is currently Senior Lecturer in Social Work at Sheffield Hallam University. She has previously worked as a probation officer, a mental health social worker in a variety of settings, a training officer and manager in social services. She is a director of Sheffield MIND and is involved in research into nurse and social work perspectives on assessment.

Ian Moore is currently a manager of integrated health and social services mental health teams in North Derbyshire. From a background in the voluntary sector, residential work and field social work, he has retained a strong commitment to work with service users in planning and delivering services. He is Chair of the Community Mental Health Team Managers Association, which provides information and support for managers at a national level.

Audrey Mullender is Professor of Social Work, Chair of the School of Health and Social Studies and Deputy Chair of the Faculty of Social Studies at the University of Warwick. She is a member of the Academy of Learned Societies for the Social Sciences and of the Sociology, History, Anthropology and Resources College of the Economic and Social

Research Council. She has over 20 years' experience of teaching and researching social work, prior to which her background was in local authority social services. She is the immediate past Editor of the *British Journal of Social Work* and has herself produced well over a hundred publications in the social work field, including thirteen books. Her chief research interests are in domestic violence, post-adoption issues and groupwork.

Theresa Nixon was involved for fourteen years in the provision of social work services for people with a learning disability in Northern Ireland both as a Social Worker and as a Children and Adult Services Manager. She became Development Manager of Learning Disability Services with the Eastern Health and Social Services Board in April 1998 and subsequently the Board's Assistant Director of Social Services for Children in 2001. She is secretary to the NHS Confederation Northern Ireland Advisory Committee on Learning Disability and is currently a member of the Supporting People Reference Group in Northern Ireland in relation to implementing this policy in 2003. She collaborates with colleagues at the University of Ulster on various research projects.

Jonathan Parker is Senior Lecturer in Social Work at the University of Hull. He has a professional background in social work and specialised in mental health and working with older people with dementia. He is also a psychotherapist by profession. He has published widely in the field of dementia care and interpersonal violence, and these areas represent his main research foci.

Bridget Penhale is a Lecturer in Social Work at the University of Hull. With a first degree in psychology, she has a professional background in social work and specialised in working with older people in hospital and community settings. She has published widely in the field of elder abuse, which remains her principal research interest.

Stephen Pugh is Director of Pre- and Post-Qualifying Social Work at the School of Community, Health Sciences and Social Care at the University of Salford. He trained as a social worker working for several years with older people. Within the school he has been responsible for the development and implementation of MA Gerontology and BSc Regulation and Inspection. In addition to these areas of interest he is at present engaged in carrying out research for a PhD that is concerned with service provision for older gay men.

Steven M. Shardlow is Professor of Social Work at the University of Salford, where he is Director of the Salford Centre for Social Work Research. In addition, he is Professor of Social Work at the Univesity of Bodø, Norway. He is founding Editor-in-Chief of the *Journal of Social Work*. Previously he has worked as a social work practitioner and manager. He has been involved in international social work, particularly in Europe through research, consultancy and development work. Current research interests are in the following areas: professional ethics; comparative social practice in the social professions; professional social work education and practice – especially in respect of practice learning. He has published widely in these fields, including eleven books – his work has been translated into several languages.

John Swain is Professor of Disability and Inclusion at the University of Northumbria. His research interests include the analysis of changing policy and professional practice from the viewpoints and experiences of disabled people. He has worked as principal researcher in a number of projects including a DH funded project, *Developing Primary Health Care for Young Adults with Learning Difficulties*. His recent publications include *Therapy and Learning Difficulties: Advocacy, Participation and Partnership* (1999) co-edited with Sally French.

Chapter 1

Specialism: A Force for Change

Jan Horwath and Steven M. Shardlow

Looking across the United Kingdom, in the early years of the twenty-first century, the social work organisational landscape is predominantly populated by social workers who are employed in specialist posts and engaged in delivering specialist practice. Prior to the 1990s, a decade of transition for UK social work, the landscape of social work contained a very different topography: one in which more generalist forms of practice predominated. The existence, of differentiated specialist forms of social work introduces a series of problems for practitioners, in particular: *how can the practitioner, securely grounded in their own specialist practice, comprehend other specialisms and work with colleagues from other specialist areas of practice?*

In this new and emerging social work landscape, social work practice is being reshaped and redefined often through the ideas, actions and polices of particular specialist areas of practice. Whilst the forging and strengthening of particular forms of specialist practice is to be welcomed, there is a continuing need to promote and encourage a wide and inclusive dialogue, across the profession as a whole. Only through such an inclusive dialogue, that embraces the similarities and differences between specialisms can the processes of *making links* across specialist forms of social work practice be realised. This book is part of that process of establishing links across specialist professional boundaries with the particular aim of helping specialist practitioners understand the roles, responsibilities and issues encountered by other specialists in order to promote effective practice across specialisms.

What is Specialism and Specialist Practice?

Before exploring any further the issues that specialist social workers might face, we need to consider how can we begin to understand the idea of specialisms in social work? In general

terms, to be a 'specialist' is, according to the Oxford (Shorter) English Dictionary, to be:

> *a person who specially or exclusively studies a branch of a subject.*

(The primary definition of 'specialist' given relates to a medical practitioner with expertise in a given area.)

While 'specialism' is:

> *restriction or devotion to one aspect of a subject or area of work.*

Turning to specifically social work notions of 'specialism' and specialist; rather surprisingly, the Dictionary of Social Work (Thomas and Pierson, 1995) contains no entry in respect of the terms 'specialist social worker', 'specialist practice' or specialism. Writing in the Blackwell Encyclopaedia of Social Work, Parsloe stated:

> *Generic practice means individuals and teams working with all client groups, from the cradle to the grave, addressing a range of problems; using all or some social work methods; covering intake and long term. Occasionally, it means working across domiciliary, day and residential settings; it can also mean working with one client group using various methods and or settings.*
>
> *Specialist practice means the opposite. It can mean either a division of labour or superior knowledge and skill about a client group, problem area, methods or settings. The specialist practitioner can be at the front line or specialism can extend up the organization.*

(Davies, 2000: p145.)

From these accounts we take it that in terms of social work, the 'specialist' is someone who focuses on a particular type or aspect of work: a 'specialism' is an area, aspect, domain, form, or type of practice. The term 'specialism' is not used in this book to automatically denote any predetermined form of specialism. Although, as will become apparent, in the twenty-first century topography of social work the notion of 'specialism' is most closely associated with dedicated work with one 'client group'.

Forms of Specialism in Social Work

Specialist practice, in one form or another, has been in existence since the end of the Second World War, it is the more usual form of social work in the UK and indeed more generally. Hence, for example, Tolson, Reid and Garvin (1994) propose that most social workers specialise in their practice with one form of system – a system being: the individual; families; groups; organisations or communities. Perhaps surprisingly, there has only been a relatively brief period when generalist practice has been the dominant form of social work – at least this is what we shall argue. Over the last fifty years specialist and generalist practice have been at opposite ends of an imaginary see-saw: either specialism or generalism is in the ascendant at any one time. We do not intend to trace the detailed history of the ups and downs of the see-saw here, rather to provide a taxonomy of the various different forms of specialism that can be found, Table 1.1 illustrates the different forms of specialism in social work.

Table 1.1 Types of Specialism

Type of Specialism	Characteristics	Issues	Strengths
Client group	Social worker practices more or less exclusively with one particular group of clients.	1) Families may have to relate to several social workers. 2) Social workers may ignore needs if these do not relate to their specialist area of knowledge. 3) Workers may ignore the impact of the service user's issues on the family	Social workers are able to develop detailed knowledge of the law, policy and practice in relation to one client group – and so provide a better service to the service user.
Community	Social worker works exclusively with a small community, other names for this specialism include: locality social work; patch based social work; neighbourhood social work.	1) Social workers may become isolated from senior management. 2) Clients may feel that the social worker knows too much – maintaining client confidentiality could be problematic.	1) Social worker has direct and continuing knowledge of people and issues living in a defined area. 2) Provides opportunities for early response and continuing involvement and mobilisation of community resources.
Expertise	A social worker may be informally acknowledged by colleagues to have a particular expertise, for example the 'office' expert on benefit legislation. Senior practitioners may legitimately be given this role.	1) Social workers with ascribed expertise but no formal employment position that validates this may resent the time spent advising other workers. 2) Experts may be reluctant to consider other forms of practice.	1) Makes good use of available skills within an organisation and provides personal satisfaction for individuals. 2) The role if formally recognised provides a remit to develop expertise.

Table 1.1(cont.) Types of Specialism

Type of Specialism	Characteristics	Issues	Strengths
Method	Exclusive or predominant use of one particular method by a social worker, for example, behavioural social work, crisis intervention; task centred practice.	Methods of intervention may be chosen according to social worker preference rather than based upon a differential analysis of client need.	1) Some methods are especially useful when applied to certain kinds of problems. 2) A more rigorous application of method to social work practice may be highly desirable.
Mode	Social worker who works with either, individuals, families, groups, or community work.	Some of these forms of practice have been vulnerable to political unwillingness to fund them, for example community work.	1) Much social work practice focusses on individuals and families: the development of expertise with larger groups is highly desirable. 2) Provides a diverse range of interventions to service users.
Organisational	The delivery of services to the public are divided according to the agency's organisational structure for example intake or reception teams and long term teams.	1) Social workers work with people according to the needs of the agency rather than the client. 2) Clients may have to change social workers for organisational reasons.	1) Ideally leads to a speedy response to need and the resolution of clients' problems within short and previously delimited timescale. 2) Workers develop specialist knowledge and skills.
Qualification	Social worker has a recognised post professional qualification in social work. For example Post Qualifying Child Care Award; Approved Social Worker, and so on.	The existence of this form of specialism may make it difficult for social workers to move to develop skills in new areas of practice resulting in inflexibility in the employment market.	1) The introduction of the Advanced Award in Social Work (AASW), and national awards in Practice Teaching, Mental Health and Child Care make possible the accreditation of knowledge and expertise.
Setting	Social worker who works in either a voluntary, statutory or private agency. This term is sometimes used to differentiate health care e.g. hospital social work from social work in an area team.	1) Social workers may approach work more from an organisational focus than a client focus. 2) Working across settings may be difficult because of differences in organisational philosophies and approaches.	Each of these settings have distinct organisational characteristics developing an ability to work in one such context may convey advantages.

Specialism by client group

Where social workers work substantially or exclusively with one group of clients, for example older people, children and families, mentally ill people and so on. This has become the dominant form of *specialist* practice in the UK. When the term specialist is used in the context of social work it is often taken to apply exclusively to this form of specialism (see below for a more detailed account of how this dominant form of specialism functions today).

Specialisation by community

In this form of specialist practice, social workers usually focus their work on one community, located within a geographical area; it was most prevalent during the late 1970s and 1980s. The development of variously termed, 'locally-based social work', 'neighbourhood social work' or 'patch based social work' makes the generic or generalist social worker a *specialist* in that they know the resources and problems of the particular patch or area. A number of detailed research projects were undertaken on the advantages and disadvantages of this form of social work (Hadley and Mcgrath, 1981). While the Barclay report articulated the rationale for community social work:

> *Community social work requires of the social worker an attitude of partnership. Clients, relations, neighbours and volunteers become partners with the social worker in developing and providing social care networks.*
>
> (Barclay, 1982: p209.)

This form of specialisation largely disappeared during the 1990s to be replaced by specialisation by client group.

Specialisation by expertise

As the name suggests, social workers may specialise by virtue of expertise in a given area of practice. Most usually, this will be based on other colleagues recognising the specialisation abilities or interest of a social worker – hence the specialisation will be informal and may not be formalised by the organisation.

Alternatively, the introduction of senior practitioner posts in some social services departments formalises expertise.

Specialisation by method

Social workers have sought to create a professional identity and specialism by delineating their practice expertise by method. Advocates of 'groupwork' for example may identify themselves as 'group workers' claiming the method of intervention a specialism and making common cause with others from different professional backgrounds practising the same methodology.

Specialisation by mode

In the 1970s, it was current practice to differentiate social workers as specialists according to their primary 'mode of intervention'; i.e. whichever mode formed the core of their practice. Hence, social workers might specialise in working with individuals, families, non-family groups or wider communities. Such a conceptualisation of specialist practice emphasises the locus of intervention, whether at individual, group or community level. It perhaps gave the strongest voice to those engaged in community workers, as being able to conceptualise their practice as a legitimate part of social work; yet one having its own distinctive methodological approach. These forms of specialist practice were more apparent when there was a strong tradition of community work practice; many community work posts, located in local authorities, were lost during the 1980s and 1990s. As a conceptualisation of specialist practice this form does not find a strong voice in current UK literature.

Specialisation by organisation

During the period, that social work was supposedly generic (during the 1970s) a form of organisational specialisation emerged. Many departments grouped social workers into short-term (some times known as intake-teams) and long-term teams. Ideally, the short-term teams would work intensively with clients from a variety of client groups and sought to resolve clients' problem within an arbitrary time period – say three months. Any people with problems at the end of a three-month period would be passed over to the long-term team. Hence, meeting an organisational need to manage workflows – while there may have been some informal specialisation in the long-term team in theory all social workers remained generic. Recently, a similar form of organisational specialism has re-emerged in some local authorities as 'reception teams', these deal with the initial client contacts with subsequent assistance provided by a specialist practitioner based upon client group.

Specialisation by qualification

There have always been opportunities for social workers to acquire post professional qualifications. During the period from the 1980s, there has been an increase in the number of national qualifications such as those in Child Care, Approved Social Work, and Practice Teaching. These qualifications validate and legitimise the specialist knowledge and skill of the social worker who has one or more of these awards. The introduction of the Advanced Award in Social Work leaves open the possibility of developing specialist practitioners who by virtue of their being more skilful than others, in a generalised sense, should provide services to people with highly complex needs.

Although, in practice, the take up of the AASW has been lower than anticipated; according to the General Social Care Council (GSCC) there were only 102 awards in 2001/02[1] (GSCC, 2002: p18). Whilst the post-qualifying awards in mental health (ASW) are steady at about 300 per annum (GSCC, 2002: p29). For the child care post qualifying award (PQCCA) there is a Department of Health target of 7,000 award holders by 2006-07 (GSCC, 2002: p32). To some extent the very existence of these qualifications for post qualifying social has begun to define the *notion* of specialism by qualification. For

example, it is now only possible to act as an approved social worker under the Mental Health Act (1983) *if* a social worker possesses the ASW. However, as the GSSC comments 'there is little employer support for post qualifying training if it is not linked to direct funding or compulsory awards' (GSCC, 2002: p18). As yet, there has been insufficient linkage between these awards and additional financial remuneration or career progression to fully embed such awards within a specialist landscape.

Specialisation by setting

The professional space occupied by social work has always been problematic. Other 'helping' or 'social' professions nudge and jostle against the boundaries delineating the area of professional competence claimed by social work. One of the most permeable boundaries between occupational groups is to be found within community mental health teams where whilst each professional group has an area of expertise there are a very significant number of tasks that might be undertaken by any member of the group. Social work, as a profession has not articulated a strong case for delineating its area of professional competence. None the less, within the professional space that might be claimed by social work, there have been attempts to delineate specialist forms of practice according to setting, for example: fieldwork – work with individuals and families or residential work – work within residential units.

One form of specialism, by setting, that has developed in most areas, is that of the EDT (Emergency Duty Team) see Department of Health (1999) for a report on the provision of this type of specialist service. Here, specialist practice is defined by the time of referral, i.e. problems that require a social worker that arise outside of normal office hours are referred to an emergency team. Social workers in emergency duty teams develop an expertise in crisis work with all service user groups. For an account of some of the problems encountered in this type of work see Clifford and Williams (2002).

---

1   This is the latest date for which figures are available – note the figures relate to England.

The Case for Specialism

Many social services departments have tended towards specialist teams and away from genericism in recent years. If specialism is the usual and dominant form of practice we may legitimately ask to what extent, this approach to social work has been researched and evaluated. Importantly, Parsloe comments that, 'There has been little research into whether the different practices [specialist and generalist practice] have different outcomes' (Davies, 2000: p145). Similarly, Fuller and Tulle-Winton characterise the literature on 'team organisation' (i.e. the organisational structure of teams including discussion of specialism) as being 'long on theoretical and conceptual debate…shorter on descriptive accounts…brief indeed on evaluation' (Fuller and Tulle-Winton, 1996: p682).

There are some investigations of the degree of student preparedness to undertake work in their particular specialism after the end of the period of professional training (see for example, Marsh and Triseliotis, 1996). Such studies tend to find that students feel better prepared for some areas of work than others: Pithouse and Scourfield (2002) found that in some specialist areas of practice almost half of recent graduates perceived their level of preparation to have been poor or less than adequate. There is a body of literature (see for example Hay, 1979a; 1979b; Vickery, 1970) that largely predates the current organisational structures which was concerned to explore the value of specialist practice and organisational forms, most notable among these being the empirical work of Stevenson (1981). Looking at more recent work, in a modest discussion, Gilders (1997) describes, evaluates and quantifies outcomes in respect of a pilot specialist post of social worker specifically for vulnerable adults in West Oxfordshire. Whilst Fuller and Tulle-Winton (1996) have compared the approaches of fifteen generic and specialised teams to making assessments of older people. The findings were complex, however, there was no easy correlation between, for example: 'specialist social work skills do not translate readily into improved outcomes for elderly clients' (p697), yet there were benefits at the assessment and planning stages.

It may well be the case that the empirical case for the adoption of specialist practice, i.e. that in some shape or form this type of practice leads to better outcomes for service users is at best unproven and at worse not significantly investigated empirically. Hence, it may be that the case for specialist practice is rather more to do with an emotive justification, financial imperatives or policy preferences. None the less there is a widely held view that greater practitioner expertise derives from specialisation (Audit Commission, 1992). As Bamford suggests, there are two assumptions that underlie the adoption of specialist practice. These are:

> First, the knowledge and range of skills required to deal adequately with the tasks required is too great for any individual practitioner. A better quality of service will therefore be obtained by focussing more narrowly on a defined group, and developing expertise in that specialist area of work. The second assumption is that not only will the quality of individual work be improved, but the organisational response to service delivery will also benefit by virtue of drawing together common needs and common service responses.   (Bamford, 1990: p20.)

Yet, Stevenson (1981) identified a difficulty that seems to be particularly strong in social work with respect to the notion of specialism. In so far as being a specialist implies that the social worker is part of some elite group who has exclusive knowledge – not a notion that fits easily with social work. This apparent possession of exclusive knowledge, according to Bamford (1990: p20) conflicts with notions of partnership between service users and social workers. Despite such observations about negative aspects of specialism, which may now be losing some of their currency, the adoption of client based specialist practice seems almost universal. However, despite the apparent desirability of specialist forms of practice it remains largely untested through empirical evaluation against other methods of delivering social work.

Current Specialist Practice in the UK

The origins of current forms of specialism in the United Kingdom

It is becoming more difficult to speak with confidence or certainty about the development of social work across the United Kingdom.

There are increasing divergences in organisational forms of social work, legal systems and implementation of policies in the countries of England, Northern Ireland, Scotland, and Wales. Hence, for example, in England local authority social services are delivered though social services departments and these departments do not have responsibility for probation services. Whilst in Scotland, services are delivered through social work departments, which have responsibility for probation. In addition, there is a different legal system in Scotland which has an entirely different structure for juvenile justice from that found in England; Northern Ireland or Wales i.e. the Children's Panel a non adversarial approach to justice for juveniles which operates in Scotland but not in the rest of the United Kingdom. Similarly, there are significant differences between the arrangements for the organisation of social work as between Northern Ireland and both England and Scotland. In Northern Ireland social services are delivered through integrated Health and Social Services Boards, ideally this should lead to greater integration of health and social care provision (for more details on these and other differences see Payne and Shardlow, 2002). In respect of policy differences, the so-called 'community care reforms', so important in the construction of current forms of specialism (see below), were introduced at different times, with some differences in content across the four countries of the United Kingdom. Indeed, they have never been formally implemented in Northern Ireland although in practice they are in operation. Hence, it cannot be assumed that there is a common approach to specialism throughout the United Kingdom; care must be exercised when making generalisations that refer to all of the countries within the United Kingdom.

Current forms of specialist practice, to a considerable extent, echo the organisational arrangements and forms of social work practice that developed between 1948 and 1971. These forms of social work originate from the creation of the Welfare State, in the years that followed the Second World War. The intellectual drive to create a more humane society derives from the Beveridge Report (1942) which identified five 'giants' that plagued the United Kingdom, these were: illness, ignorance, disease, squalor and want. To destroy the reach of these 'giants', Beveridge proposed the creation of a universal system of state welfare to apply 'from cradle to grave', based on a social insurance scheme. His report identified key elements to underpin the new welfare state, these were:

- A system of social insurance and assistance.
- The provision of family allowances.
- A comprehensive national health service.
- Policies to maintain full employment.

A series of Acts of Parliament were introduced to bring into being these elements of the welfare state:

- The National Insurance Act (1946) introduced social insurance contributions and provided benefits for a range of groups.
- The National Assistance Act (1948) gave local authorities the responsibility to provide accommodation needed by the population on the grounds of age and infirmity.
- The National Health Service Act (1946) created a comprehensive National Health Service.
- The Children Act (1948) gave local authorities a general responsibility for children deprived of a normal home life and set up arrangements for boarding out and reception into care.
- The Education Act (1944) gave Local Education Authorities responsibilities to ensure the quality of primary, secondary and higher education.
- The Criminal Justice Act (1948) laid out provisions for dealing with young offenders.
- The Mental Health Act (1959) defined mental illness and how people with mental illness and learning disability[2] should be given care.

---

2. Then termed 'subnormality'.

During this period from the end of the Second World War until the early 1970s, social work services were delivered principally through two separate departments (The Children's Department and The Welfare Department) in each local authority, through which specialist social workers[3] were employed and provided specialist services. By the mid-1960s, growing dissatisfaction was evident with these organisational arrangements, as Sainsbury commented some twenty-five years ago:

> *...as social legislation became increasingly wide in scope, and departments were given powers to extend their services to promote the general welfare of client-groups and the prevention of distress, so the problems of overlapping services and of the demarcation of responsibilities increased. Services were competitors for resources, irrespective of their common concern with welfare; and frequently the aims and values which they held in common made co-operation difficult rather than easy.*
>
> (Sainsbury, 1977: p73-74.)

As a consequence of this state of affairs the Seebohm Committee was set up in 1966 and duly reported in 1968 (Seebohm Report). The report famously commented:

> *There is a realisation that it is essential to look beyond the immediate symptoms of social distress to the underlying problems. These frequently prove to be complicated and the outcome of a variety of influences. In many cases, people who need help cannot be treated effectively unless this is recognised. Their difficulties do not arise in a social vacuum; they are, have been, or need to be involved in a network of social relationships, in social situations. The family and the community are seen as the contexts in which problems arise and in which most of them have to be resolved or contained.*
>
> (HMSO, 1968: p44.)

The organisational consequences of this comment for the development of specialist practice and the mode of delivery of social work within the United Kingdom were profound. As, when Social Services

Departments were created in England and Wales[4] on 1st April 1971 (based upon recommendations contained within the Seebohm Report), the majority of the United Kingdom began its experimentation with forms of delivery that centred upon the 'generalist' or 'generic' social worker.[5] This was one of the most important consequences of the Seebohm reorganisation – an almost universal rejection of specialisation and the invention of the 'generic' social worker. Curiously, Seebohm did not advocate the abolition of the specialist worker and took the view that there should be specialist workers within generalist teams. The creation of a single social services department in each local authority purported to unify previously disparate professional groups and refashion social work along generalist or generic principles. This reorganisation contained an expectation, in some quarters, that 'generic' social workers would be able to deal with all forms of problem and with all groups of clients.

In theory, generalist practice remained the dominant form of social work from 1971 until 1990. Despite this apparent dominance of one paradigm, some forms of specialist practice re-established themselves quite speedily within local authorities. For example, although never constituting a large group 'fostering and adoption' social workers could be found in many 'Seebohm style' departments. These departments were centralised and often perceived to be bureaucratic in character. The philosophy that underpinned the approach of these departments to service delivery was 'universalist welfare provision' i.e. everybody should be entitled to the same services. This notion of extensive and universal services was dependent upon the continuation of sustained economic growth such that in time social services provision would have the same universalist characteristics as health care or education. The economic strains of seeking to

---

3. Levels of professional qualification were not always high especially among those working with adults: nor would the term social worker have been widely used. Terms such as 'children's officer' or 'welfare officer' would have been more common.
4. Scotland and Northern Ireland were recognised in 1972.
5. The 'generalist' (the US term) or 'generic' (the UK term) social worker was assumed able to deal with a range, maybe even all, clients – whatever their problems.

provide a universalist service were fully evident in the mid-1980s; these strains provided one factor that inclined toward the development of different paradigm of practice, which reopened the possibility of specialist practice re-emerging on a substantial scale. A specialist practice that was grounded in detailed and extensive assessment of need and the provision of a selective service.

Prior to the re-emergence of the 'full blown' specialist paradigms during the 1990s, now largely forgotten 'experiments' developed with different forms of specialism to those that now prevail; these were specialisms that were highly generalist in character – an apparent paradox.[6] These forms of practice, were known by a variety of terms: 'community social work'; 'locally based work'; 'neighbourhood social work'; 'patch based social work' – each term might imply a slightly different type of practice. The key aspect of these forms of practice was that social workers, worked singly or in small groups that would provide all the core social work tasks for the population within a defined modestly sized geographical area. Often the social work office would be based within the geographical community served, either as a small independent office perhaps in a private house or within a community centre or GP surgery. This model of social work has much in common with the way that primary health care services are delivered through GP practices. The then Conservative government, in October 1980, set up a working party under the chairmanship of Peter M. Barclay: the final report was published in 1982 (Barclay, 1982). This report described the nature of community social work practice and for a few short years provided a paradigm for practice. If some of the forms of community social work, described in the report have lost their significance, i.e. locally based social work practice, then other principles in the report remain as powerful and relevant as when first written, hence for example:

> *Citizens who give and receive services should have opportunities to share in decisions which affect their lives. This partnership is the essence of what we mean*

> *by community social work and depends upon an* **attitude of mind** *in those in the statutory and voluntary sectors.* (Barclay, 1982: p202.)

The community social work approach, attracted a considerable amount of interest amongst the research community and there were several attempts to evaluate particular examples of these forms of practice (see for example, Bayley, Parker, Seyd and Tennant, 1987; Hadley and Mcgrath, 1981). By and large the published accounts were favourable and espoused the virtues of this form of practice. None the less the final demise of generalist practice was heralded in 1988 with the publication of the government commissioned report under the chairmanship of Sir Roy Griffiths (Griffiths, 1988), which proposed that a 'managed' approach be developed to the provision of care in the community. Following the publication of this report, Mrs Thatcher's Conservative government introduced a White Paper, *Caring for People* (Department of Health, 1989), which substantially adopted the proposals of the Griffiths Report. These principles were enacted into legislation through the National Health Service and Community Care Act 1990. This watershed Act imposed a new framework for the provision of 'care in the community', and thereby social work practice, by separating the *purchasing* from the *provision* of community care services, and introducing the care management[7] system of social work (Payne, 1995). These two changes facilitated a massive transfer of resources from state social work to the private and not-for-profit social care sectors. The result being a 'mixed economy of welfare', where, most usually, the assessment of individual need would be made by the state (local authority employed social workers), with the provision of services by the cheapest provider. The establishment of this new system derived not only from the Thatcher government's desire to introduce competition, drive down costs in the public sector and emulate US systems of social welfare, but also from a series of research led demonstration projects (notably Davies and Challis, 1986). These reforms

---

6. Social workers working in defined geographical areas were expected to work with all clients and with any problem.

7. This had been previously known in the US as the *case management* system.

created two domains of specialism, those who purchased services, 'care managers' and those who provided services. Importantly, these changes modified the role of the social worker and pushed them, in many cases, most notably when dealing with adults-in-need-of-services to become the organiser and manager of the services. This role might often include financial monitoring. The legislative changes induced changes in practice which gave birth to a new specialist paradigm.

As a consequence of this shift in the nature of social work during the 1990s, various forms of specialist practice emerged in different areas, care managers might only work with one client grouping, for example older people or disabled people. The divide between the organisational and practice forms of social work with 'children and families' and social work with 'adults' has strengthened and deepened – leaving an increasing sense of specialisation for social workers in these respective fields. This growing divide recreates some of the divisions in social work organisation and practice that existed prior to 1970. As different legislative arrangements apply to those who work with children and families to those who work with adults. In addition, those who work with children and families are less likely to become solely the organisers of services – as they have retained aspects of their practice that are concerned with service delivery.

Specialism: the current position

The current dominant form of specialist practice in the UK has two major characteristics: an organisational division between social workers who purchase from those who provide services, and an additional specialist practice division between social workers providing services for different client groups. This practice division has a strong 'fault line' between those who provide services for adults and those who provide services for children. These divisions have organisational, financial, educational, skill and ideological dimensions. The consequence of these divisions is that individual service users or families may be in contact with social workers from several different types of specialism.

Some of the complexities of current patterns of service delivery can be seen using a case example. Figure 1.1 illustrates the process of referral following the expression of concerns about a child who is believed to be at risk of significant harm. This process of assessing and meeting the needs of the child involves the child and their family having contact with social workers working in different settings who use different approaches in their work with the child and family. To be effective with the family, social workers in such situations have to work with colleagues from a range of social work specialisms. A case example well illustrates some of these issues:

Case example

Jade is a ten year old girl. A referral has been made to the social services child and family access team by a social worker from the community mental health team. The worker is concerned that Jade's mother, Gwen, is unable to care for Jade. Gwen has been compulsorily admitted to a psychiatric unit under section 2 of the Mental Health Act (1983) by the mental health social worker (acting as an Approved Social Worker). Gwen has been in hospital for four weeks. Jade's maternal grandmother has been caring for Jade with assistance from an outreach team attached to social services family support services, while Gwen was in hospital. Jade's grandmother has a hearing impairment and cares for her husband who is disabled with multiple sclerosis. Gwen is about to be discharged and is keen to look after Jade once more. Jade's father Ben misuses alcohol and has a history of physical violence towards both Jade and Gwen. Jade is very depressed and withdrawn and has been referred to the child and adolescent mental health service by her GP.

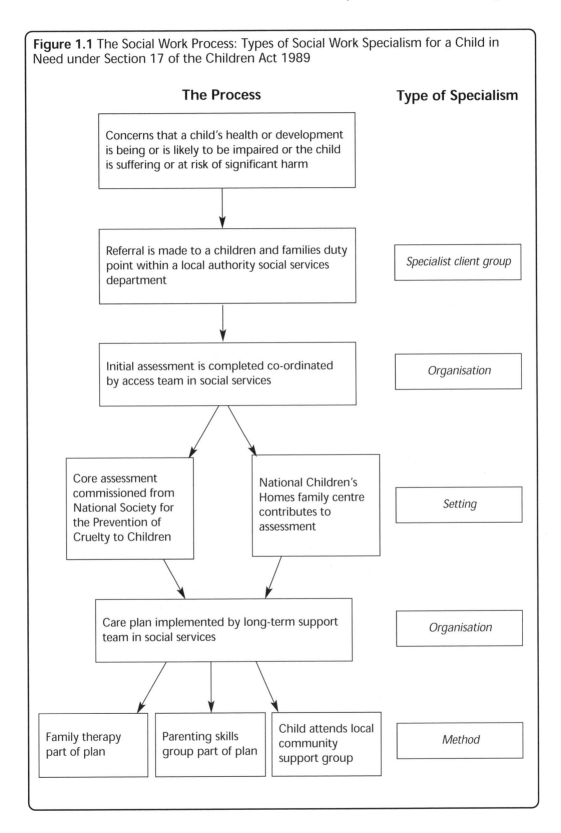

Figure 1.1 The Social Work Process: Types of Social Work Specialism for a Child in Need under Section 17 of the Children Act 1989

This example highlights the number of different social workers who could be involved in an assessment of Jade and her family using the *Framework for the Assessment of Children in Need and their Families* (Department of Health et al., 2000). A child and family social worker from a social services department would be responsible for working with other professionals to assess: the developmental needs of Jade; her carers' capacity to meet these needs; the effect of family circumstances; and social environmental factors that impact upon the capacity of the family to meet Jade's needs (see Chapter 8 for further detail). This might mean that the child and family social worker from the access team will work with:

- the approved social worker
- social workers from the alcohol advisory service
- social workers from a family centre who could be asked to assess Gwen and Ben's parenting skills
- social workers from the outreach family support team
- a specialist social worker for people with hearing impairments
- a social worker from the team for people with physical disabilities
- a hospital based social worker
- the social worker from the child and adolescent mental health service

In circumstances such as those illustrated by the case of Jade and her family, it is easy to assume that because the social workers involved will have experienced qualifying training, leading to the same professional award, and share the job title 'social worker', that they will share common approaches to practice. In reality, this is highly *unlikely*, as the context in which social workers operate greatly influences their approach to working together across social work specialisms. Although, these contextual differences are frequently recognised when social workers work with other professionals across *social care and health* disciplines (Leathard, 1994; Hallet, 1995; Brechin et al., 2000), such differences are more likely to be forgotten when working across *social work* specialisms. Helpfully, Hudson (1999) has explored some of the contextual issues that can influence inter-

professional relationships. These issues are considered below in relation to social work specialisms.

Different patterns of employment and accountability

Social workers work in a range of multidisciplinary settings. Hence, for example, social workers are members of: primary care groups; community mental health teams; and youth offending teams. In these situations, social workers may be employed by the local authority but work alongside colleagues employed by education, health services, probation and police. It is possible, in these multidisciplinary social teams for workers to lose sight of social services priorities and to accept instead priorities determined by any of the other agencies. For example, the approach adopted by social workers towards service users may be different in multidisciplinary community care teams to those adopted by social workers who are centrally based within the social services department's team, predominantly consisting of social services personnel.

Different decision making loci

Social workers, depending on their work context, will take different approaches to decision making. For example, the approach to decision making is likely to vary between those employed by statutory and voluntary agencies. Social workers employed by social services departments are likely to make decisions based on the organisational procedures using 'rules as tools' (Eguland, 1996). While social workers in the voluntary sector, for example in a women's refuge may be expected to make decisions based on the majority opinion of the co-operative running the refuge.

Different perceptions of costs and benefits

Working as a social work specialist implies that social workers may work with just one particular type of issue, such as adults with drug issues. Such an approach to practice can result in 'tunnel vision' where the costs and benefits of assessing and planning for a service user are understood in isolation rather than in the context of the service user's family and community. For example, Cleaver et al. (1999) note that social workers working with parents who misuse drugs do not always understand the impact that the parental drug using behaviour can have on the parent's ability to meet the needs of their child. Social workers in this situation may tend to perceive the costs and benefits of intervention solely in terms of the needs of the parents – their service user.

Different professional cultures

Differences in social work cultures are reflected throughout this book. For example, probation officers have moved from being grounded in a social work ethos, with an emphasis on identifying and meeting needs in a welfare context, to a public protection and punishment ethos with an emphasis on risk and public protection (see Knight Chapter 9). Mental health social work has made a similar shift (Moore Chapter 10). By contrast, the approach towards meeting the needs of children has shifted from a narrow focus on safeguarding children to both safeguarding and promoting the welfare of children and their families (Horwath Chapter 8).

As a result of these contextual differences, social workers who work together may have different perceptions of task, roles and responsibilities. This can result in a number of problems. Workers may misunderstand or hold different perceptions of the task leading to either a partial response, the duplication of or the omission of activities. Alternatively, if social workers are unclear about their roles in relation to the task, situations can arise where workers can become precious regarding their responsibilities and reluctant to share tasks with other workers. This can occur if they believe they are the experts and do not trust other practitioners. In this situation, practitioners may attempt to address all of the service user's issues resulting in a vague low-skilled generalist response (Loxley, 1997) or workers may take actions that conflict with the work undertaken by other specialists. Lack of clarity regarding roles and responsibilities can also result in poor working relationships with for example, workers blaming each other for failing to complete tasks. As described above, specialist social workers

will have different service priorities. Under these circumstances, a professional hierarchy may develop with one specialist perspective dominating and the views of other specialists becoming marginalised.

Underlining all the issues described above are communication difficulties regarding the clarity of task, roles and responsibilities. These difficulties can occur at individual and organisational level. They can to some extent, be avoided if there are established frameworks for effective practice across specialisms. Morrison (1996) has identified a number of factors that need to be in place for effective inter-agency practice. These are as applicable for social workers collaborating across specialisms and are dependent on positive leadership – with senior managers from the specialisms actively encouraging joint working and collaboration. This is most likely to occur if the senior managers model effective practice across specialisms through establishing the following:

- Shared value base: creating a common understanding as to the benefits for service users of collaboration. This can be achieved by members from the specialisms working together to develop a mission statement.

- Clear mandate: staff need a specific remit to work across specialisms. This enables workers to appreciate the fit between the core business underpinning their specialist service and the core business of other specialist services.

- Systems, structures and joint protocols that provide a framework for practice. These should ensure that both managers and practitioners are clear regarding the roles and responsibilities of different social workers when working together. Policies and procedures also offer clarity regarding accountability and reporting arrangements.

- Systems of support and supervision from managers. These should include systems for conflict resolution and criteria for prioritising tasks.

- Resources to promote effective joint working.

- Quality assurance mechanisms: enabling both practitioners and managers to evaluate the effectiveness of current arrangements in terms of promoting better outcomes for service users.

- Training and staff development. As described in Chapter 13 effective inter-specialist training can clarify roles and responsibilities and promote effective communication across specialisms.

The Sainsbury Centre for Mental Health (2000) evaluated the literature on partnerships amongst professionals working in mental health. They concluded that attitudes and beliefs towards working together will have a significant influence on policy and practice developments. In order to develop the policies and systems described above senior and operational managers and practitioners must see joint working as a priority and be committed to achieving this despite any obstacles. 'Starting out with the positive attitude and a solution-orientated approach of 'how can we do this 'rather than 'can we do this' is important' (The Sainsbury Centre for Mental Health, 2000: p37).

Education for specialism

High quality and most importantly *relevant* professional education for social workers is fundamental in the preparation of social workers for effective and efficient practice that meets the requirements of those who use social work services and those who employ social workers. Yet, what is relevant professional education? Is it a professional education that is generalist, preparing newly qualified practitioners to be able to practice, with a basic level of competence, in all, or at least most areas of professional practice? Alternatively, might it be an initial specialist professional education. Whichever form of initial professional education is provided for new entrants they must have the opportunity to develop a firm grounding in the current realities of practice. If the basic education is generalist then opportunities need to be provided soon to develop specialist expertise after qualification. If the basic education is specialist then there must be flexibility and mechanisms to allow practitioners to change their professional focus and to develop expertise in alternate professional areas. Whichever form of professional education is adopted, and there are arguments in support of both, it is highly desirable that students, new entrants to the profession and experienced practitioners develop and maintain an awareness of other

forms of specialism within the discipline of social work. Not least because the experiences and needs of clients cannot be neatly parcelled between specialisms.

Many of the issues regarding training social workers to work across specialisms may result from attitudes that begin to develop on professional qualification training programmes. For example the precursor to the current basic professional qualification in the UK, the CQSW was a generalist qualification. The introduction of the DipSW in 1989 (CCETSW, 1989) initiated a shift towards a more specialised form of training, although this was denied officially. In practice the introduction of specialist pathways for students completing the Diploma in Social Work has had an impact on students' attitude towards practice (CCETSW, 1995). Students were able to complete a social work course without having experience of a broad range of groups of clients. For example, under the DipSW regulations it has been perfectly possible for a student to gain experience solely with adults who use social work services. This is well illustrated in the work of Marsh and Triseliotis (1996) who studied social workers and probation officers' views of initial professional education (DipSW) and found that students considered that they were prepared for particular areas of work, *but not others*, as encapsulated by the comments of two students:

> Well. I'm a specialist aren't I. I only know about working in my own area.

> I don't feel that I can work in other areas like adult services.

> (Marsh and Triseliotis, 1996: p95.)

The students were unsure as to whether their skills were transferable

> I think there are some things you could apply to any of the other areas you're working in…but there are a lot of things I am ignorant about.

> (Marsh and Triseliotis, 1996: p95.)

Our experience as educators indicates that many students commence their studies with very clear views regarding their areas of interests and can be selective in assessing the relevance of learning as preparation for practice in their chosen specialism. For example, within the context of the DipSW, students completing the children and families pathway often question why they should learn about ageing. Moreover, taking a broad approach can also create difficulties; for example, Mullender (1996) highlights that conflicting messages can be given when educators attempt to take a broader approach to social work education by integrating topics such as domestic violence into the curriculum.

Basic professional education for social work is currently being changed. Following various reports by consultants J.M. Consulting, an extensive review process, involving key stakeholders in the educational enterprise, and entitled the 'Reform of Social Work Education', the Department of Health has endorsed the implementation of a three-year social work undergraduate[8] qualification, with a first intake in England 2003.

The systems and structures, although similar are somewhat different in the various countries of the United Kingdom.[9] This marks a change from the past when one central body, the Central Council for Education and Training (CCETSW) specified the rules and regulations that obtained throughout the United Kingdom. Now, for example, in the England the new arrangements will apply from the intake of students in September 2003; in the other countries of the UK this is likely to be one year later. There are also more substantive differences: for example. Students in Northern Ireland are likely to have three full years as undergraduates (in Scotland this will be four years) and then a protected year in practice before being deemed competent as compared with other countries in the UK which may not make such substantial arrangements to protect the first year of practice. However, there are core elements that will be the same; most notably the new system is based upon the premise that to qualify as a social worker, it will be usual to study for three years as an undergraduate.[10] No central body will specify the detail of the curriculum taught, as with the DipSW. Instead, Higher Education Institutions (HEIs) will we accredited by the various Care Councils, in each country within the UK, to

provide social work education. The professional qualification will thus be a degree from a HEI rather than an award from a professional body, as was the case of the predecessor award, the DipSW. Guidance is available to HEIs about what should be taught in the shape of the Quality Assurance Agency's (QAA) National Benchmark Statement for Social Policy and Administration and Social Work (QAA, 2000), which states the expectations concerning: subject knowledge: teaching, learning and assessment methods; standards expected of them at the point of graduation (QAA, 2000: p10).

In addition, the Training Organisation for the Personal Social Services (TOPSS England) has, in the National Occupational Standards, (TOPSS, 2002) specified the baseline to define the standards that are expected of qualified social workers. This statement identifies six key roles for social workers:

- Key Role 1: Prepare for and work with individuals, families, carers, groups and communities to assess needs and options to recommend a course of action.

- Key Role 2: Plan, carry out, review and evaluate social work practice, with individuals, families, carers, groups and communities and other professionals.

- Key Role 3: Support individuals to represent their needs, views and circumstances.

- Key Role 4: Manage risk to individuals, families, carers, groups, communities, self and colleagues.

- Key Role 5: Manage and be accountable, with supervision and support, for your own social work practice within your organisation.

- Key Role 6: Demonstrate professional competence in social work practice.

Taken from the Department of Health (Department of Health, 2002).

---

8.   There will be a postgraduate entry route.
9.   For full details of the respective approaches see: England http://www.doh.gov.uk/swqualification/new requirements.htm; Northern Ireland http://www.niscc.info; Scotland http://www.sssc.uk.com/SSSC.Web/index.aspx; Wales http://www.ccwales.org.uk
10.   There will also be some two-year masters level courses for those who have an undergraduate degree.

Moreover, The Department of Health has also stipulated that social workers will be assessed on five key dimensions of practice, these are: Law; Partnership Working; Communication Skills; Assessment, Planning, Intervention and Review; Human Growth, Development, Mental Health and Disability (Department of Health, 2002: p8).

These trends which locate basic professional education as being more generalist than previously are evident in one of the most important aspects of the new system of professional education, i.e. the part that is concerned with practice learning. According to the statement of requirements issued by the Department of Health:

> *Students must spend at **least** 200 days gaining required experience and learning in practice settings.*

and

> *Each student must have experience:*
> ● *In **at least** two practice settings.*
> ● *Of statutory social work tasks involving legal interventions.*
> ● *Of providing services to **at least** two user groups (e.g. child care and mental health).*
> (Department of Health, 2002.)

In addition to these specific requirements, Universities that provide social work education will be expected to conform to the guidance that the QAA has issued in respect of all courses that provide periods of practice learning

Therefore the QAA *Benchmark Statement*, combined with the TOPSS statement of *National Occupational Standards* in conjunction with the Department of Health statement of *Requirements for Social Work Training* (Department of Health, 2002) and the QAA *Code of Practice for the Assurance of Academic Quality and Standards in Higher Education : Placement Learning* combine to construct a complex set of rules, requirements and statements of guidance that will shape the new form of social work education. The General Social Care Council (GSCC) accredits approves and inspects the providers of social work education in conducted in England – in the other countries of the UK other arrangements apply.

These regulations and guidance documents in respect of practice appear to provide a more generalist qualification than the predecessor DipSW, which had specialist pathways. The requirement that students under the new arrangements have a more diverse range of practice experience will shift some of the practice that had gown up under the DipSW. Under this award there was no requirement that students would have placements with different client groups. It was possible under the DipSW regulations for students to choose to specialise at the start of their professional education and have all of their practice with one client group. Hence, the diversity occurred in the *setting rather than the client group* (for example, a student could have had two 'mental health' placements, one in a Community Mental Health Team and the other in a Residential Unit for Mentally Ill People). Under, the new arrangements students will be expected to experience a broader range of practice. These changes will have implications for the development of subsequent specialist practice, but until there are examples of the new arrangements readily available it will not be possible to determine the impact upon the development of specialism across the UK.

The key question is how *all* of these developments will affect the education and training of specialist practitioners. There is an apparent paradox. The world of practice is tending to become more specialised, evidenced if in no other way, by the nature of jobs advertised in the professional press. Yet, simultaneously, basic professional education appears to tending to the generalist – at least as far as can be surmised from the published requirements prior to the introduction and delivery of programmes under the new regulations. Moreover, embedded within the structure of the new regulations is the embryonic notion that basic professional education should be at undergraduate level, and that post basic professional education should lead to a masters level qualification. This structure resonates strongly with that in the US where there is a firm conceptual divide between the baccalaureate (undergraduate level) and the masters levels and there is a strong association between the level or type of job and qualification possessed. It remains to be seen whether in the UK such an association might develop. It would be dependent upon a more carefully thought out relationship between undergraduate and post-graduate qualifications in social work.

Unresolved at present is the relationship between new forms of basic professional practice and the integration of the developing number of post basic qualifications in social work (for example: AASW, the CCA, the ASWA and so on). To provide education for professional practice, at all levels, there will need to be a very clear approach to these issues. It is clear that the new professional qualification will have a greater emphasis than previously upon multi-professional working, especially across the health and social care divide (see for example Ministerial statement 22.05.02). Furthermore, the Department of Health has demonstrated its continuing commitment to reform post qualifying education in social work and in the Spring of 2003 launched a major review. Whatever the outcome of this review there will be a need for the basic professional qualification to educate social workers to work across other specialisms. Moreover, whatever new framework emerges as a result of the review process there will be a need for the basic professional qualification to address the need to educate social workers to work across specialisms.

In order to promote a positive approach to working together across specialisms, educators should consider the following:

- How are students who complete a specialist pathway made aware of practice within other social work specialisms in order to achieve a common understanding when working together?

- How are issues that affect specialist areas of practice taught to students so that they are aware of the importance of multi-specialist assessment, planning and intervention?

An Overview of the Contents of the Book - Outstanding Issues

The book is divided into two separate thematic sections. Part one consists of issues that can be found within a wide range of social work practice. For example, anyone of any age, in

any set of social circumstances, may have HIV/AIDS – albeit that certain groups within the population are at higher risk than others of contracting the HIV/AIDS. Likewise, anyone may be a carer, have a disability or be a substance abuser and so on. These are common and universal issues. Part two consists of a series of chapters that are concerned with particular groups of people, for example children, older people, people with mental ill-health and so on, and the forms of specialist practice that cohere around these groupings. Very often, there are specialist social workers employed by local authorities to work with people from each of these groupings. Hence, rather loosely these groupings might also represent some of the key traditional organisational structures (i.e. by client group), that are to be found within social work as provided by the state through the local authority. For example, fieldwork teams working with children and families. The final chapter in this part of the book is a little different to all of the others and discusses educational and training issues in respect of specialist practice.

Each chapter in the book is both particular and general in scope. Particular, in that the chapter refers to a given specialist area of practice and as a consequence the core issues that are central to that particular field of practice are explored. Moreover, each chapter approaches the subject matter slightly differently. Generally, in that all chapters raise a series of issues and questions that can be examined by the reader in relation to each of the other specialist areas of practice. Moreover, taken cumulatively the authors address a very wide range of issues and concerns about current and developing social work practice. The details of the chapters are as follows:

Chapter 2

Sally French, Maureen Gillman and John Swain examine the way in which society constructs 'chains' that bind and constrain disabled people, through institutional, structural, environmental and attitudinal discrimination. By addressing these forms of discrimination, in partnership with disabled people, social workers can, through an increased awareness of disability, challenge the 'chains that bind'. A key theme being to promote and enable disabled people's opportunities to exercise choice over their desired lifestyle: the authors suggest that this can be achieved through mechanisms such as goal clarification; identification and removal of barriers to goal achievement.

Chapter 3

Substance abuse may affect all individuals across society, whether as substance abusers themselves or as those who live with the consequences of abuse. Phillip Guy and Larry Harrison highlight the differences in the ways that people abuse substances (typified by what they term the mid point in the spectrum of substance abuse, i.e. the person who is employed but is a heavy drinker) and the evolving shifts in government policy towards those who abuse substances. They explore the use of motivational interviewing and the application of Prochaska and DiClemente's (1984) model of change (a model that resonates through several of the chapters in the book).

Chapter 4

Di Hart also explores some of the policy shifts that have occurred in the governmental response to the management of HIV/AIDS. She comments that one of the unique features of the development of services is that they have developed outside of mainstream provision – a consequence of the moral panic that accompanied the first recognition of the HIV/AIDS in the West. She presents a thorough and detailed picture of the way in which social services, health care and he voluntary sector are interlinked in the provision of services. A key moral issue that arises from practice concerns the maintenance of confidential information which is held by professionals about clients' lives. She concludes with a statement of the principles of good practice, based upon the need for; a clear local policy, a family focus, clear procedures, multi-agency working, participation and staff support.

Chapter 5

Caring for others is something that the majority of people will experience at some point in their lives. For some this is perceived as a normal part of the life-cycle, for others they may care for others for only brief periods during their lives. However, currently, there are a very significant number, according to Christine Heron, some 5.7 million who support others with social care needs. She charts, beginning in the 1980s the growth of the idea of carers having needs. Furthermore, she highlights that one of the most important services that carers need is the provision of high quality accurate information about available services to enable them to access those services that they may need. The mechanisms for the assessment of carer need and the recognition that carers are a very heterogeneous group are key themes – the implications for practice of 'career need' are explored in this chapter.

Chapter 6

Catherine Humphries and Audrey Mullender examine the nature of domestic violence and provide a very full account of the current state of the legislative framework that exists to protect, or otherwise, individuals from domestic violence. Despite the existence of this legislative framework the authors demonstrate how this issue is often invisible or ignored; although known about in a particular case it maybe treated 'informally' and not included in formal reports. Moreover abusers may appear highly plausible, to professionals. Most importantly, they highlight 'the direction of good practice' which should include key elements such as: the inter-agency context; careful monitoring and screening to ensure that domestic violence is not minimised or obscured; to avoid 'traps' in the way that assessments are conducted ; the promotion of joint working and the need for inter-agency training.

Chapter 7

This chapter is conceptually close to the previous chapter in that it concerns those adults who are vulnerable and who may be abused or neglected. Yet, work in the field of abuse of vulnerable adults has developed as a conceptually distinct specialism. As in the case of several other specialist areas, it is only relatively recently (i.e. during the 1990s) that professional interest in protecting vulnerable adults has developed as a specialist area. Moreover, there is no significant legislative framework in existence to protect adults (see for example Williams, 2002). Bridget Penhale and Jonathan Parker explore the meaning of abuse of vulnerable adults and examine notions of prevention – particularly using Browne and Herbert's (1997) tripartite typology of prevention. From this base the authors develop a framework for protection, identifying the elements that are currently present; this includes the importance of professional education; the need for public accountability; national guidance and collaboration across specialist boundaries. They discuss some practice dilemmas and examples of good practice. One ethical issue that impinges strongly upon this area of practice is the need for a balance between protecting the individual at all costs yet preserving individual dignity and the right to be self-determining.

Chapter 8

This is the first chapter in the second part of the book. In this part of the book we focus upon more specific areas of specialist practice. Jan Horwath begins by tracing the development of legislative policy and practice shifts on the delivery of child protection services; it is impossible to understand this area of practice without a full account of these historical changes. Work with children and families is one area of specialist practice in which inter-disciplinary work across professional boundaries is institutionalised and required by government – as operationalised through the *Framework for the Assessment of Children in Need and Their Families*. The author describes the operation of this framework and then explores ways in which child protection issues interact with a range of other areas of specialist practice such as substance abuse, learning difficulties and so on. This leads to important discussions about assessment and intervention and how

specialists and non-specialists can work together in this area of practice.

Chapter 9

Charlotte Knight reveals the centrality of the assessment process in work with offenders. A very structured approach to assessment is one of the characteristics of this area of work. Current social work practice is strongly influenced by evidence-based practice. In the context of work with offenders this may be characterised as the 'what works' movement. Central to good practice in this area of work is the identification of a programme of intervention for each offender that will minimise the risk of future offending. The author discusses the nature of risk and how a range of assessment tools can be used with offenders. As might be expected, practice with offenders places the practitioner in situations where the resolution of moral and practice issues deriving from, *consent*, *voluntarism* and *coercion* are central to good practice.

Chapter 10

Sam Mello-Baron, Aileen Moore and Ian Moore have forcefully located the construction of mental health practice within the contested contexts of government policy and broader ideological constructions about the meaning and nature of mental health. The chapter reveals and explores the diversity of need amongst those with mental ill health - the challenge being to respond appropriately to those who require compulsory institutional care as well as those, a much large number, whose symptoms are less severe, and who pose no danger to themselves or others and who can and do live with the support of others in the community. Fundamental to mental health practice is the Care Programme Approach (CPA) – the nature of this approach is explored, its correspondence with care management and most importantly the multi-professional structures that embrace this approach and make it viable.

Chapter 11

Roy McConkey and Theresa Nixon examine the meaning of learning disability making clear that it is no 'unitary form' of disability. They employ the social model of disability, elaborated in chapter two, as a basis for the need to re-conceptualise learning disability. The authors review the range of services available to people with learning disability throughout the life span before reviewing the particular contribution made by social workers to the field of learning disability – it should not be forgotten that a range of other professionals are actively involved in this field and that working across specialisms is also concerned with working with other professional groups. The particular contribution that the authors identify from social work is concerned with: person-centred planning; care management; multi-disciplinary working; protection of vulnerable adults; carer support and in the case of offenders with learning disability acting as an 'appropriate adult'.

Chapter 12

Ageism is a pervasive and pernicious influence in our society. Stephen Pugh exposes the impact of ageism in a most illuminating manner by exploring the different experiences of those who belong to different 'age cohorts' and yet might be placed into the category of being regarded as 'older people' by others. This analysis is further developed to reveal the differences of experience according to gender and sexuality. Building upon this analysis the author examines some of the current debates in respect of the provision of care for older people and identifies some of the most important themes, including; the emergence of a contract culture; the dichotomy over the provision of support in the home or through residential care and the importance of developing an rights based approach to social work with older people.

Chapter 13

The final chapter of the book is a little different to the other chapters in that it does not explore one particular specialist area of practice. Rather, Jan Horwath and Steven Shardlow pose the questions as to how far professional education can help overcome the obstacles to working across specialist boundaries. They

take a series of exercises designed, in partnership with several of the authors within the book, to reveal some of the complexities of work across specialist boundaries. These exercises can be used as they are or adapted to meet more specific educational needs.

Throughout the book, a number of themes emerge consistently across different chapters. First, Sally French, Maureen Gillman and John Swain explore issues of disability in so doing the authors, in their analysis, emphasize the importance of structural issues to promote an understanding of current policy and practice. They make a powerful argument for the development of a model of disability that takes full account of the social construction of disability and the consequences that such an understanding imposes upon the nature of service provision. Their analysis should remind us that each of the forms of specialist practice within the book needs to be fully located within its unique and particular structural context. For example, the introductory section of the chapter by Sam Mello-Baron, Eileen Moore and Ian Moore contains a very full discussion of the policy context of the specialist practice in respect of mental health, all specialist areas of practice should be fully located in their policy context. If the level of detailed analysis that you, the reader, require is not to be found in each chapter then apply the arguments found in this chapter to other areas of specialism. Some authors have concentrated more upon the practice issues rather than the structural. Second no doubt, one of the most difficult aspects of practice for specialists is to make assessments and to exercise professional judgement outside of the boundaries of their specialism. Throughout the book, the authors have provided a range of insights into the way that specialists in particular areas formulate their assessments. There is much that is common – nonetheless, there is also much that is different. A third major issue that permeates the book concerns how specialist practitioners may differently or similarly approach the identification and management of risk. This is a highly contentious aspect of professional practice and one where individual practitioners have been vulnerable, to post hoc counter factual statements suggesting that they ought to have acted differently to the way that they did - especially for example in respect of failures in child protection practice. However, risk is equally prevalent in other areas of practice, for example: vulnerable older people living alone in the community; the management of people who abuse substances; the risk to community in allowing offenders to remain within community rather than be punished elsewhere; the risk within the family of one member abusing another. Bridget Penhale and Jonathon Parker take risk to be the key element of social work, as they suggest, 'social work gains its meaning from its role within protection'. The approach to risk is one of the defining features of specialist practice. It is because specialists are finely attuned by experience and knowledge to the primary constituents of risk within the given area of practice that they are able to make pertinent and reasoned judgements about the level of risk in any particular case. However, they are equally unlikely to fully appreciate the subtle gradations of risk in respect of other areas of professional practice. Herein lies a danger of specialist practice, in that risk outside of the specialist's own area may not be fully recognised. Even if it is recognized, the specialist may not have the knowledge about risk management in other areas of practice.

Debate about the nature of specialist practice will continue, as will debate about specialists can work together to promote better practice. This book is a contribution to those debates.

Chapter 2

Disabling Chains and Enabling Links

Sally French, Maureen Gillman and John Swain

Introduction

Oliver and Sapey state:

> ...the major criticism is that social workers, like all other professionals, have largely operated with inappropriate models or theories of disability.
>
> (1999: p12.)

This criticism, which is the fundamental challenge to the provision of social work for disabled people, provides the focal point for this chapter. We begin by contrasting the individual model of disability with the social model. The former has dominated current practice in the field with disabled people, their families and carers. Within this orientation, the adjustment of the individual to their limitations, the assessment (by professionals) of needs, and the provision of interventions aimed to care for or cure the individual have underpinned policy and practice.

By contrast, the development of the social model, with its roots firmly within the burgeoning Disabled People's Movement, has provided the most significant alternative perspective. From this orientation, people with impairments are disabled by the barriers they face in a physical and social environment produced by and geared for non-disabled people. The experiences of disabled people are understood in terms of institutional discrimination, which denies disabled people access to full participation and citizenship in society. It is a viewpoint that has offered a basis for analysing recent developments in social work practice in respect of disability and the changing legal, economic and political context. The social model offers, in addition, a basis for an overall evaluation of the significance of recent changes. We conclude the chapter by arguing that, the social model of disability, offers central principles of good practice, through which specialists can work together with disabled people towards the empowerment of disabled people.

The Chains of Disability

In this part of the chapter, we will explore the ways in which conceptions of disability are translated into practice and restrict and confine the lives of disabled people. We will first look at two major and conflicting models of disability and then we will turn to the concept of institutional discrimination.

Models of disability

The individual model of disability is based upon the assumption that the problems and difficulties disabled people experience are a direct result of their individual impairments (Swain et al., 1993). This view has been promoted by the health and welfare professions and is often referred to as the 'medical model of disability'. In this model disability is viewed in terms of disease process, abnormality, and personal tragedy, with the assumption that both the problems disabled people experience and the solutions lie within disabled people themselves – rather than within society. This view is seen to operate in the medically based assessments that are used by most health and welfare professionals. Ryan and Thomas state that:

> Medical model thinking tends to support the status quo. The subnormality of the individual rather than the subnormality of the environment tend to be blamed for any inadequacies.
>
> (1987: p27.)

In direct contrast, the social model of disability has emerged from the collective experience and views of disabled people themselves. Whereas from the individual model, disability is viewed as stemming from the functional limitations of impaired individuals, disabled people believe that their difficulties stem from the failure of the social and physical environment to take account of their needs and rights. Disabled people's views constitute a social model of disability, where the problems are seen, not within the individual disabled person, but within society (Oliver, 1990). Thus, for example, the physically impaired person is not disabled by lack of muscle strength or balance but by inaccessible buildings, rigid work practices and patronising attitudes. Finkelstein (1981) has argued that non-disabled people would be equally disabled if the environment was not designed with their needs in mind. The social model of disability, though recognising numerous barriers, is liberating to many disabled people as it locates the problems they encounter within society where change is possible.

The social model of disability has broken the accepted causal link between impairment and disability. This can be seen in the definition of impairment and disability provided by The Union of the Physically Impaired Against Segregation (UPIAS):

> *Impairment*
> *Lacking part or all of a limb or having a defective limb, organ or mechanism of the body.*
>
> *Disability*
> *The disadvantage or restriction of activity caused by a contemporary social organisation which takes no or little account of people who have physical impairments and thus excludes them from the mainstream of social activities.*
>
> (UPIAS, 1976: p14.)

The word 'physical' is now frequently excluded from this definition so as to include people with learning difficulties and those who experience mental distress. With the growing influence of the Disabled People's Movement and the persistent demand for civil rights from disabled people over the past twenty years, the social model of disability has gradually become more influential leading to the passing of the first Disability Discrimination Act in the United Kingdom in 1995. The Act, at least in principle, establishes new rights for disabled people in the area of employment rights in respect of the provision of goods and services, and buying and renting land and property. Employers are expected to take 'reasonable measures' to ensure that they are not discriminating against disabled people. The legislation is complex with many caveats. Oliver and Barnes note that:

> *The Act gives only limited protection from direct discrimination…because not all disabled people are covered by the Act and employers and service providers are exempt if they can show that compliance would damage their business.*
>
> (1998: p90.)

Although the legislation is weak, with numerous exemptions, Gooding (1995) describes its introduction as 'a fundamental shift'. The Act provides the most comprehensive anti-discrimination legislation in the UK to date but it does not amount to full civil rights legislation. The Act is full of loopholes and phrases such as 'if it is reasonable' and ill-defined words such as 'substantial'. Cost can be taken into account as well as health and safety regulations. It is not as robust as the Sex Discrimination Act (1975) or the Race Relations Act (1976) and has been dubbed the 'Doesn't Do Anything Act', by disabled people themselves (Trade Union Disability Alliance, 1997).

It is therefore, legal to discriminate against disabled people and discrimination can be justified, for example by employers, in ways that cannot be justified in the Sex Discrimination Act and Race Relations Act. A major limitation of the Act is that there has been no commission, i.e. no body to take up people's complaints. A commission, comparable to those of the Sex Discrimination Act and Race Relations Act was, however, put in place in April 2000.

Institutional discrimination

Institutional discrimination can be defined as:

> *Unfair or unequal treatment of individuals or groups which is built into institutional organisations, policies and practices at personal, environmental and structural levels.*
>
> (Swain et al., 1998: p5.)

The notion of institutional discrimination has played an important role in the development of theories of disability. It is also a concept that links the experiences of people from minority or oppressed groups together (Thompson, 1997). Disabled people face institutional discrimination in a social and physical world that is produced by and geared for non-disabled people. This prevents their full access to and participation within organisations and the wider society.

Institutional discrimination can be understood in terms of attitudinal, environmental and structural barriers. Attitudinal barriers are constructed from environmental barriers which, in turn, are founded on structural barriers. Essential to understanding discrimination as being institutionalised is to reject individualised, or victim blaming explanations of unjust treatment.

The structural level of discrimination

Institutional discrimination is founded on the social divisions within society and, in particular, hierarchical power relationships between groups (for example disabled and non-disabled people). Inequalities in the distribution of resources (particularly economic) underpin hierarchical relations, with many disabled people being marginalised from open employment and condemned to poverty. At a structural level, institutional discrimination is built into British society in what might be called the macro-systems, for example, the economy, education, employment and welfare.

Poverty underlies the marginalisation of disabled people within the UK. For many disabled people poverty is central to the substantially poorer quality of life they experience compared to the rest of the population. The statistics from a succession of surveys (such as Burchardt, 2000) highlight considerable disadvantage. The statistics in relation to income testify not only to the high levels of unemployment among disabled people but also to substantial underemployment. In her paper analysing the employment opportunities for visually disabled people, French (1998) documents statistics from two surveys showing that visually disabled people in employment are far less likely (approximately 70%) to be in professional jobs than non-disabled people.

Explanations of unemployment, underemployment and poverty can focus on all three levels of discrimination – structural, environmental and attitudinal. Oliver (1991) argues, however, that disabled people are primarily excluded from labour market participation because of changes in the work

process that occurred with the coming of industrialised capitalist society. The crucial importance of the structural level is emphasised, too, by Finkelstein (1993) who believes that low levels of employment and lack of participation in the creation of social wealth is 'the predominant factor' in the creation of disability.

The environmental level of discrimination

At the environmental level, discrimination is encountered by disabled people in their daily interactions with the physical world of non-disabled aids and physical barriers, such as cars parked on the pavement, the placement of furniture in a classroom, lack of parking spaces, curbs and so on. The picture is complex in that the needs of disabled people are diverse (for instance, lack of curbs is problematic for blind people who use them to differentiate the road from the pavement).

Institutionalised discrimination is experienced by disabled people when they encounter so-called 'public' buildings, transport and facilities which they cannot enter, cannot use, or provide so-called 'special' provision and 'special' backdoor arrangements. Shops, 'public' houses and restaurants, theatres and cinemas, sport and leisure venues, town halls and law courts – the list of inaccessible buildings is well known to many disabled people. Furthermore, inaccessible housing is a key barrier to 'independent living'; it has been estimated that a quarter of a million people with physical impairments are inadequately housed and there is much evidence that large numbers of disabled people are excluded from many transport systems (Liberty, 1994).

Ideologies of normality and independence are inherent in the construction of disabling barriers within the environment – with little account being taken of human diversity. These ideologies are manifest in all the rules, regulations, patterns of behaviour, social organisation and aids to daily living that marginalise disabled people from the mainstream of society. Wendell states that:

> *Much architecture has been planned with a young adult, non-disabled male paradigm of humanity in mind. In addition aspects of social organisation that*

take for granted the social expectations of performance and productivity, such as inadequate public transportation…communication systems that are inaccessible to people with visual or hearing impairments, and inflexible work arrangements that exclude part-time work or rest periods, create much disability.   (1996: p40.)

The attitudinal level of discrimination

Attitudinal discrimination refers to negative feelings, beliefs and behaviours (including stereotyping) of non-disabled and disabled people towards disabled people such as staring and overprotection. Attitudes are complex. They are generally seen as having three components: i.e. a cognitive component, that is knowledge and understanding of disability; an emotional component, i.e. the feelings provoked by disabled people; and a behavioural component, i.e. how people act and react towards disabled people.

Attitudes are complicated further, because there is a loose connection among these three components; our understanding, our feelings and what we do about things do not necessarily relate closely to each other. Nevertheless, each of the three components is seen to play a part in negative attitudes. A negative attitude towards a deaf person might include a lack of understanding about deafness, fear of deaf people and negative labelling which may, in turn, lead to discrimination in, for example, social services or employment. Professionals, including those in the health, welfare and education fields, are seen as possible contributors to such attitudes in that they further a specific medical or individual model of disability (Swain and Lawrence, 1994).

Disability as personal tragedy

The literature written by disabled people testifies time and again to what we regard as the most fundamental challenge to non-disabled people generally and those who work with disabled people in particular: i.e. for many disabled people disability is not a personal tragedy but may, on the contrary, enhance life or provide a lifestyle of equal satisfaction and worth (Swain and French, 2000). The following are two examples from many we could have chosen:

As a result of becoming paralysed life has changed completely. Before my accident it seems as if I was set to spend the rest of my life as a religious sister, but I was not solemnly professed so was not accepted back into the order. Instead, I am now very happily married with a home of my own.

(Morris, 1989: p120.)

I cannot wish that I had never contracted ME because it has made me a different person, a person I am glad to be, would not want to have missed being and could not relinquish even if I were 'cured'.

(Wendell, 1996: p83.)

Yet, the dominant view of disability in our society is that it is a personal tragedy. The policies, practices and interventions of non-disabled people are justified and rationalised by this non-disabled view of personal tragedy. The tragedy is to be avoided, eradicated or non-disabled (normalised) by all possible means. As Wendell states:

This is reflected in the assumption that potential disability is a sufficient reason for aborting a foetus, as well as in the frequent statements by non-disabled people that they would not want to live if they had to use a wheelchair, lost their eyesight, were dependent on others for care, and so on.

(1996: p54.)

The erroneous idea that disabled people cannot be happy, or enjoy an adequate quality of life, lies at the heart of this response. The disabled person's problems are perceived to result from impairment rather than the failure of society to meet that person's needs in terms of appropriate human help and accessibility of facilities.

In this section, we have touched on some of the barriers that deny disabled people access to organisations and society generally. In understanding the construction of institutional discrimination, it is important to recognise the integral nature of the barriers. Segregated education, inaccessible transport, inaccessible 'public' buildings, unemployment and underemployment all reinforce each other and are cemented through ideologies of normality and independence (Swain and French, 1998). Furthermore, from the viewpoint of disabled people, help in its various forms of charity, welfare and professional intervention, can itself be part of institutional discrimination. Wendell expresses this succinctly:

Disability is also socially constructed by the failure to give people the amount and kind of help they need to participate fully in all the major aspects of life in society.

(1996: p40.)

Disabled writers have consistently argued that such participation begins essentially with disabled people having control over the kind and amount of help they receive (see for example, Morris, 1993; French, 1994).

In the next section, we focus our analysis on professional help. We concentrate mainly on social work, but in general terms our analysis is applicable to all types of professional intervention.

Constructing and Deconstructing Chains

The 1980s and 1990s have witnessed massive changes to the profession of social work. The imposition of a competency based paradigm upon social work education and training, the attack upon its value base, and the permeation of market forces (in the form of privatisation of services) have all contributed to the devaluation and dilution of anti-oppressive practice. The drive towards social work as a profession has led to what Hugman describes as:

...the separation of ideological and technical control...In the growth of hierarchies the caring professions have maintained their technical autonomy at the expense of ideological control through the objectives of the employing agency. Technical control becomes unnecessary because in this process the goals of the professionals become subordinated to those of the organisation.

(1991: p81.)

The reorganisation of social work training in the 1980s saw the introduction of competency based learning and assessment. Dominelli suggests that:

Competencies in social work are a set of highly technical, decontextualised practice skills which can be broken down into smaller and smaller constituent parts that can be carried out by personnel trained to a specific level.

(1996: p154.)

The following are some consequences of competency based training:

- It fragments and reduces social interaction and social problems.

- It reduces social work to a set of performance criteria.

- The breaking down of competencies into smaller and smaller elements allows less highly qualified individuals to take on social work tasks for less pay. Those tasks have traditionally been associated with the provision of services to older people and disabled people (see, for instance, the different levels of assessment offered within the NHS and Community Care Act 1990).

- There is less space for professionals to exercise flexibility, autonomy or discretion.

- It separates out various forms of oppression and adopts an individualistic approach. Individual workers and users of services address oppression only as it is experienced by an individual.

These structural changes to the education of social workers have implications for the kinds of service that disabled people receive. Such an approach reduces social work to a formulaic activity in which both the worker and the service user are disempowered.

Values, which are central to the practice of social work, have also been under attack, and there has been a change of emphasis from social justice and anti-oppressive practice to an equal opportunities approach to discrimination. This is evident in the revised version of the Diploma in Social Work (CCETSW, 1995) which Vass asserts:

...curtailed references to anti-discriminatory and anti-racist practice and focused, instead, on an Equal Opportunities statement limited to four paragraphs. It redefined the purpose, knowledge, values and skills of the profession.

(1996: p3-4.)

These developments, together with the development of competency based training, were associated with the individualisation of problems and interventions. The individual approach to discrimination is antithetical to that of the social model of disability that promotes collective action against oppression and the fight for civil rights. Such moves in the development of the social work profession represent a serious threat to the goals of disabled people to work in partnership with social workers to combat institutional disablism.

Disabled social workers

Institutional discrimination is experienced by disabled people as professionals as well as clients. Many disabled people have experienced institutional discrimination when attempting to gain entry to social work training (James and Thomas, 1996; Baron et al., 1996). Once qualified, some disabled social workers have had to overcome significant barriers to employment and promotion (French, 1988). Much has been written about the institutionalised racism and sexism that excludes women and black people from the higher echelons of social work management. In contrast very little has been written about the discrimination experienced by disabled professionals. In French et al. (1997) there is a case study of Alan Dudley who is blind and a senior social worker. The barriers he faced began in gaining access to training when he received ten rejections before he was offered a place on a course. Once qualified he had similar difficulties finding a job. He said:

> I was told by many local authorities 'Well if you want to work with blind people we'll offer you a job, but if you don't, we're not prepared to.' I can actually remember crying tears of frustration over this issue.
> (1997: p57.)

This is compatible to the findings of French's study of the experiences of disabled health and welfare professionals. She concluded:

> A sizeable minority…had experienced some degree of negative discrimination either as a result of their colleagues' attitudes or lack of understanding. Most of these problems occurred when attempting to gain access to training and during training.   (1988: p584.)

Baron et al. found that there were many disabling barriers to recruitment and training on the Diploma in Social Work programmes. They state that:

> A lack of experience of disability issues was evident as well as the absence of an active approach to arrange support at all levels of the programme…
> (1996: p175.)

James and Thomas (1996) undertook a programme to give greater prominence to work with disabled people on a Diploma in Social Work course and to attract more disabled students to social work training. They found that many practice teachers in voluntary and statutory settings were reluctant to recruit disabled students and cited fire regulations, or the fear that they would be vulnerable to violent or aggressive clients as justifications. It is clear that discrimination and oppression occurs (albeit sometimes unintentionally or subconsciously) within professionals' own agencies and is embedded within such everyday practices as student recruitment and training.

This case study illustrates many aspects of institutional disablism and oppression of disabled people at a variety of levels. At the structural level, the social support required by disabled people is regarded by the local authority as 'special needs' rather than civil rights. Dominant discourses, such as prioritisation and assessment of need, are used by the workers to carry out the local authority's role of distributing resources, and denying many disabled people resources needed to live an ordinary life.

Case vignette: A Local Authority Community Care Team

We will now provide a brief synopsis of a Local Authority community care team, which works with people over the age of eighteen years, who require assistance that falls within the remit of the NHS and Community Care Act. The account is based on a group interview with members of staff working as part of the team. Team members include qualified social workers, social service officers (SSOs), a team leader and occupational therapists who also work with other teams in the borough. The role of the team is to carry out assessments of need within the community, which includes the allocation of a range of domiciliary services, day, residential and respite care. The team operates a 'care management process' which, Dave, the team leader suggests is:

> …to carry out assessments within the community. To produce an assessment document which identifies the needs people have and which they receive a copy to keep. Then to produce a care plan that shows how those needs are going

to be met, or sometimes not going to be met. We implement the care plan...monitor that care plan to see whether services are appropriate and then... review the care plan and make changes.

There is a much higher proportion of unqualified staff in the community care teams compared to the child care and mental health teams. One member of the team, Ann, commented:

There is quite a big emphasis on unqualified staff in these teams and I think it is changing even more so to that...most of the short term workers are the SSOs and the long term workers are social workers, so I would agree that most of the time we try to put the cases where the skills are. It's often the case of whoever has time to do it and sometimes they are taking on things that are unseen. In an ideal world they may not have been asked to do that at all.

There is a degree of ambivalence in the team about the introduction of the care management system. Some of the criticisms include the erosion of the social work role and the reduction in staff coupled with the raised expectations of the public in relation to community care. Another concern stems from the current emphasis on individual assessments and care plans which have restricted social work activity, such as representing the views of oppressed groups within the community. Dave said:

We don't meet with groups as much as we used to and put forward their ideas. It is not seen so much as a social work task now. The social work task is to assess people.

Others in the team felt that service users do not understand the care plans that are drawn up by the professionals but are prepared to 'sign anything' in order to get assistance or services. In addition, care plans are not produced in a form accessible to some visually impaired people. Ann made the point that although the team members have received training in producing care plans, the users had not:

...they don't know why we are writing something in here...You get them signed and that means that they have agreed to it, but I think that people in that situation will often sign anything because they're pretty desperate, they want some services. I know that I often don't explain fully and if you ask people where their care plan is the majority don't know. I think it is about the professional side thinking that you have to have a nice piece of paper.

The positive aspects of care planning identified by the team included the notion that it makes workers more accountable for what they write about service users, it directs the worker's attention towards certain aspects of a person's life, and it provides workers with clearer parameters around entitlement to assessment, assistance and services.

There is no restriction on the size of workload carried by each worker but staff are encouraged to close cases or to pass them on to long term workers as soon as possible. Bombardment of work is managed by a priority system drawn up by the local authority. Cases are categorised according to these priorities by the team leaders. The team leader explains:

Priority one represents a situation where the situation has collapsed or is about to collapse imminently and you are required to provide some kind of care package where they would be safe and secure in their own home, and be fed, or provide them with residential or nursing care because their carer has become ill. Priority two is a situation which is going to break down and should be dealt with, in theory, within two weeks...Cases in priority one and two get done, because they have to be. Priority three is supposed to be dealt with within twenty days and it is where people could use some help – the classic is assistance with bathing – it may require a bath board and seat and rails. We all accept that they need that but it is not life and death, it is not urgent and you could have a sponge down anyway – it's not me saying this you understand – but that's it, and priority four don't get done.

An example of a request that would be categorised as priority four is, according to Ann 'for equipment that would improve their quality of life'. Another would be a request for help with managing bills.

The team was aware of changes in legislation to allow disabled people to receive direct payments, so that they can organise their own personal assistance. Ann is currently working with someone who has requested direct payment:

I'm working with a person who is going to be one of the first to get direct payment...The feeling from consumers is that the majority don't want to take it on. I don't think it is going to be a lot of people who want that sort of control because they feel it is going to be too much bother. The biggest problem the council seem to have with it is how do they monitor it? What's been spent and where?

The offices occupied by the community care team are not open to the public and personal callers are discouraged. The building is inaccessible to some disabled people and the staff are unaware of any potential employees who might have been prevented or discouraged from working there. Service users can contact staff by telephone but their initial requests for assistance must be made to a 'customer service centre' in the borough. Some of these centres are not accessible to disabled people. Dave, who is blind, said:

In terms of people who can't see very well, many of the buildings are difficult to find. There are no signs up there that could identify this is the council office. You have to ask for that and even when you get into them, someone has to tell you where the queue starts and ends and you rely on people to tell you when the queue is moving.

Access to information about services is limited. While some information is available to visually impaired people on audiotape, very little is available in braille or produced in large print. The borough does employ interpreters for deaf people but they are not easily accessible because they are so much in demand. Some of the staff in the team has expressed an interest in learning to sign but no offer of training has been forthcoming. Laura felt that the local authority was no longer interested in supporting requests for professional development per se but prioritised training needs that supported service delivery.

There has been a devaluation and dilution of anti-oppressive practice and the subordination of the profession's goals to those of the organisation (in this case the local authority). As Dave pointed out, social workers are no longer allowed to represent the collective voice of disabled people in their community, and professional practices/organisational procedures, such as individual care plans, prevent social workers from intervening at a community or societal level. Professional autonomy and discretion have, therefore, been reduced.

On the other hand, it could be argued that the diminution of professional power allows disabled people more freedom to organise their own care. The introduction of direct payments to disabled people is one example. Oliver and Zarb (1992) found that disabled people who received direct payment had more freedom to participate in employment and leisure activities of their choice. They could arrange to receive the kind of help they wanted at a time that would fit with their requirement and schedules. Such flexibility allowed disabled people to follow the lifestyles of their choice. From his research with the Derbyshire Centre for Integrated Living, however, Priestley (1999) suggests that some disabled people require support in managing

their own package of financial support, such as the information, advocacy and peer support provided by organisations of disabled people.

The notion that personal assistance should be provided by trained and qualified personnel has also been challenged by disabled people:

I'm not looking for professional qualifications, nurses are definitely out, I'm looking for people who are enthusiastic...I want to train them in my own way.

(Morris, 1991: p32.)

As long as local authorities retain the right to determine the needs of disabled people and how these are to be met, there will always be tensions between social workers and disabled people. Social work practices such as interpretation of legislation and assessment of need are used in the service of distributing scarce resources. Oliver and Sapey argue that social workers should adopt strategies such as empowerment and self-assessment in order to support disabled people to achieve their goals. In addition, they suggest that social workers should adopt the position of:

...determined advocate...(which) implies not making judgements about whether the request...is correct to some normative criteria, but to advocate...without reservation. This is not to relinquish any form of

professional judgement…the advice and experience of the social worker may be of immense value in helping disabled people develop their strategies in self-assessment.

(Oliver and Sapey, 1999: p181.)

Counselling skills may also be employed in the service of enabling disabled people to overcome disabling barriers or to counteract painful and oppressive experiences at the hands of a disabling society. However, counselling disabled people to 'come to terms' with the 'limitations' of their impairments or the lack of resources to achieve a desired lifestyle are inappropriate if social workers wish to practice within the social model of disability.

At the environmental level disabled people are discriminated against on a number of fronts. Local authority reorganisation within the borough has led to the dismantling of the old social service department into a number of 'functions', community care being one of fifteen. In the past, service users had access to their local social services office. Now, the local offices are not open to the public. Social workers appear to have become distanced from their local community. Such measures seem to be a way of managing bombardment of demand. Laura[1] explained that, in addition, reorganisation has meant that much of the information about location of services is out of date:

We get a lot of calls on duty where people have accessed five or six numbers for the information that they needed because there has been so many changes in procedures and departments over the past four years.

This case study demonstrates that the thinking of those who have power to plan and implement policy is not influenced by awareness of disabling barriers, or of practices that exclude and marginalise disabled people. Institutional disablism is embedded within such organisations and is evident in the design and implementation of policies based on the assumption that consumers are non-disabled.

The case study also highlights the environmental barriers experienced by disabled people who wish to work in such organisation, or who would like to train as social workers. James and Thomas (1996) argue that disablist culture permeates and influences both education and employment organisations. They go on to say that:

…there are subtle connections too between the culture of an organisation, especially in relation to its employment practices and its service delivery. It is doubtful that a lack of commitment to one will allow a full flowering of the other. This seems to hold good for both educational institutions and providers of social services.

(1996: p45.)

Discrimination at an attitudinal level can be identified within this case study. Within the profession of social work, working with disabled people is not perceived as high status work. Stevens observes:

Where social workers have expressed a preference for work within particular client specialisms they have most often chosen to work with children or offenders or to do mental health work rather than work with elders or people with learning difficulties or a physical disability. (1992: p12.)

As the team leader observed, the staff in the community care team are perceived by their colleagues as '…carrying less complex cases', a view that is disputed by the team members. Research also indicates that the proportion of unqualified staff in such teams is higher than those teams working with children and families (Burke, 1990). Moreover, career development opportunities and promotion prospects are also poor (James and Thomas, 1996). Others have noted that the workforce within these teams is predominantly female, with a much higher proportion of men working in the high profile areas of child protection and mental health (Hugman, 1991; Dominelli, 1996). Here the dominant discourse of women as carers is inextricably bound up with the medical model of disability that perceives disabled people as in need of care.

These attitudes to disability are also reflected in the curriculum of professional social work training where disability issues are marginalised. In 1991, CCETSW expressed concern that:

…disability will be seen by courses as of marginal special interest because of the small numbers of students currently wishing to opt for work with disabled people.

(1991: p20.)

Recent research seems to suggest that this is the current state of affairs within DipSW

---

1.   See case vignette above.

programmes. Baron et al. found that, all the DipSW programmes in their survey, allocated CCETSW's minimum requirement of two days to disability issues and that:

> *...the compartmentalisation of disability in the timetable led to tutors seeing it as having been 'covered' and therefore not an issue to be discussed in other aspects of the curriculum.*
>
> (1996: p370.)

Linking Specialisms to Break Chains

While professionals may feel constrained by their agency role or the administrative procedures required in carrying out an assessment, there usually remains some degree of flexibility in which professionals can look for opportunities to work in partnership with disabled people. For example, professionals can share power by sharing 'expert' knowledge and information. They can also encourage clients to actively participate in the writing of reports and case files so that their voices are heard and their viewpoints represented in 'official' documents.

Information about services and resources should also be in an accessible format for disabled people. Visually impaired people may, for example, require large print or audiotape and people with learning difficulties may communicate best through pictures and symbols. Social workers should examine their own information sources for clients for evidence of discrimination against disabled people. Raising the awareness of those who produce leaflets, forms and so on within their own agencies is a legitimate role for social workers working within a social model of disability.

Awareness of disability by all those who work in social services departments can be encouraged and developed through disability equality training which is run by highly trained disabled people. Disability equality training:

> *Is primarily about changing the meaning of disability from individual tragedy to social oppression; it emphasises the politics of disability, the social and physical barriers that disabled people face, and the links with other oppressed groups.*
>
> (French, 1996: p121.)

This is in contrast to disability awareness training which attempts to facilitate awareness in non-disabled people of what it is like to be disabled.

Such training is characterised by simulation exercises in which non-disabled people are required to use wheelchairs or wear blindfolds in the hope that this will help them understand the experiences of disabled people. This approach has been criticised by those who adhere to the social model of disability (see for example, Swain and Lawrence,1994) on the grounds that it concentrates on individual impairment rather than disabling barriers and that it ignores the fact that disabled people develop skills and strategies which the blindfolded non-disabled person would not possess. There is also little evidence to suggest that disability awareness changes attitudes (French, 1996).

Another way in which specialist and non-specialist staff can work in partnership is by recognising and acknowledging the disabled person's expertise in relation to the meaning and experience of being disabled. This means encouraging disabled people to exercise choice of services appropriate to their desired lifestyles. Social personnel can work in partnership with disabled people by seeing themselves as a resource (expertise, information, advocacy) so that clients can work towards achieving their desired lifestyles. This would include:

- Clarifying the goals to which the disabled person aspires.
- Identifying the barriers which may prevent the realisation of those goals.
- Working towards removing the barriers.

Social workers and managers can actively encourage disabled people to become involved in forums where they can influence the development of relevant services. This includes ensuring that meetings are held in accessible venues and that disabled people are not excluded by lack of transport or inappropriate mediums of communication.

At a wider level, the expertise of disabled people should be allowed to influence the development of services. However, Finkelstein and Stuart observe that:

> *Disabled people and their organisations are still almost completely absent from any real decision making in the planning and delivery of services or public utilities that they may use...Information about appropriate services then, arising out of the experience and perspective of disabled peoples' lifestyles, is very limited.* (1996: p171.)

Social workers, as well as non-specialist staff, need to consider how they and their agencies respond to those people who belong to more than one oppressed group. Many disabled people are, for example, elderly and experience the simultaneous oppressions of ageism and disablism. There is evidence to suggest that elderly, visually impaired people are given low priority in relation to mobility training (Bruce et al., 1991) based on the ageist assumption that elderly people do not go out very much. Black disabled people have also been given low priority in health and welfare services (French and Vernon, 1997).

From the perspective of the social model of disability, professional power should be used to highlight the shortfall in resources for disabled people, to ensure that the subjugated voices of disabled people are heard and responded to, and to encourage and support people to assert themselves so that their expertise about disability is at the centre of the development of services and support. It is important that social workers and all other staff in social services departments make a conscious decision to heighten their awareness of disability as an area of enquiry.

Social workers should be aware of the possibility that any client may be disadvantaged, during interviews and the process of assessment, by the assumption that the client is non-disabled. Some disabilities are not obvious and many disabled people have found ways of concealing or denying their disabilities because of the prejudice and discrimination they have experienced in the past. It is not always possible or appropriate to hand over the case to a specialised worker, especially when the reason for the referral is not the person's disability (for example, a child protection or mental health issue). On the subject of visual disability, James and Thomas argue that:

> *Visual disability occurs in all groups in society. This suggests that all social workers should undergo some basic instruction on working with visually disabled people. The case is stronger still for those choosing to work with old people or where management is the intended career.*
>
> (1996: p37.)

Disability may not be the major focus of social work intervention but ignoring it may seriously inhibit the possibilities for working in partnership

Conclusion

Professionals, and all who work with disabled people, need to become informed about disability in its widest sense and about the many factors which constitute institutional discrimination. Such an understanding can, to some extent, be achieved through professional education and a non-disabling ethos within professional organisations. The dismantling of institutional discrimination is such, however, that people working towards this goal on their own are unlikely to succeed.

Anti-oppressive practice requires social workers, and all those who work with them, to move away from the traditional casework approach to 'helping' and to work with a much broader brief. They need to join forces with the Disabled People's Movement and to use their professional power in collaboration and partnership with disabled people to dismantle every aspect of institutional disablism to further the fight for full citizenship of disabled people. Dismantling institutional discrimination is a major political enterprise which involves enormous energy and struggle.

Further Reading

Albrecht, G.L., Seelman, K.D. and Bury, M. (2001). *Handbook of Disability Studies.* London: Sage.

Barnes, C., Mercer, G. and Shakespeare, T. (1999). *Exploring Disability: A Sociological Introduction.* Cambridge: Polity Press.

Begum, N., Hill, M. and Stevens, A. (1994). *Reflections: Views of Black Disabled People on their Lives and Community Care.* London: CCETSW.

Campbell, J. and Oliver, M. (1996). *Disability Politics: Understanding our Past, Changing our Future.* London: Routledge.

Priestley, M. (1999). *Disability Politics and Community Care.* London: Jessica Kingsley.

Shakespeare, T. (Ed.) (1998). *The Disability Reader.* London: Cassell.

Chapter 3

Evidence-Based Social Work with People Who Have Substance Problems

Philip Guy and Larry Harrison

Background

At the beginning of the 1960s, when concerns were raised about illicit drug use, cannabis smoking was largely seen in those ports where there was a regular supply: Bristol, Liverpool and London. There was no organised, nationwide distribution network for cannabis or any other illicit drug, and injecting drug use was extremely rare. Forty years later, surveys indicate that one in three UK adults of working age has used an illicit drug at some time in their life (Ramsay and Percy, 1996; Ramsay and Spiller, 1997).

Anyone who had predicted an increase of this magnitude in 1960 would have been dismissed as a fool. It is one of the greatest cultural changes of the second half of the twentieth century. In effect, cannabis smoking and the use of opiates (for example heroin,) stimulants (for example cocaine and amphetamine), hallucinogens (for example LSD), volatile inhalants (for example butane gas), and sedatives (for example barbiturates), have been added to the traditional drugs used in the British Isles, alcohol and tobacco, to produce an extended menu of psychoactive substances[1] which are available in the illicit and licit markets.

This expansion in the range of available psychoactive substances was not achieved at the expense of alcohol sales. In Britain, as in many other countries, the volume of alcohol consumed increased by over 50 per cent between the end of the Second World War and 1980 (Edwards et al., 1994). Like all countries that saw an increase in alcohol consumption, Britain witnessed a concomitant rise in the health and social problems associated with drinking. The number of male and female deaths directly related to alcohol consumption doubled between 1985 and 1995, while other indicators of alcohol-related harm also rose substantially (Office of National Statistics, 1996).

It is perhaps not surprising that the UK personal social services have failed to keep pace with change on this scale. In the 1960s and early 1970s, when many of today's directors of social services were undertaking their professional training, substance problems were a relatively low priority and were hardly mentioned on qualifying courses. Moreover, training was still dominated by a view that had become popular in the nineteenth century, of alcohol and drug dependence as an intractable disease (Berridge, 1989). The diseases of 'alcoholism' and 'drug addiction' were seen as afflicting a small minority of individuals, who were possibly vulnerable for genetic reasons. The course of the disease was irreversible, and unless patients achieved abstinence they could be expected to deteriorate progressively.

The majority of people who develop problems with their substance use do not seek professional help, however most eventually recover, or 'mature out' of their problems, without specialist intervention (Drew, 1968; Vaillant, 1995; Temple and Leino, 1989). Help seeking populations are often highly atypical minorities, and theories based on people in treatment – such as the notion of the 'addictive personality' – do not always generalise to people in the community (Nathan, 1988; Williams, 1976). There are similar findings for depression and anxiety-related disorders: people who get referred to specialist psychiatric services are more likely to be suffering from severe psychiatric disorders, and to represent the extreme end of a continuum (Goldberg and Huxley, 1992).

Although people from all walks of life may choose to use illicit drugs, it is clear that social disadvantage plays a role in deciding who is

---

1. Any substance taken by the user that changes their mood or perception. Usually regarded as meaning street drugs, alcohol and tobacco but can include a wide range of natural, household or commercial products.

more likely to consume substances in a hazardous way, to develop problems with substance use, and to relapse following treatment. It follows that interventions aimed at improving social circumstances have the potential to make a major impact on substance-related problems. Indeed, Vaillant (1988) found that US probation officers, who provided heroin dependent parolees with supervision, support for job-seeking, and accommodation had more success than hospital treatment programmes. Similarly, Azrin (1976) demonstrated the importance of intervening in the social, occupational and marital functioning of clients through a highly structured Community Reinforcement Program. Far from substance dependence being the preserve of the medical profession, as many social workers believe, intervention requires inter-disciplinary collaboration, and social casework is one of the essential components of success. The Department of Health (1999: p14) recognised the need for what it calls 'shared care' in the treatment of drug dependence in its Guidelines on Clinical Management, and specifically included social workers as one of the professional groups that should be involved.

Policy Responses to Cultural Change

As ideas about the nature of substance problems have changed, so have the policy responses. Where alcohol is concerned, the policy process in the 1970s was relatively open to influence from biological and social scientists (Harrison et al., 1995). Led by research findings on the relative effectiveness of intense and brief intervention, there was a shift away from reliance on hospital in-patient treatment, which had been established as the treatment of choice for 'alcoholism' in the 1960s (Ministry of Health, 1962), towards the provision of a wider range of community services for people with drinking problems (Department of Health and Social Security and the Welsh Office, 1978). Responding to drinking problems was 'everyone's business' and an effective national response depended on the mobilisation of those responsible for primary health and social care, including local authority social workers (Department of Health and Social Security, 1981).

There was also a move away from an exclusive concern with dependence, towards a broader focus on a wide range of problems, including public disorder and drinking and driving. In the wake of the 1977 White Paper Prevention and Health, an attempt was made to emphasise the prevention of alcohol-related problems, and to develop the role of primary health care and the social services in promoting local community initiatives (Department of Health and Social Security, 1977). In a linked development, and one which was associated with a fundamental change in social attitudes towards risk (Beck, 1992), there was a shift from explanations predicated on the concept of causation to those centred on the notion of risk. The target for intervention switched from people who could be diagnosed as alcohol dependent, to those demonstrating at risk drinking behaviour – those who, while free of problems, were judged to be drinking at potentially hazardous levels. This was paralleled, in the drugs field, by a focus on risky practices or routes of administration, such as potentially harmful injecting procedures, or hazardous techniques for inhaling volatile substances.

Drug-related policy

Where illicit drugs were concerned, the rapid growth of the illicit market from the mid-1960s led the UK government to a number of de facto policy shifts, but for much of the time the drugs policy agenda was dominated by criminal justice rather than health concerns. First, a series of restrictions were placed on the so-called 'British system' of maintenance prescribing, which permitted people who were dependent on illicit drugs to receive regular supplies from the National Health Service. The right of general practitioners to prescribe cocaine on a maintenance basis was removed. The prescribing of heroin was made subject to strict licensing. Subsequently, most maintenance prescribing and prescribing directed towards abstinence was limited to oral methadone, a synthetic opiate.

The penalties for the possession and supply of drugs like heroin were increased progressively. In the 1980s, a growing awareness of the risks to the public health from blood borne pathogens like HIV helped slow the movement towards more punitive policies on injecting drug use, and re-emphasise the principles of harm minimisation, which had been implicit in the 'British system'. Instead of abstinence being the sole objective of intervention, from the mid-1980s it became acceptable to pursue harm minimisation goals again.

Alcohol-related policy

While the combined study of alcohol and other drugs has yielded many scientific insights, there are issues that differ at the service delivery level, while at the national level alcohol and drug policies have developed independently. Unfortunately, policy segregation has meant that the treatment of alcohol-related problems has been the 'Cinderella service', even though alcohol generates greater social costs than illicit drugs (Maynard, 1989). The separate development of alcohol and drugs policy has led, therefore, to some logical inconsistencies. Where alcohol is concerned, policy has focussed on demand side measures, such as health education. There has been little attempt to tackle alcohol-related problems by restricting supply; indeed, in recent years there has been a series of measures aimed at liberalising the liquor licensing laws and increasing the availability of alcohol. Where illicit drugs are concerned, however, the policy agenda has been dominated by 'supply side' measures, such as laws to prohibit possession, and enforcement measures aimed at severely restricting the supply of drugs on the streets. Until relatively recently, there was no sustained effort to educate people about drugs. Thus, supply side measures were viewed as ineffective or unnecessary in relation to the prevention of alcohol problems, but were endorsed as an effective means of preventing drug problems.

On the whole, formal government policies on illicit drugs have been far better developed and articulated than those on alcohol (Hodgson, Raistrick and Ritson, 1999). In 1994, the government produced a drugs strategy for England, *Tackling Drugs Together* (Lord President, 1995), and related strategies were introduced in Scotland (1994) and Wales (1996). In an echo of *Drinking Sensibly* (Department of Health and Social Security, 1981), the first and only government discussion document dedicated to alcohol policy, *Tackling Drugs Together* had three key objectives; reducing

drugs-related crime, reducing the availability of drugs to young people and reducing the health risks related to drug use. These objectives were to be achieved through improved inter-organisational co-ordination at the local level. The government's strategy for England was developed further in the White Paper *Tackling Drugs to Build a Better Britain: The Government's 10-Year Strategy for Tackling Drug Misuse* (Lord President, 1998). In this policy statement, the government went beyond the exhortation that had characterized *Drinking Sensibly* and *Tackling Drugs Together*, and specified the mechanism through which this was to be achieved: the establishment of local Drug Action Teams (DATs) to co-ordinate the activities of local agencies. The DATs bring together representatives of the local health, education, welfare and law enforcement agencies. The representatives are expected to be senior personnel, who are in a position to ensure the support of their organisation for the DAT's local strategy. The updated strategy, which focuses on England, but which the government believes to be 'relevant' for Wales, Scotland and Northern Ireland, has four objectives:

1. Young people are to be helped to resist drug use in order to achieve their full potential in society.

2. Communities are to be protected from drug-related anti-social and criminal behaviour.

3. Treatment should enable people with drug problems to overcome them and live healthy and crime-free lives.

4. The availability of illegal drugs is to be stifled. (Lord President, 1998: p2)

Unlike *Drinking Sensibly*, which had explicitly rejected calls to improve the co-ordination of alcohol policy at a national level, claiming that the existing Whitehall mechanisms worked perfectly well (Department of Health and Social Security, 1981: p67), the need to co-ordinate government activity on drugs has been recognized. The Cabinet has established a Sub-Committee on the Misuse of Drugs which involves ministers from all relevant Departments of State: principally the Home Office, the Departments of Health, Education and Environment, the Ministry of Defence, the Foreign and Commonwealth Office, and the Northern Ireland, Scottish and Welsh Offices.

The Minister for the Cabinet Office chairs the Sub-Committee and is supported by the Cabinet Office's Anti-Drugs Co-ordination Unit. An Anti-Drugs Co-ordinator (popularly known as the 'Drugs Czar') reports directly to this Sub-Committee.

Co-ordination at a local level remains one of the cornerstones of the government's drugs policy. The drive for local co-ordination also led government to introduce the Crime and Disorder Act 1998, which placed obligations on local authorities, housing authorities, social services, education authorities, the police, health authorities and probation to co-operate over local strategies for tackling crime, including drug-related crime. The Act requires agencies to adapt or develop existing policies on crime, in co-ordination with other local agencies. More emphasis has been placed on the role of local authority social services as part of a local crime prevention strategy, through their child protection and family support services; and through funding social care for drug users, including residential rehabilitation, under the Community Care legislation.

A similar desire to improve the co-ordination of local agencies featured in *Our Healthier Nation*, where health authorities were directed to lead local alliances in translating the government's 'aims, priorities, targets and contracts' in action (Department of Health, 1998: p40). In case there should be any reluctance to co-operate with these arrangements, a duty of partnership is placed on the NHS and on local authorities (Department of Health, 1997).

Practice Issues

Service user profile

The contemporary social worker is likely to be working with substance-related needs that span a broad and diverse continuum of professional practice. At one end of the service profile are the needs of novice and recreational users of substances, whose problems are likely to be connected with unexpected intoxication, school exclusion, high risks of a fatal overdose, or the threat of criminal prosecution. Such clients are being initiated into substance use at an earlier age. They seek help at an earlier age; they now tend to use more than one substance at any one

time, and they now tend to get into trouble with the substance at an earlier stage of their substance using career (Williams, 1996). As Williams points out after identifying these trends, young clients are difficult to help within most existing services, not least because of the contact with adult substance users that attendance within adult orientated services makes almost inevitable. With the exception of cocaine users (Brain et al., 1998), the younger substance user is also more likely to be female than in the past.

The young age of current substance users formed a central concern of the most recent government policy statements. Nevertheless, legally, beyond the general principles of the Children Act 1989, social work with young substance using clients remains a grey area. Neither Parliament nor case law has yet clarified difficult areas of practice; for example, the content and parameters of the advice and information that can be given to young people, or how syringe exchange services should respond to juveniles (McHale, 1991; Mounteney and Shapiro, 1997: p71). Mechanisms and protocols that can facilitate child protection measures without driving young substance users away from services, and possibly further into a substance using lifestyle, have also yet to be developed. This issue, if the current trend in youthful substance users extends into even younger age groups, is likely to pose social work with a significant challenge.

The mid-point of the needs continuum consists of a large number of relatively stable substance users. Typically the middle range substance user will be employed and be a heavy drinker, rather than one whose life revolves completely around alcohol, or an occasional, holiday, or weekend only drug user. The other end of the continuum can be characterised as containing those with multiple problems, which may decrease but not be resolved if the client stops using substances. Many such clients have a specific psychiatric diagnosis, and often a history of sexual abuse, of trauma induced by a poor parenting experience, a criminal life style or other problems of social adjustment.

The social work response

The response to this continuum has usually taken two broad forms. The first of these is casework, the goal of which has traditionally been total abstinence from substance use. In many contemporary forms, casework goals now include safer or controlled substance use. The second strand of social work activity has a more community orientated rationale. Since the mid-1980s, this has taken a harm minimisation and community safety approach, through outreach projects and the provision of clean syringes (O'Hare et al., 1992; Power et al., 1995).

Self help manuals and information in leaflet form are useful and popular in the context of harm minimisation. Based on the sound principles of clarity and the balanced presentation of controversial topics, such manuals are particularly useful in helping middle range substance users, those who are hesitant to engage fully with services, require dispassionate and balanced information and those able to manage their problems themselves. This is a reflection of the legal status of some substance use, the stigma that is attached to it, and the positive role that sound information can play in an area of activity surrounded by myth and rumour.

Substance services and specialist social workers have moved away from an exclusive concern for the substance user. The needs of non-substance using children, parents and partners are now also a focus of many service specifications and social worker roles as described in Chapter 8. Partly because many agencies are part of the non statutory sector where innovation is a strong point, services for substance users can be quite varied and might include day centres, residential rehabilitation, youth justice services, outreach teams, supported housing, adult fostering, pathways to employment, community and residential detoxification and residential rehabilitation specifically aimed at families. A particular feature of services that do not require community care funding has been their low threshold character. However in many parts of the country, specialist services for substance users are non-existent, or offer few choices beyond counselling.

In deference to the client's felt needs for confidentiality, a relative degree of geographical and professional isolation has developed for those who work within specialist services. Mindful of the need to attract clients by stressing high levels of confidentiality, the specialist agencies often find it difficult to work with other agencies. The fault does not lie completely with the specialist agencies. With law enforcement forming the focus of most media coverage of substance issues, many people expect agencies to have a punitive approach to clients. The non-judgmental approach that is proven to be a prerequisite when helping substance users is out of kilter with the prevailing social discourse on substance use, and with many people's personal reactions to it.

Agencies and the social workers within them have been left to develop services and practices on their own. Without a mechanism to promote existing good practice, innovation often remains local, whilst bad practice goes unchecked. Moreover, not all of these services have embraced the notion of evidence-based practice. Residential rehabilitation in particular has been criticised in this regard (Harrison, Guy and Sivyer, 1995).

Even if we take the most conservative of estimates of how many problematic substance[2] users there are amongst the general population, or in the existing caseloads of social workers, one further issue is apparent. Be they concerned with alcohol or drugs, including gases and solvents or all substances, the numbers involved in substance use are such that the specialist agencies and their social workers are unlikely to have the capacity for the task. Thus there will always be a vital role for the non-specialist social worker.

Facilitating Change and Motivation – A Practice Objective

A major issue for the non-specialist is when a client should be referred to a specialist.

Referring some clients too early can stigmatise them as drug users, place them in touch with other, more committed drug users and confirm their self-image as a drug user. The central question is what the new service can offer that

---

2.   Any threat to social, psychological or physical well-being that is predicated on the use of a substance.

the present one cannot (Mounteney and Shapiro, 1997: p74). If the referral process is not smooth and seamless, this is a point at which clients may drop out of the system.

Clients may raise real difficulties that lie in the way of change, or they may be wildly optimistic. Imagine what it must be like trying to give up a substance when others in your home, such as brothers, sisters, or partners, are going to continue. Often a client's concerns will focus on issues relating to withdrawal symptoms, when what really needs to be placed on the agenda is the social support the client can enrol on their own behalf, and how they are going to achieve their goals. Clients should not be placed in a position where they exchange dependence on a substance with dependence on their social worker. Judgements often have to be made between doing things for the client in order to facilitate change and enabling the client to do things for themselves.

Whether they are the clients of a specialist social worker, the non-specialist or acting without help, people stop using intoxicating substances or change to a more controlled pattern of use when they believe that the advantages that can be obtained through change outweigh the benefits accrued through their current behaviour. There are many life events that might make a drug or alcohol free lifestyle more attractive to a client. Perhaps the client has a new partner, the chance of a new job, has come to terms with an emotionally troubling past or has run up a large debt with a drug dealer.

What the social worker needs in this situation is some clarity in order to help the client move forward. What the client may need is some clear 'thinking space' where the conflicting pressures and emotions of a substance sustained life can be harnessed to encourage change. Social workers can provide problematic substance using clients with a confidential, non-judgmental arena in which to weigh up the pros and cons of drug use. We can also provide psychological and material support to tip the balance. If this is what the client is searching for, then as social workers we can make a significant contribution to the welfare of substance users and the wider community.

Clients with substance problems can often appear confused, contradictory and ambivalent about their situations, as this interview carried out by one of the authors makes clear.

I don't really know what to do. I want to get off it I want a job. I want my girlfriend to take me back. Cos I have been in this game a long time. Everybody knows me. They don't mess with me, know what I mean? No one has ever given me anything, know what I mean? Taking it, that's what it's all about getting money for drugs, fighting and doing the business, everyday is like an adventure and drugs are part of the buzz.

Prochaska and DiClemente (1984) outline five stages of thinking that clients go through when considering themselves, their situation and their motivation to change substance using behaviour. These five stages are: pre-contemplation, contemplation, action, maintenance and relapse. In the pre-contemplative stage it is not the case that the client lacks motivation, rather this is a period when motivation is directed towards continued substance use. The pre-contemplative stage is characterised by an uncertainty about continued substance use. In this stage, it is appropriate to consider ways of reducing risk and improving the health of the client by, for example, providing basic health information and clean injecting equipment. The stages of contemplation, action and maintenance can also contain ambivalence about needs, goals and intentions. It is, however, in these stages that the resolve to make changes is supported, the planning and action occurs, and the ways in which change can become permanent are the focus of any intervention.

In the contemplative stage, the client's ambivalence can be resolved using motivational interviewing. Motivational interviewing is a highly structured cognitive behavioural approach that builds on the contradictions within a client's view of themselves and their drug use (Miller and Rollnick, 1991). To undertake motivational interviewing a social worker requires empathetic abilities, basic skills in restructuring the versions of events that clients give them, and skills in reflecting and providing feedback to the client (see Chapter 9 for more detail).

In Prochaska and DiClemente's stage of contemplation, the client will consider the advantages and disadvantage of lifestyle change. This kind of deliberation may lead to a continuation of existing behaviour, or it can lead on into an action stage. It is in the action stage that a client might begin a methadone programme or change risky injecting practices to safer ones. The clients might either enter a detoxification programme or detoxify themselves.

The maintenance stage implies that successful action has been taken and the client needs to maintain this. Maintenance might involve help in learning to deal with the behavioural cues that lead directly to substance use. This could require an exploration of the client's lifestyle, friends, places and the feelings and emotions that have led directly to drug use. Many clients have never experienced a substance-free life as an adult, and at any stage after pre-contemplation a client may relapse to an earlier stage. It can be important to recognise the difficulties this might pose. Relapse is a situation in which the client may not have achieved their goals. The client may have restarted substance use, although this may not follow the previous pattern and the social worker's task with the client in this time is to help the client to learn the lesson that can be drawn from their experience and build motivation for a fresh start.

Using motivational interviewing with clients who are considering change is not about imposing a version of reality or a goal upon the client. It is, rather, about helping the client to understand their behaviour and getting them to take responsibility for it, reinforcing through conversation the positive things that the client says about themselves and reinforcing, but not suggesting, the notion that a changed lifestyle may have advantages and is attainable as described in the case vignette 'Kelly'.

As Miller and Rollnick comment, motivational interviewing is not simply an exercise in semantic word games. The things that clients say are a strong indication of their perceptions and can have a direct bearing on their actions. Self-motivating statements are the verbal indications that the client is cognitively engaged with their problem. The client's expressed concerns are signs that the client is engaged at an emotional level, and the social worker's aim should be to draw out those parts of the client's story that are positive about change, and build on these by building up self-esteem.

Although these are relatively complex techniques that involve behavioural insights of some depth, the principles of good practice are shared across social work. Jenner (1998: p21) suggests that good outcomes are predicated on co-operation, harmony between clients and staff, and shared responsibility. The existence of cliques in any agency, and of high levels of tension and low participation on the part of clients and staff, are implicated in poor outcomes. These are principles and good ways of working that are recognised, for example, in child protection, mental health and the care of older people.

Case vignette: Kelly

Kelly, a nineteen year old woman with an eighteen month old daughter, has been using amphetamine for about five months. There were concerns about Kelly's commitment as a parent because she spent long periods out of the family home enjoying her busy social life. However, Kelly's drug use was unknown to her social worker. Kelly financed her drug use through her job on a supermarket checkout. At first her use of the substance occurred on her days off from work and caused Kelly few problems. Several times during the second month of her substance use Kelly needed a day off work to recover. Moreover as time passed, these days off became more frequent.

Eventually, Kelly's substance use became obvious to those around her including her social worker, and Kelly's deteriorating work record led to the loss of her job. Kelly's mother was not very pleased but at least Kelly still had a partner to support her, her child and her substance use. Amphetamine was still a good 'buzz'. When her relationship ended, Kelly began financing the purchase of amphetamine by stealing money from her mother. This led directly to Kelly and her daughter being thrown out of the family home.

Kelly and her daughter were living in a hostel, where, as Kelly pointed out, there was not even a lock on the bathroom door. As is often the case, Kelly's drug use was not initially the main focus of concern in terms of the quality of the parenting that she provided. The issue of neglect had always been the concern. With a lifestyle that was beginning to revolve around drug use and without the support of her mother, Kelly's amphetamine use became much more of a child protection issue.

A referral was made with Kelly's co-operation to a specialist agency. Initially this was for an assessment of the role that drugs played within Kelly's lifestyle. The reality of Kelly's situation was clearly out of step with her own perception of the kind of person she was and her aspirations. Once the issues had been clarified, it was clear to Kelly that she had much to gain from giving up amphetamines; reunion and reconciliation with her family, the potential for moving back into the family home, and the possibility of achieving her ambition to become a hairdresser through a course at the local college. These were all items on the inventory that Kelly and the specialist social worker drew up. A preparedness to work on her drug use was also seen by Kelly as one way of keeping her daughter. There were also losses as well, not least of which was the loss of face in having to admit to herself and her family that Kelly's actions had not always been wise. Moreover, amphetamine still made Kelly feel good and provided an easy way to remove herself from her situation.

The specialist social worker made the initial contact with Kelly's mother because Kelly felt she could not. The approval of Kelly's mother was a major gain for Kelly and a source of psychological and material support. With this and the support of both social workers, Kelly stopped using drugs. There were two occasions when Kelly used amphetamine during this process but each time her specialist social worker approached this as a learning experience for Kelly. Kelly learned to deal with the feelings and situations that led to her drug use. It was important at this stage that her return to amphetamine use was not allowed to confirm in Kelly's mind that failure was inevitable. Kelly's enrolment at college was a major gain and was achieved through her own efforts. Kelly moved on from her amphetamine use because she was able to experience positive rewards from change.

Drawing Research and Practice Experience Together

The trends over the last four decades suggest that social workers in all fields are likely to have those with substance problems amongst their caseloads. To work effectively with substance users a social worker needs to have some basic knowledge about such substances, but does not need to be a walking encyclopaedia on pharmacology. It is more important that information is balanced and objective and is communicated in an even-handed way.

This area of work is about improving the client's quality of life through motivation and change. The potential for gain and loss should be mapped out with the client. This can be an exercise in clarity for the client and the social worker. The potential to lose from change is important to the client. Social workers who openly downplay the benefits those clients feel they get from alcohol or drugs will lose the confidence of the client. Change may involve false starts and relapse. However, these events can be used in a positive way. Being in charge of the process of change is one potential gain for the client, the value of which should not be underestimated. To a client, the gains to be had from change may not be transparently obvious they may need to be explored. This is a task that social workers are ideally placed to facilitate.

Further Reading

Barber, J. (1995). *Social Work with Addictions*. Houndmills, Basingstoke: Macmillan.

Davies, J.B. (1997). *The Myth of Addiction*. Amsterdam: Harwood.

Thom, B. (1999). *Dealing with Drink: Alcohol and Social Policy: From Treatment to Management*. Free Association: London.

Van Wormer, K. (1995). *Alcoholism Treatment: A Social Work Perspective*. Chicago: Nelson-Hall.

Chapter 4

A Holistic Approach to Working with HIV and AIDS

Di Hart

Background

There are over 2,000 new HIV infections reported each year in the UK and the recent encouraging decrease in mortality rates coupled with significant ongoing rates of new infections is likely to lead to a doubling of the numbers of people living with HIV over the next 10 years. The epidemic has not gone away.

(Neil Gerrard MP, All-Party Parliamentary Group on AIDS, October 1998).

We cannot afford to be complacent about the impact of HIV/AIDS: it continues to take its toll on the estimated 41,200 adults infected with the HIV virus in the UK, who are living with differing degrees of illness (Unlinked Anonymous Surveys Steering Group 2002). For every person *infected* with HIV there are many more *affected*, whether as partner, carer, relative or friend. Services must continue to be developed which meet the needs of those infected or affected in a time of considerable change.

Epidemiology

The Public Health Laboratory Service receives voluntary notifications of cases of diagnosed HIV infection in the UK. At the end of September 2002, they had received 52,729 reports including 18,972 people who had progressed to an AIDS diagnosis, many of whom have died (PHLS, 2002).

What do we know about the people who are infected? Although men who acquired the infection through sex with other men are still the largest group of those with an AIDS diagnosis, they are followed by heterosexually infected black Africans who now exceed the numbers of injecting drug users. The 'traditional' population of those affected by HIV is therefore changing. Rates of *new* infection are declining amongst injecting drug users, remaining stable amongst gay men and increasing amongst heterosexuals. Men still outnumber women

by approximately four to one but this will change if the increase in heterosexual transmission continues.

The changes are reflected in the prevalence of HIV infection amongst children. There had been notifications of 1,232 infected children to the end of June 2002, 914 who have survived and are living with the infection. Initially, most children in the UK were infected as a result of receiving infected blood products or by vertical transmission from mothers who were injecting drug users. This has changed dramatically and over half of children with AIDS in the UK are now of black African origin whose mothers were infected through heterosexual activity.

The population of those infected, and therefore needing services, is not evenly distributed, with over 60 per cent living in or near to London. This is particularly true of black Africans, 86 per cent of whom live in this region. Outside London, there are areas of high prevalence in the North West and parts of Scotland, mainly as a result of drug use. This is not to say that other areas of the UK are unaffected. Moreover, there may be particular difficulties in developing services where the need is less obvious.

It cannot be predicted how the patterns of infection will change in the future. There are now dramatically rising levels in West and Southern Africa and the Indian subcontinent. This shift in epidemiology may affect the UK depending on changing patterns of immigration. We also cannot know how many new infections there will be in the future or how many people are already infected but undiagnosed. The most recent information as a result of anonymous screening suggests that only two thirds of those infected are aware of their status and, within this overall picture, only half of those infected through heterosexual sex (Unlinked Anonymous Surveys Steering Group 2002).

Legal and policy context

The legislation of most universal relevance to those infected by HIV is that which determines services to people with an illness or disability; the NHS and Community Care Act 1990 and the Chronically Sick and Disabled Persons Act 1970. People who are infected by HIV are entitled to an assessment of their needs by the local authority and, if eligible, the provision of a range of services. The Carers (Recognition and Services) Act which came into effect in 1996 placed a duty on those carrying out community care assessments to also assess the support needs of carers, and the Carers and Disabled Children Act 2000 extended this to those caring for disabled children.

Other legislation may be relevant depending on the particular circumstances of the person infected. People with HIV infection may, along with the general population, suffer from mental illness but are at increased risk in view of the stress of their diagnosis or AIDS related dementia. The Mental Health Act 1983 may be of relevance. The NHS (Venereal Diseases) Regulations 1974 and the Data Protection Act 1998 provide a legislative framework for the disclosure of information. Disclosure of HIV status must be on a strict 'need to know' basis and with the informed consent of the person infected, except in exceptional circumstances. Many of those infected of African origin are seeking asylum and face difficulties with their immigration status. The changes to benefit regulations in 1996 may result in their being ineligible for public funds and their basic subsistence needs are currently being met by the new National Asylum Support Service or local authorities through the provisions of the National Assistance Act 1948 or, if there are children involved, the Children Act 1989.

The Children Act determines the provision of services to 'children in need' i.e. those whose health or development would be impaired without the provision of such services. Although the Act does not specifically mention HIV, infected or affected children are likely to meet the criteria: children with AIDS could be classified as 'disabled' but asymptomatic children or those whose parent or carer is ill are also vulnerable because of the many practical and emotional difficulties they face. In 1992, the Department of Health issued guidance for local authorities in respect of children both infected and affected by HIV/AIDS (Department of Health, 1992a). This described the principles which must underpin service delivery and outlined the practice which should be adopted in respect of issues such as confidentiality, testing and prevention. Although this guidance is currently out of print, there are plans to update and re-issue it shortly.

This government has launched a wide range of new initiatives, many of which will have an impact on HIV services, such as Tackling Drugs To Build A Better Britain (Department of Health, 1998a) and Saving Lives: Our Healthier Nation (Department of Health, 1999). In respect of children, the Quality Protects programme is of particular relevance (Department of Health, 1998b). Many of these initiatives fall within the broader goal of tackling social exclusion which must resonate with people infected by HIV, given the stigma which is still attached to the illness and the predominance of the infection amongst minority groups. A somewhat conflicting message stems from the Immigration and Asylum Act 1999, which made provision for asylum seekers to be dispersed within the UK. This has given rise to concern that HIV affected African families may be isolated from suitable treatment and support.

The All-Party Parliamentary Group on AIDS (APPGA) published a report in October 1998, based on submissions from a wide range of organizations and individuals and making a number of recommendations to government. These ranged from the need for stronger national leadership through to specific recommendations about benefits, treatment, social care and prevention. In response, the government announced that it would draw up a national strategy for HIV/AIDS, subsequently expanded to include other sexual health issues. *The National Strategy for Sexual Health and HIV* (Department of Health, 2001) is currently the subject of consultation and makes a series of proposals to reduce rates of infection, to improve sexual health in general and to develop better services for those infected.

The final policy initiative of significance is that relating to vertical transmission i.e. transmission from mother to child. A Working Party was established by the Royal College of Paediatrics and Child Health to consider this issue and reported in April 1998 with a number of recommendations aiming to reduce the numbers of babies infected by HIV (Intercollegiate Working Party, 1998). This was followed by a directive from the NHS Executive which states that Health Authorities must develop systems for offering all pregnant women an HIV test and sets targets for the uptake of such testing (NHS Executive, 1999).

Overview of Practice

Impact of HIV

A study undertaken between 1988 and 1990 of the social care provided to people with HIV/AIDS (The Hull–York Research Team, 1993) found that the diagnosis affected all aspects of everyday life. This was not necessarily related to level of illness and included effects such as rejection by work colleagues, reduced income, difficulties with family relationships and changes in sexual behaviour and lifestyle. The challenge for agencies was to develop services that could respond to this social and psychological impact of an HIV diagnosis as well as all the physical needs arising from a life threatening illness.

The 'special' nature of HIV/AIDS

HIV/AIDS services have largely developed outside the mainstream for a number of reasons. It is sometimes suggested that there has been an over-reaction to HIV/AIDS and that there are many other diseases that have a devastating effect without requiring a 'special' response. When the illness was first identified, there was a degree of moral panic and those infected risked stigmatisation and rejection. A distinction was drawn in the media between those who had brought the illness upon themselves (the 'gay plague') and those who were 'innocent victims' such as haemophiliacs and children. There were fears of a major epidemic and a poor prognosis for those infected. Service users were likely to be from minority groups, either gay men or injecting drug users, and this contributed to their marginalisation. As a consequence of these factors, HIV was considered to be somehow outside the remit of 'normal' services and deemed to require a specialist approach. Since 1988, central government has made money available specifically to develop HIV/AIDS services. This has contributed to their location outside the mainstream. Health authorities were given money for treatment facilities and local authorities for social care through what is now the AIDS Support Grant. What are the specialist services which have been developed and what part do they play? The Hull–York study found that people turned to social services when they wanted information, advice or practical services but tended to seek support from informal networks and the voluntary sector.

Social services departments

Social services departments were not immune to the panic. There was some reluctance to provide services because of fears about the risk of becoming infected or of having insufficient skills. Therefore, specialist social work teams and/or posts were created, as described in Chapter 1. With the introduction of the NHS and Community Care Act and the Children Act in the early 1990s, most social services departments restructured to provide separate adults' and children's services. They also began to separate the functions of purchasing and providing services and increasingly looked to the private and voluntary sector to act as the providers. Although the number of designated social work teams dealing purely with HIV/AIDS is now declining, the most common model within social service departments is to have specialist HIV social workers located within the adult/purchasing sector. Social workers (or care managers) are predominantly engaged in assessing the community care needs of those infected and purchasing packages of care. Although people may be referred to social services when diagnosed, they are unlikely to receive a comprehensive assessment unless they became symptomatic. This model is reasonably effective as a response to needs which arise from HIV related illness, but is more problematic where there are multiple needs, for example where there are also concerns about mental health or the welfare of other family members. This will be considered in greater detail below.

Social services departments have had more difficulty in resolving how to deliver a service to HIV infected children. Numbers of infected children are small and have not generally warranted the creation of specialist teams. Lothian did create specialist services in the 1980s including a fostering scheme, but subsequently reintegrated services into the mainstream. Some specialist social work posts do exist in areas of high prevalence and the issue then arises as to where those posts should be located. They may be attached to hospital social work teams, disabled children's teams or adult HIV teams.

Health care

The provision of health care is a universal need for anyone with HIV infection. Again, the model of service delivery is dependent, in part, on prevalence within Health Districts, with London having a number of specialist treatment units. Because many infections were sexually transmitted, health services have usually been developed within Genito-Urinary Medicine. The appropriateness of this is open to debate, particularly in view of the need to reduce stigmatisation, and a recent decision by the NHS Executive (1998) to classify HIV services as a specialism in their own right was welcomed. However, the National Strategy now proposes a more integrated approach, with all sexual health services being integrated into the new Primary Care Trusts.

The initial moral panic linked with, as was the case until recently, the poor prognosis for anyone who was diagnosed with HIV infection, led to controversy over the value of having an HIV test. The consequences of a positive test result were socially and psychologically devastating and there was little to offer in the way of treatment. Health Authorities responded to this dilemma by providing opportunities for pre- and post-test counselling to anyone considering an HIV test. This model has continued with Health Advisers and/or counsellors being employed to support people attending for HIV testing and treatment. Health Authorities are therefore providing not only a diagnosis and

treatment service but in many cases have taken on part of the social care function.

Again, the situation regarding children is more complex. In areas of high prevalence, i.e. London and parts of Scotland, paediatric HIV infection has become a specialism and treatment centres have been established. In other hospitals, children are managed by general paediatricians and there are a variety of shared care arrangements which have been established between local and specialist units.

Voluntary sector

The voluntary sector responded rapidly to the challenge of HIV/AIDS and established a number of innovative services ranging from drop-ins, support groups and 'buddy' schemes through to respite and home care. Many of these initiatives have not survived or have been absorbed into larger organisations but there is still a thriving network of voluntary organisations operating on both a local and national level. In addition to the direct services provided, these organisations act as a lobby to ensure that the issue of HIV/AIDS remains on the political agenda: most notably, the Terrence Higgins Trust and the National AIDS Trust. Many of the early organisations were developed by gay men who were themselves HIV positive or touched by the impact the infection was having on their community. This made them perhaps less accessible to the other infected groups. Positively Women and Positive Partners/Positively Children were set up in response and, more recently, there have been initiatives by African community groups.

Preventative services

There was a public education campaign in the 1980s based on a tombstone with the epitaph 'Don't die of ignorance'. Subsequent initiatives on prevention have been targeted at specific groups thought to be particularly vulnerable and much of this more focussed work has been undertaken within the voluntary sector supported by funds provided through local Health Authorities. There have been criticisms that this has resulted in a piecemeal approach and it was recommended by the APPGA that there was a need for a national strategy for health promotion. There is particular concern that young people are receiving insufficient information and do not believe that HIV/AIDS is an issue for them. *The Sex and Relationship Education Guidance* produced by the DfEE (July 2000 DfEE 0116/2000) acknowledges that teaching about safer sex is a key strategy for reducing the incidence of HIV and sexually transmitted diseases but the social aspects of HIV infection are not specifically addressed within the National Curriculum. They could usefully be included within the Personal, Social and Health Education programme and teaching on 'citizenship' but teachers may be inhibited by their own lack of knowledge or from fear of discussing homosexuality because of Section 28 (Local Government Act, 1988).

A framework for addressing the needs of drug users was already in existence before the arrival of HIV. This facilitated an early response to the spread of infection and services were developed to minimise the risks of intravenous use. Needle exchange projects were established and there was a shift in emphasis within drug treatment programmes away from detoxification and abstinence from drug use towards continued but safer use. It was recognised that many people using drugs were not realistically going to become drug free and that it was preferable to acknowledge this by offering long term maintenance treatment rather than accepting a cycle of rapid reduction followed by relapse. There has been a problem, however, in tackling the spread of infection inside prisons both from sharing injecting equipment or sex between men. The National AIDS Trust (1999) have recently suggested that insufficient funds are being provided for prevention campaigns among gay men although they still constitute the largest group of those infected.

Issues Arising from Practice

The case vignette, *Ruth*, illustrates many of the issues relevant to current practice.

Confidentiality

Confidentiality has remained a central issue for practitioners, which is perhaps surprising given that all those using services are entitled to expect that their confidentiality will be maintained. Professionals who thought they were aware of the imperative to maintain confidentiality have been taken by surprise when they realise, too late, that an individual's HIV status may be a secret from partners or between parent and child. Why is confidentiality such a sensitive issue with regard to HIV? It is increasingly suggested that HIV is an illness like any other and should be

---

Case vignette: Ruth

Ruth contracted HIV infection when she was raped by soldiers in Uganda. She fled to the UK requesting asylum and has been given temporary accommodation and subsistence by her local authority. Shortly after her arrival, she discovered she was pregnant as a result of the rape and her son, James, is now 2 years old and also HIV positive. Ruth was extremely depressed for many months and was slow to form an attachment to her child but they have recently become much closer. She finds the strain of coping with a sick toddler, in cramped accommodation and with little money, overwhelming at times but has been reluctant to seek help in case her HIV status becomes known. The Home Office has just refused her application for refugee status but James could remain in the UK because he was born here. Ruth knows that they will not have access to the recent improvements in treatment in Uganda when their health deteriorates and feels James might have a better future if he remained here but doesn't want to place her child in the care of strangers. Ruth has a social worker from the HIV team, but a worker from the children and families' team has also been involved at times to arrange day care or respite fostering. An approved social worker was asked to assess Ruth's mental health shortly after her diagnosis when it was feared that she may harm herself.

'normalised' but this can only take place when there is wider acceptance of those infected. Stigmatisation still exists and the fears about the consequences of disclosure are based on reality. It is certainly true that people are still afraid of contracting HIV through social contact in spite of information to the contrary. A unique feature of HIV/AIDS, when it occurs in children, is that a disclosure of the child's status is inextricably linked with that of the mother.

Treatment

In the latter half of the 1990s, there has been a dramatic improvement in the treatments available. It was found that giving drugs in combination was more effective than using drugs singly and 'combination therapy' is now offered to people with HIV/AIDS when there is evidence that their immune system is failing. The treatment involves taking a complicated cocktail of toxic drugs within a rigorous regime that can produce a range of side effects. If successful, it reverses the progress of the disease and has led to a significant fall both in the numbers of people developing AIDS and in the mortality rate. Whilst there were a peak of 1,533 AIDS deaths in 1994, this reduced to 565 in 1997 and 266 in 2000. Although treatment has undoubtedly improved the quality of life for many people, HIV organisations are concerned that it should not be seen as a panacea: some people are not able to tolerate the regime or do not respond. It is also possible that the drugs will become ineffective over time and the disease will be reactivated. Meanwhile, it is undoubtedly the case that people with HIV infection are likely to be in better health than ever before. The immediate impact on services has been:

- **Cost:** Combination therapy is expensive and has resulted in a huge increase in the treatment budget. This will continue as treatment is offered at an earlier stage of the disease; people develop resistance and need more drugs; new drugs are developed, and there are fewer deaths. The additional cost has been met by reducing other aspects of HIV expenditure, particularly in-patient beds and grants to the voluntary sector. Several

projects have been unable to continue or have reduced their level of service and there is concern that this will have an adverse impact on those who are not getting better or those who may relapse in the future. The National Strategy proposes that the treatment budget for HIV will not continue to be ring-fenced indefinitely, which is also causing concern to Health Authorities.

- **Changing expectations:** People who were anticipating their imminent death now have to adapt to the prospect of living for an indefinite period. This may not be the straightforward benefit that it appears, with some people reporting feelings of depression and confusion:

  So, it's all over bar the shouting is it? Thanks to those gifts of the gods, the miracle working combination drugs, we can forget about death and plague…Then there are the psychological side effects of success – the coming back to life, what Americans are calling the 'Lazarus Syndrome'.

  (White, 1999: p33.)

- **Adapting services:** It also means that services must adapt: the long established residential unit at London Lighthouse has closed and several organisations are developing skills training for those wishing to return to work. Social services must also adapt from offering a service to those who were terminally ill to those who are 'better' but facing an uncertain future of chronic illness. Service users may find themselves being reassessed and losing services on which they had become reliant, partly because they are no longer considered to need them but also because there is less money available.

- **Babies:** The process by which mothers infected their babies was initially little understood. It was thought that, not only were unborn babies at considerable risk of becoming infected, but that pregnancy was likely to exacerbate the mother's HIV disease. Women were advised not to become pregnant or to consider having a termination if they were already pregnant. The position has changed radically and it has now become known that the risk of vertical transmission is not only less than was originally thought (15-25% where women do not breast-feed) but that it can be reduced by medical intervention to two per cent or less (Department of Health, 2001b). Women who are known to be HIV positive are advised to take medication before the birth, to consider having a Caesarean delivery, to allow the baby to be medicated and to avoid breast-feeding. This has highlighted the fact that, although anonymous screening indicates that 300 babies are born to HIV positive women every year, HIV infection has not always been detected ante-natally. The position in 1998 was as follows:

In the UK, over three-quarters of HIV infections in pregnant women remain undiagnosed at the time of birth, and often women only discover they are infected when their child develops AIDS.

(Inter-Collegiate Working Party, 1998: p2.)

This resulted in urgent action to increase the testing of pregnant women for HIV infection and the most recent information suggests that 73 per cent of women in the high prevalence areas of London and Scotland are aware of their status by the time of delivery (Royal College of Obstetricians and Gynaecologists, 2001). It has also raised the question of whether women who refuse to follow the advice offered are putting their babies at risk of significant harm.

- **Child protection:** The point at which refusal to accept treatment is a child protection issue is controversial. It is generally accepted that unborn babies have no legal status in the UK. The High Court did rule in 1992 that a woman in labour must undergo a Caesarean section in order to save her life and that of the baby (Re S Adult: Consent to Treatment All ER 671) but this ruling was controversial and condemned by the Royal College of Obstetricians (Dyer, 1994). A similar decision taken in 1996 using powers under the Mental Health Act was deemed to be unlawful on appeal (Re S Adult: See Community Care 14-20 May 1998). There should therefore be no question of legal intervention to force a pregnant woman to have an HIV test, medication or a Caesarean delivery. However, following the birth, the baby acquires legal rights of their own and it could be argued that an HIV infected

mother is then putting the baby at risk of significant harm if she breast-feeds or refuses monitoring for the baby. In a recent case, the High Court was asked to rule on whether an infant born to an HIV infected mother should be tested against the wishes of the parents (Re C: Child 1999). The Judge decided that the baby should be tested but that he could not rule to prevent the mother from breast-feeding. It is also feasible that a refusal to agree to a child receiving combination therapy could be considered as a child protection issue. This is causing concern not only to parents but also to those supporting them and is likely to become of increasing importance if the efficacy of treatments becomes proven.

African communities

Services were initially developed to meet the needs of the population seen to be most affected: gay men and drug users. Although there have always been people who did not fit these categories; it is now apparent that those of black African origin are a significant minority requiring a very different approach.

- **Multiplicity of need:** Black Africans are likely to be facing many problems more pressing than HIV infection. These are well documented and include uncertain immigration status, traumatic effects of civil unrest, poverty, language and cultural differences, stigmatisation and isolation (Tan, 1993; BHAN, 1995; Chinouya-Mudari and O'Brien, 1999).

- **Shame:** Although the situation is changing, HIV infection is seen as shameful within some African communities, particularly in view of the fact that it is usually sexually transmitted. Once someone is diagnosed with HIV, questions arise as to how they became infected and who is to 'blame' for spreading the infection. Africans in the UK are afraid that, if their HIV infection becomes known, it may interfere with their immigration status or become common knowledge within their community and be reported to family back home.

- **Access to services:** Africans may be reluctant to access diagnostic services, consequently, they may only become known when their illness is relatively advanced, reducing the possibility of being able to benefit from combination therapy. This is of particular concern in relation to ante-natal testing and the reduction of vertical transmission rates. African families may also be bewildered by the way social care services are organised, particularly in respect of the roles of different professionals:

Many African families we have worked with find the concept of a multi-disciplinary approach to their psycho-social care very confusing. Often each 'professional' has a defined role or function that is rarely explained or understood.

(The Local Authority Associations' Officer
Working Group on AIDS, 1995: p23.)

African organisations are attempting to open up discussion within their communities, both in order to prevent the spread of infection and to assist those who are already infected. Individuals who are infected are volunteering to speak in public about their experiences in an attempt to reduce the stigma.

Children

Children carry a particularly heavy burden in families where there is HIV infection. Cultural difference is particularly highlighted where there are children. The concepts of sparing children from domestic responsibility or empowering them to participate in decisions are alien to many African parents. This may give rise to conflicts as to their 'rights', including the right to information.

- **Secrecy:** This is not unique to African families and other children have described their distress and isolation at being unable to discuss the issues of HIV because the adults in their lives are 'protecting' them. The requirement within the Children Act to elicit the wishes and feelings of children may be difficult to implement under these circumstances. At a conference held in London to consider this issue, children were able to deliver their own testimony about their wish to be told the truth:

My mum said to me, 'Sorry, I've been lying to you about your dad. He never had cancer, he had AIDS,' and I started crying because she had lied to me.

(Africare, 1998: p30.)

- **Stigma:** At the same time, children who are aware of their own or a family member's infection may be unable to discuss it openly because of the continuing stigmatisation attached to HIV/AIDS. One thirteen year old boy reported:

I haven't told anyone outside my family that I'm positive. Not even my best friend, who I play football with every day…I know he'd have a bad reaction, look at me weird, be afraid to play with me. At school I can never relax: I always have to watch what I say. If HIV comes up and people start talking about being able to catch it by touching someone, I'll correct them but I always add, 'in my opinion' so they won't wonder about me. It's like having two personalities, being infected.

(Time Out, March 18-25 1998: p10-1.)

- **Loss and bereavement:** Children may have experienced the death of one or more family member and be fearful that they too are going to die, or they may see their parents' health deteriorate and wonder who is going to look after them. More difficult to identify but equally distressing may be the loss of a carefree childhood.

- **Parental incapacity:** In addition to these emotional burdens, children may be assuming an inappropriate level of responsibility as young carers (see Chapter 8 for more detail). In some families there is a tacit expectation that the older children will be able to take over the care of younger relatives when their parents die, which the children may or may not be aware of. Apart from increased domestic responsibility, children may experience reduced opportunities for play or outings as a result of their parents' ill-health.

- **Planning for future care:** The issue of planning for the future care of children is of widespread concern. There are many reasons why parents may postpone consideration of this, not least the pain of acknowledging that they are facing a premature death. Parents may be 'hoping for the best': that they will live long enough for their children to reach independence or that someone will come forward who is able to care for the children. In order to plan effectively, they will need to tell others about their HIV status and risk their disapproval and rejection. They will also be faced with the dilemma of what to tell their children and there may be differences of opinion between professionals and parents as to the 'right' time to involve children in discussions about what will happen. A further deterrent, particularly for African families, is the legal complexity of placing children with alternative carers. The fact that carers must be formally approved and the emphasis on adoption as a preferred option is bewildering to families who have no experience of bureaucratic involvement in family life.

Families have difficulty understanding the differences between concepts like child minding, short-term foster care, long term fostering and adoption. Some expect one service to extend into another; for instance that the child minder could also care for the child overnight if the need arose, since she or he already knows the child. To many families the legal implications and regulations are not familiar and seem to make no sense in terms of their children's needs.

(Matovu et al., 1998: p20.)

The consequences for children if plans are not made are considerable. They will have been denied the opportunity to prepare themselves for the loss of their parent and may be placed with unfamiliar and possibly unsuitable carers. There have been initiatives, notably the Barnardo's Positive Options project, to assist families in planning for the future and in collecting material which will ensure the child has something to remind them of their parents and family history.

(Fratter, 1993).

Service delivery

The current model of local authority social work is based on the individualisation of need with separate teams for different client groups, which have separate planning and management structures and, crucially, provide services from separate and fiercely protected budgets. This has caused considerable

difficulty where there are multiple needs within a household. There is no right or wrong model for delivering services to those affected by HIV as long as this complexity can be recognised and provided for:

● **Adults, children or families?** The issue of how best to structure services to families is complex. The needs of adults with HIV related illness are usually assessed by specialist HIV social workers who then organise a package of care. If the adult is also a parent and requires a service for their child, it may be defined as the responsibility of the children's social work team to assess and meet this need. The interface between an 'adult' and a 'child' need is a contested area. If the need arises because of parental illness, for example, they are too ill to take the child to nursery, it could be argued that this is a daily living task and within the remit of a community care assessment. It could also be argued that this is a 'child in need' who requires the stimulation provided by the nursery and that a service should be provided within Section 17 of the Children Act. Time and energy may be wasted on this debate while the family waits for a service.

● **Specialism or genericism?** There are advantages in HIV specialists providing the service. They will know about the illness and its progression, and not be overwhelmed by medical jargon; they will understand the social and psychological impact of an HIV diagnosis and the need for an unusual degree of confidentiality and will be able to access a complex array of resources. They may also have more time to do the work. It may be the case that the HIV specialist can meet all the individual or family's needs. There are a number of risks, however. Having an HIV social worker immediately reveals the service user's diagnosis and may contribute to stigmatisation; workers may be less familiar with 'ordinary' children's needs and services and contribute to the sense of difference which many families fear; some tasks may be outside their expertise, for example mental health assessments, child protection investigations. It could be argued that HIV work should be brought back into the mainstream but there are some pragmatic difficulties with this approach. For example, Children and Families social work teams are bombarded with referrals and it is understandable that child protection and children 'looked after' cases are given priority in allocation whilst 'children in need' may be offered a Duty appointment. Complex assessments do not lend themselves to this approach and there are complaints about lack of consistency, insensitivity, and poor communication. Even where cases have been allocated, there have been issues about social workers having little information about the illness or its social consequences and not being able to provide adequate resources. Because other services to this client group are often specialist, the social worker can be made to feel very much an inexperienced outsider and to be scapegoated for the perceived lack of appropriate help. They, in return, may be resentful of the privileged position of HIV staff who may be seen to have access to additional resources or to be 'precious'. The situation is particularly unclear regarding affected children. Do they require a specialist HIV service or should they be considered primarily as 'children in need'? Perhaps the key is to accept that the complexity of current social work practice requires a range of responses. It is important for all social workers, whatever their specialism, to recognise the limitations of their own expertise and to involve colleagues who can assist them, either by offering advice or becoming directly involved in joint working.

- **Co-ordination:** There are some cases where appropriate services have been provided across teams but service users have found it difficult to negotiate having two (or more) social workers. People with HIV already have to relate to many professionals (such as Health; Housing; Benefits Agency; Education; possibly Home Office and Asylum seekers team and interpreters). This is bewildering and adds to their fears about breaches of confidentiality. It must seem unwieldy to have one social worker organising help in the home but to be told that another social worker must get involved if this help is to extend to your

child. The HIV social worker may have been involved for some time and service users will want to channel their requests for services via that person. Although this issue arises most commonly in the interface between HIV and children's social workers, it may equally arise where drug or mental health specialisms become involved. It is essential to clarify the basic question: who is doing what?

Family focussed resources

The above fragmentation of service delivery has resulted in fragmented resources, which may not meet the needs of the family as a whole, and the following resources need further development. This is particularly the case in areas of low prevalence where families may experience real isolation:

- **Flexible care:** A 'typical' family affected by HIV is likely to be a single mother who defines her needs as having someone to come in the morning, help get the children ready, take them to school, do the shopping on the way back and then do some housework. In times of illness, she would like the carer to stay overnight to care for the children and may also want increasing periods of respite care, possibly with a view to permanent alternative care for the children. Such a service could be developed but would require a family focussed approach difficult to envisage with services structured as they are at the moment. It would also require a creative response to childcare regulations, which require different processes to be followed for different types of care.

- **Accessible resources:** HIV services are perceived as being relatively well resourced as a result of the AIDS Support Grant, but this relatively generous provision is not geared towards families, who may be reluctant to access specific HIV services for fear of being identified. There are also issues of taking children to an HIV project if they do not know about the diagnosis. African communities have set up several advocacy projects although again some users are reluctant to be referred for fear of being identified.

- **Direct support for children:** Both infected and affected children have considerable support needs, both practically and emotionally. These needs may be overshadowed by those of their parents, or may be difficult to address because of secrecy about the diagnosis. There have been initiatives within the voluntary sector to offer peer group support, such as Teen Spirit or PPC's 'Young People who Know' project, but little within the statutory sector or outside London. Children living in areas of low prevalence are particularly at risk of isolation.

Principles of Good Practice

The changing needs of service users combined with the above developments have implications for the social work task. It is no longer enough to offer an individualised service to 'your' client: consideration must also be given to the needs of other family members. A package of home care may be successful in resolving practical difficulties but does not address the fears of a child that her mum will die and leave them alone. It may also be the case that HIV infection is only part of the story: an individual may be more in need of help in coping with the results of war trauma, or treatment for heroin dependence. Where cases are held by an HIV specialist, they will need to consider whether they can address these other issues and, if not, seek the contribution of colleagues from, for example, the Children's or Substance Misuse service. The situation may also be reversed: a social worker undertaking a child protection investigation may discover that a parent is HIV positive. The same principle will apply, whereby the social worker acknowledges the need for a contribution from an HIV specialist. There is still a tendency to panic when faced with an HIV diagnosis and it is important to be well-informed in order not to over-react. Anecdotally, there have been reports of non-HIV specialists making assumptions that the infected individual has only weeks to live, or inadvertently breaching confidentiality. Having unravelled the social work service into specialisms, we now need to consider how to knit it together again. The following is suggested as a model for good practice.

Clear local policy

It is suggested that local multi-agency policies be developed relating to HIV/AIDS that describe the principles that will underpin the service and which all agencies can adhere to. This would need to include the issues of confidentiality, cultural sensitivity, anti-discriminatory practice, health and safety, entitlement to services and the paramountcy of children. Such a policy would clarify the expectations and responsibilities of both workers and service users so that they would 'know where they stood'.

A family focus

It is suggested that a family focussed approach is adopted whereby the social work team receiving a referral is required to identify the needs of all members of the household. For example, although it may be inappropriate for an HIV social worker to undertake a full assessment of the children in the family, it should be an expectation that they identify whether they are 'children in need' and, if so, request the involvement of a children and families social worker. This reflects the new *Framework for the Assessment of Children in Need and their Families* (Department of Health et al., 2000) and should avoid a situation where families have to pass through separate duty systems, repeating their story at each stage, in order to receive each aspect of the service they need. Instead, there would be a key worker with responsibility for co-ordinating an entire care package, with contributions from other workers as necessary.

Clear procedures

If this model is adopted, there will need to be procedures as to how teams work together to meet the needs of those infected and affected by HIV. It is suggested that this should be within the framework of joint responsibility so that teams move away from a focus on their aspect of the service and consider needs holistically. The process for involving and working in partnership with social workers from other teams should be clarified, including mechanisms for the exchange of information, network meetings, and key worker system and written care plans. Some of these processes may appear to be obvious; for example, a requirement that social workers communicate with each other when closing a case, but experience shows that 'best' practice is not always attained unless formalised.

Multi-agency working

People with HIV/AIDS are likely to have multiple needs and to require involvement from several agencies. Service users have reported feelings of being overwhelmed rather than supported by the number of people trying to 'help' them and co-ordination between agencies is essential. This should be facilitated by improved working practices at social work level but will need to be mirrored by joint working amongst those who plan and commission services. A seamless or 'joined up' service cannot be offered until there is an overview of needs. Services should then be commissioned to meet those needs rather than developing on an ad hoc basis.

Participation

Service user involvement is essential to the delivery of a good service. People with HIV/AIDS may have particular difficulty in making their views known because of the stigmatisation which is associated with their illness and because of the disparate nature of those infected; gay men, black Africans, injecting drug users, and children. A model of service user involvement that relies on public meetings is therefore unlikely to achieve a representative voice and it is important that other means of participation are sought. Service users particularly likely to be marginalised are those living in areas of low prevalence or who wish to keep their HIV status a secret. We particularly need to hear from children who may be doubly disempowered.

Staff support

Working with people who have a life threatening illness is inevitably distressing. Where that person is also experiencing a range of other problems, including rejection by society, workers are likely to be particularly stressed. If they do not specialise in HIV work, they may feel anxious that they do not have the necessary expertise to do a good job. Similarly, HIV social workers may feel uncertain about their ability to consider the needs of children. As social work has become increasingly bureaucratised, we risk losing sight of the strong impact such situations may have on staff. It is important that social workers are given the opportunity to acknowledge this impact and offered support either within supervision or elsewhere. If we are asking social workers to move outside their specialism and to take on a broader perspective, we also owe it to them to make sure they have adequate training to do the job.

Conclusion

HIV services have been seen as separate from the mainstream, which has had advantages in ensuring that a stigmatised group with complex needs received a service. It is now essential, however, to make links between HIV/AIDS specialists and other social work teams, particularly those involved with children. The imperative for this arises not only from the notion of good practice but is clearly directed by Parliament:

> *The specific needs of children living with or affected by HIV need to be addressed in a co-ordinated way to deliver appropriate care with a high level of continuity. Social work with families must ensure that work with children and adults with HIV in the same family are well co-ordinated.*

> (APPGA, 1998: p6.)

Further Reading

Department of Health, Department for Education and Employment and Home Office (2000). *Framework for the Assessment of Children in Need and their Families*. London: The Stationery Office.

Children with AIDS Charity (2000). *Voices of Children*. London: Children with AIDS Charity.

Aggleton, P., Hart, G., and Davies, P. (Eds.) (1999). *Families and Communities Responding to AIDS*. London: UCL Press.

Chapter 5

Working with Carers:
A Specialism that Crosses Boundaries

Christine Heron

Introduction

For thirty years I was his wife, now I'm his nurse and his minder. We had planned our retirement together but now it's all so different. Twenty-four hours a day, seven days a week responsibility. That's what my life has become.

(A carer who looks after her husband with dementia.)

Work with carers, unpaid relatives or friends who support people with social care needs spans the majority of disciplinary boundaries. Out of the estimated 5.7 million carers in Britain, approximately 1.7 million spend more than twenty hours a week on caring responsibilities. Of these, some 855,000 people devote more than fifty hours per week to caring (Department of Health, 1999). The involvement of carers can be found in all the main adult groups in need of care: people with mental health problems; older people; people with disabilities; and people with learning difficulties. Furthermore, carers are also involved with children; either as carers of children with disabilities or as young carers caring for parents, for example, with terminal illness. Workers in both adult and children's services will need to be aware of and respond to the needs of carers, even though their main focus is the service user. Organisations may not have addressed the structural issues that can stem from this dual need.

Perhaps one of the major difficulties in integrating support for carers and service users is the inherent tension that potentially exists between the person requiring, and the person giving care. In most cases, the tensions are those of any people in a close relationship, perhaps exacerbated by additional responsibilities and constraints. In extreme situations, tensions can result in abuse, of the person requiring care by the carer or vice versa. For both the policy maker and the individual practitioner, there is a constant challenge to achieve a balance between the needs and the rights of all people in the caring relationship. The potential for tension is particularly evident within some of the social work specialisms; this will be a recurring theme as we examine good practice in the provision of support for carers.

Carers are not a homogeneous group of people. While carers may have many general needs in common, their particular needs will be different. For example, the specific needs of parents with a child diagnosed with severe learning difficulties will be significantly different from those of a working man who is trying to care for his mother who has dementia. Similarly, the child of ten who feels she needs to watch her father in case he tries to commit suicide will need different support to the Chinese woman who is isolated from her community, speaks little English and is caring for her husband who has had a stroke. Take the complexities of each service user group and multiply this by their carers and this gives some idea of the diversity of carers' experiences and needs.

At the same time, working with carers has developed into a clear specialism in its own right. A major contribution to this has been from the voluntary sector and the self-help movement in which a wealth of support groups, carers' centres and carers' networks have developed. By contrast, statutory services often focus on assessment and provision of direct services, such as care in the home or short term breaks. This distinction is supported in the National Strategy for Carers (Department of Health, 1999), which identifies voluntary organisations as appropriate providers of information, advice and emotional support for carers. At its best, this cross-sector approach results in complementary services in which the needs of carers are addressed, with professionally based and self-help services contributing to a full spectrum of support. At its worst, if the systems are not working together, carers will lose out through lack of information or failure to access the appropriate level of help.

In this chapter, policy developments and research findings currently shaping the provision of support and services to carers are considered, focussing particularly on the implications for social care practice. Carers play an indispensable role in the provision of social care services and there are vital issues that must be addressed to ensure that they receive the support that they need.

The Policy Context

Work with carers is a 'late entry' to the field of social care, with carers only emerging as a major care group in their own right in the 1980s. While some areas of work, such as mental health, had developed a number of approaches to working with families, the focus of this tended to be on how people could help relatives with mental health problems, rather than considering the carer's own needs. In terms of service provision, while there were local pockets of good practice in which the needs of carers were recognised and addressed, the presence of a carer, especially women carers, invariably meant that the service user received far less support. At this stage, the role of carers in national policy or in resource allocation was barely recognised.

Although a late arrival, the consideration of the needs of carers has quickly become part of the national agenda for social care. The increasing numbers of older people over the age of seventy-five means that caring is close to home for many people. Nearly all of us will know or be carers at some time in our lives, which means that the cause of carers is well understood by society as a whole. Therefore, carers have gained increasing priority on successive government's agendas for social care. In addition, unlike some other groups such as people with disabilities, there is also one clear national lobbying movement – Carers UK, formerly the Carers National Association, which is focussed on the needs of carers as a whole with the intention of achieving change at a national level.

The national carers' movement is working to improve carers' lives in the widest sense. This is taking place not just in the UK but in other countries in the West, where carers are questioning society's assumption that they will continue to care – no matter what the personal cost to themselves. In summary, their aim is to achieve appreciation of the contribution that carers make to society, backed up with remuneration so that carers do not suffer financially or face social exclusion. This includes elements such as improved benefits, opportunities to gain employment, pension rights and flexible working arrangements.

The first landmark development for carers was specific legislation which acknowledged that carers had needs in their own right and gave local authorities the duty to assess these needs – the Carers (Recognition and Services) Act 1995. With this Act, local authorities are clearly obliged to consider the needs of carers when arranging services for the service user. One of the most significant features of the 1995 Act and associated Guidance is the statement that authorities should not assume that carers would be willing to continue with some or all of their caring responsibilities. This is a change in emphasis from an approach that focussed solely on enabling the carer to care, to acknowledging that there may be circumstances in which this is not what the carer wants or is able to do.

The second major development for carers is the National Strategy for Carers (Department of Health, 1999) which sets out a number of measures through which the government intends to encourage support for carers. In addition to new social care initiatives, there is financial and employment support. For instance, the time spent caring will give some carers an entitlement to pension rights above the basic state retirement pension. The government is also promoting flexible 'family friendly' employment, such as job share or flexi-time, and special schemes to enable carers to retain or regain employment. Collection of information about carers will also be improved, with a duty for local authorities and primary care services to identify carers (Department of Health, 1998a). A new question on carers was included in the 2001 census.

A further important development accompanying the National Strategy is that, as part of the modernising social services agenda (Department of Health, 1998b), local authorities have been given additional funding to support carers. The Carers' Special Grant

every day – their break is from the caring tasks not from the person.

Services which support carers

It is important to be aware that services that benefit service users will also have a significant impact on carers. One of the most important features of services for carers is their reliability – if services such as transport are late or do not turn up at all, the carer's time may be wasted and their opportunity for a break or to do some essential task lost. Similarly, services need to be as flexible as possible – while some carers need a service on a regular basis, others may need less provision but one which can be accessed at short notice. Another extremely important factor is having emergency back up should anything happen to the carer. Given that many carers are older people, emergency services that can take on the caring role if the carer becomes ill are essential to ensure peace of mind. Sometimes the carer dimension of services is neglected by people responsible for developing services or evaluating their quality, and it is important that this situation is redressed by all services formally evaluating how they can best serve the carer as well as the user.

In addition to services for the user, some carers will benefit from support such as counselling or stress management. This type of service is important because it focuses on the carer and their own emotional and practical needs and may be a rare opportunity for the carer to pay attention to their own situation.

Involving carers

Involving carers in service planning and evaluation must be an integral part of social care developments and all authorities need mechanisms in place to ensure that the views of carers are heard and acted upon. It is interesting to note that the emphasis placed upon consulting with carers by the Department of Health is arguably greater than for the user groups. For example, plans for the carer's special grant were assessed on how far they demonstrated consultation with carers.

For individual carers, however, the main issue of involvement is likely to be the relationship between themselves and the workers who they meet on a regular basis. An interesting distinction in the ways workers view carers has been made by Twigg and Atkin (1994). Workers may treat carers as 'co-workers', as 'co-clients', as a 'resource' and as 'superseded'. It is important that such preconceptions are not a barrier to effective support. Perhaps the best way of describing the ideal relationship between worker, carer and service user is as a partnership based on respect for each person's expertise. While the worker may have professional expertise, it is certain that the carer, and user, will also have expertise based on personal experience.

Assessing Carers' Needs

Assessment is the first and crucial stage in any intervention, determining subsequent service provision. The importance of assessment for adult service users is enshrined in the NHS and Community Care Act 1990 (NHSCCA) and its Guidance. The Carers Act supplements this legislation, giving carers who provide *substantial and regular* care the right to an assessment, on request, of their ability to care and to continue caring. Carers' assessments are not undertaken in their own right but are connected with an assessment or review of the needs of the person receiving care, mainly through the NHSCCA or, in the case of parent carers and young carers, through the Children Act 1989.

In 1998, the Social Services Inspectorate (SSI) undertook an in-depth inspection of seven social services departments to determine how they had implemented the Carers Act. While much good practice was found, the overwhelming result of these inspections was that carers were subject to a 'lottery of location' (SSI, 1998: p3). There were inconsistent approaches between authorities, but also, significantly *between teams within authorities and between members of the same teams*. These findings reinforce work commissioned by Carers UK which has identified that carers are not being informed of their right to assessment and that assessments take place on an ad hoc basis (Holzhausen, 1997). Carers' assessment is now an indicator in the social services performance assessment framework and monitoring information by the the social services inspectorate confirms that at 21%, the proportion of assessments is low (SSI, 2002). Modern social services demonstrate a commitment to reform (The Annual Report of the Chief Inspector of Social Services 2001–02, SSI DoH, 2002).

According to the SSI, social services departments may not have procedures to ensure satisfactory implementation of the Carers Act 1995, or where there are procedures these are not always implemented. This means that some front line staff responsible for assessments and their line managers are unsure about the responsibilities of their departments to assess carers. The reasons for this inconsistency are complex and multifaceted; here we examine some of the issues which may have contributed to this problem and consider ways of resolving this.

The legislation itself can be seen as lacking clarity in certain areas, a factor which may have contributed to the difficulty local authorities experience in achieving consistency in relation to services for carers. Most prominently, no national definition is given of 'substantial and regular care' in the Carers Act 1995, or the National Strategy. Rather, 'it will be for local authorities to form their own judgement of what amounts to 'substantial' and 'regular' and to make their views known' (Department of Health, 1996).

If these concepts are not defined, practitioners and carers are left with no parameters within which to exercise judgement about what is appropriate. The difficulties of defining these concepts lie in ensuring an appropriate balance between too tight a definition, which would exclude carers who need help, and one which is too wide, which may raise expectations and in which authorities may find it difficult to meet demand. A rule of thumb of twenty hours per week spent caring has been proposed as a guideline, but organisations need to consider a number of factors to arrive at a picture of which carers will be eligible. For instance, acknowledging that carers do not need to live with the person needing care and that care should not be confined solely to personal care. Such an exercise is clearly best undertaken involving front line staff and local carers and their organisations to arrive at an agreed consensus.

Historically, a number of authorities operated the practice of not allocating services where carers were involved. The new approach of considering carers' needs and allocating resources to meet these may not have been 'worked through' by the organisation, leading to ambivalence in policy and practice. This situation has been exacerbated where authorities have experienced severe budgetary limitations leading to prioritisation and tight eligibility criteria, and it is the person with no carer who is often seen to be in greatest need.

Another contributing factor, as we have seen, is the services for carers across organisational boundaries. For example young carers may require services from both adult and children's services. This situation can result in, no one worker having responsibility for ensuring that the different strands of working with carers are properly co-ordinated.

In order to address these problems, organisations need to have clear policies that show how carers should be supported. Furthermore, there need to be procedures for addressing how carers' issues will be managed across specialisms. These should not be just paper exercises but brought alive in the organisations through regular training and review until supporting carers becomes an *automatic* part of the assessment and service provision by all social workers. Organisations need to allocate clear responsibility to a named individual for ensuring a co-ordinated approach to supporting carers.

Good Practice in Assessment and Care Planning

It is good practice to provide information to service users, ahead of an assessment, about what to expect from the process, and related but distinct information should also be available for carers. One method is to give carers a list of issues for them to consider, such as how their health is being affected, whether they have opportunities for social and leisure activities and any particular aspects of caring which cause them problems.

As part of the community care assessment, the care manager or social worker must reinforce with the carer and service user that the carer has a right to an assessment and explain what this would entail. The latest practice guidance has indicated that workers must inform carers that this can take place separately from the user if preferred (Department of Health, 2001c). It may be that there is insufficient information at the initial assessment to determine the extent of the carer's role. In such situations a tool such as a carer's diary sheet, completed by the carer over a period of a couple of months can provide a clearer picture of need. This information could be considered at the first review of services. When a carer's assessment is completed a carer should receive a copy of their assessment and care plan. Regrettably some authorities and workers have a 'but we're doing it already' attitude when carers are clearly saying 'but nothing is happening.'

The final area of lack of clarity may be in the relationship between the carer's assessment, the user's assessment and the subsequent service provision. Guidance in respect of the 1995 Act indicates that both users' and carers' assessments should be taken into account in designing the care plan, and that this should show how services delivered to the user will benefit the carer:

> *Views and circumstances of users and carers may be distinct but the nature of caring requires that they are considered together and reflected in the services to be provided to the user.*
>
> (Department of Health, 1996: p3.)

Sometimes services are allocated that are of benefit to carers as well as users, but this is not clarified or documented. A standard example of this is to be found where day care is part of an individual's care plan, but it is not recorded that as well as providing therapeutic activities this also provides a break for the carer. It is vital that the negotiations with users and carers, when forming the care plan, should make clear the purpose of any intervention. Similarly, written care plans should *record where services are of benefit to carers*. Without this, the carer may be unaware that they are receiving any support.

Legislative changes in the Carers and Disabled Children Act, will certainly provide an additional impetus to encourage authorities to adopt a thorough approach to carers' assessments. At the same time, it may well reinforce the potential conflict between carers and service users. Most people's relationships involve tension and disagreement at some stage, but that between the carer and cared for has more potential for this due to the intrinsic stress that can be involved in giving or receiving care. In relation to service provision, this will be played out in the balance of rights between the user and the carer. For example, if the carer is assessed as needing a break from caring but the service user refuses to take such a break, how can the situation be resolved? In such situations, the worker will need skills in negotiation to try to help those involved come to an acceptable solution. In some cases, such as dementia, where the user is not able to make an informed choice, but their preference appears clearly not to take a break, it may be necessary to decide on their behalf that their long term well being involves allowing the carer some free time. Such decisions can be stressful for the carer as well as the user, and practitioners need to be able to offer support, both to the carer who may feel guilt and to the user who may experience rejection.

As can be seen, the dimension of working with carers means that practitioners from all agencies have to be able to work in a complicated area with tact and sensitivity and to employ skills such as negotiation. This is far removed from any view of care management as a mechanical process for deployment of resources. Within this area of practice, the attitude of workers and organisations towards carers is of major importance. At the same time, while the principles of working with carers apply universally, it is important that differences between the needs of specific groups of carers are acknowledged. In this final section, four specialist areas are considered, in which the needs of carers and the relationship between carer and service user require particular consideration and expertise from practitioners (for further discussion of specific care groups see Heron,1998).

Needs of Specific Carer Groups

Carers from ethnic minorities

When we consider the response to the needs of carers from ethnic minority groups, factors such as language barriers, lack of cultural understanding and the potential for racism may all be operating. It is inappropriate to generalise about the particular issues facing carers from ethnic minorities since these will vary according to the language, culture, and individual circumstances of the carer. However, some overall principles can be applied to inform practice. Perhaps most important is that practitioners must be careful to avoid applying cultural stereotypes which contribute to denying that carers require support. Some commonly held views are that Asian people will look after elders within the family setting and that Asian and Chinese people will not wish to receive public welfare because of a strong ethic of self-help. While these may indeed apply in some situations, it is extremely dangerous to act as if they are relevant in every case. Some people from ethnic minorities live alone without extended families. Increased involvement of Asian women in work may mean a lack of carers or additional pressure on women who have the traditional caring role. Many carers may be desperate for help but unable to access support because of lack of knowledge of services and systems due to the absence of proactive communication from agencies.

There are also issues about the carers' understanding of the illness or disability of the person needing care, such as a particular cultural view of the nature of mental health issues which differs from prevalent views held in the UK. Similarly, in some situations, particularly where adults cannot communicate easily in English, young carers may be under particular pressure to undertake a role as spokesperson for the family – as well as being a carer. In order to address such situations, it is helpful if, wherever possible, the worker involved should be from the same cultural background and speak the same language as the family. Furthermore, it is essential that services are as appropriate as possible for the service user's needs viewed from a culturally relevant perspective, since carers will be unwilling for their relatives to accept services which conflict with such perspectives.

Some of the most desperate situations for carers exist amongst ethnic minorities; it is vital that organisations and practitioners do not mistake lack of demand for lack of need.

Young carers

Young carers are children and young people under the age of eighteen who have a caring role, generally for a member of their family, who may be a parent, sibling or grandparent. There are no exact figures for numbers of young carers in the UK, but estimates indicate that there may be over 50,000 of whom 10,000 are primary carers (Mahon and Higgins, 1995). Carers may be as young as primary school age and some may undertake the same range of caring tasks as an adult. A repeated pattern seen in young carers associated with young carer's projects, is that many have parents who have mental health or substance abuse problems.

Experience from the field of working with young carers indicates that adult care managers may sometimes fail to recognise the level of care that young carers provide and the effect this has upon the child. This may be because of the worker's lack of experience in working with children but can also be because the family wants to present a united front, minimising the child's contributions to care. Occasionally, this may be because the family fears intervention from social services, but generally it is through a need to be seen as coping and being a 'normal' family.

The responsibility is therefore for adult workers to adopt a child centred approach when dealing with young carers. Care managers need to make routine enquiries about the role any children or young people take in caring for a relative, even if they are not the sole carer (this is discussed in detail in Chapter 8). They also need to be aware of services for young carers locally, and have written information to hand so they can promote these positively to the young carer and their family.

The skill in working in this area lies in supporting parental rights and responsibilities while ensuring that the child's health and development is not detrimentally affected by caring responsibilities. Workers may need to involve colleagues both from the child's school and also children's social services. From the other perspective, if children and family social workers are supporting young carers they also need to be mindful of any community care needs of the adults who are receiving care and refer these individuals for appropriate support.

It is essential that all authorities have clear procedures detailing how support for young carers can be managed most appropriately when two separate sections of social services departments may be involved. Assessment procedures designed for adults are unlikely to be appropriate for young carers who will need information written in accessible language, which focuses on their areas of need such as, how their schoolwork or ability to make friends is being affected. Many authorities use separate, child focussed, assessment forms for young carers, and have looser eligibility criteria reflecting national guidance that young carers should not be expected to provide the same level of care as adult carers (Department of Health, 1996).

Many areas have a young carer's project and the National Carers Strategy has emphasised the importance of maintaining specific services for this group. Young carer's projects provide leisure, social and developmental activities on a group and individual basis to equip young carers to develop socially and educationally. For example, some projects provide homework clubs for children who do not get quiet space at home and individual counselling where children have emotional problems. Projects can be invaluable in giving the time and specialist support to young carers, which it is generally not possible to provide through a fieldwork or care management process.

Mental health

The field of mental health presents a particularly complicated picture in relation to the role of carers with a number of factors that may affect service provision. These include:

- A strong movement by families of users of mental health services to promote help for their family member, perhaps at the expense of looking at their own needs; this approach may also be taken by workers.

- A history of attributing a causal link between family behaviour or heredity and mental health problems – this can lead to prejudice about families from workers.

- Carers of people with mental health problems generally provide a different type of care to the majority of carers. Rather than physical care this tends to be emotional support, supervision or dealing with challenging behaviour or risk.

- There is a significant potential for conflict between carer and service user, such as the service user refusing to allow contact between services and their carer.

- Confidentiality can be an area of considerable contention between families and workers.

The role of carers *as carers rather than simply family members* has been recognised in the National Service Framework for mental health. Authorities need to bring a carer dimension to mental health services through improved awareness raising, policy development and training (Department of Health, Sept, 1999). The national development of family support workers will have a positive impact on carers' lives (*Developing Services for Carers and Families of People with Mental Health*, Department of Health, 2002).

In addition, organisations that provide general support to all carers need to consider developing expertise in supporting carers of people with mental health problems as well as other care groups. Some information is already available, for example, The National Schizophrenia Fellowship has designed a pack for people who care for people with schizophrenia (NSF, 1999).

Transitions – parents to carers

As children with severe or complex disabilities grow up, the role of parent generally evolves into that of parent carer. Similarly, when the child reaches adulthood such families will cross over from receiving children's services to adult services. This transition can be a particularly challenging time for service users and carers, as it means making new relationships with professionals and services and coming to terms with a new stage of life. This is particularly evident if there are basic ideological differences concerning issues of independence between workers, carers, users and groups who advocate for people with disabilities. While tensions between the aspirations and views of service users and carers can be found in all user groups, one of the areas in which disagreements most frequently surface is with people with disabilities and their carers. The focus of this conflict is generally about risk and independence.

The parent who questions whether their child who is nineteen years of age has the right to contribute to decisions about their future may be an extreme example, but some parents find it difficult to acknowledge that their children have become adults and will be seeking to extend their lives and become more independent. This will affect their aspirations for their child's future, which may emphasise their safety to the detriment of any challenge or risk. It will also determine what they expect from service provision – services to protect the individual and keep them well cared for. For practitioners this can lead to a complex situation when working with the service user and carer. Carers of children and adults with disabilities have similar needs to other carers and the right to an assessment of their needs. At the same time, the main responsibility of the worker is to support the service user and to work towards them achieving as much age appropriate autonomy as possible.

In addition, most practitioners will be aware of situations in which the relationship between the young person and their family has become more complicated, through the income associated with their disability benefits becoming inextricably linked with the families' budget. This can lead to disincentives to encourage the person with a disability to look for employment or live independently.

The long term solution to such issues are for children's services to work with adult services according to joint principles so that all parents are supported from the earliest stages in working towards helping the child maximise independence. It is also useful for workers with adults to gain an understanding of the issues that face parents who bring up a disabled child. It is easy to become judgmental about attitudes, which may be considered overprotective without understanding the family's history and perspective. The skills involved in working in this field may involve

family work and can go beyond that which is normally required in supporting carers, but within this it is important not to lose sight of the fact that parents are also carers.

The Way Forward for Supporting Carers

In all the above specialisms, if the needs of users and carers are clearly in conflict or if there is a complex family situation, it can be appropriate to have a different worker from the care manager involved with the service user to make the carer's assessment. In other situations it can be useful if advocates are involved, to speak on behalf of or negotiate for the individuals – service user or carer.

There is now a clear national direction for improving services and support for carers and the challenge lies in implementing this within available resources. Perhaps the most important message is that supporting carers must become an integral and automatic component of work in all sections of health and social care. One practical method of achieving this is suggested in the Carers' Compass, an audit and performance guide for addressing the needs of carers, which indicates that carers' issues should be built into the job descriptions of all managers (Banks et al., 1998). Responsibility for carers must be owned across authorities and across all staff:

> *All front-line workers have a responsibility to respond to carers – not just specialist carers support or development staff.*
>
> (SSI, 1998.)

Further Reading

Department of Health (2001). *A Practitioners Guide to Carers' Assessments under the Carers and Disabled Children Act 2000*. London: Department of Health.

Heron, C. (1998). *Working with Carers*. London: Jessica Kingsley.

Weightman, G. (1999). *A Real Break. A Guidebook for Good Practice in the Provision of Short-Term Breaks as a Support for Care in the Community*. London: Department of Health.

Assessment and Role Across Social Work Specialisms in Working with Domestic Violence

Catherine Humphreys and Audrey Mullender

Introduction

Domestic violence is everywhere and nowhere within social work. All social work agencies, whether they recognise it or not, work with women and children who are living in, or escaping from situations of domestic violence, and many agencies now belong to inter-agency forums through which they make public statements about their increased awareness of the problem. Yet, the effectiveness of responses to domestic violence continues to vary markedly, both in and between agencies, and, crucially, no statutory agency or department in the personal social services has the needs of abused women and their children as core business. Domestic violence survivors therefore tend only to be the subject of resources and practice attention when they 'fit' into an organisation's priority categories via a different route, for example as a child protection or mental health referral. As a result, domestic violence itself may become lost as an issue.

This chapter will follow a brief overview of relevant legislation and policy development with an exploration of how domestic violence is reaching the social work agenda. The barriers and limitations to good practice will be discussed, as will indicators for the promotion of safer and more effective work.

The Extent and Impact of Domestic Violence

Domestic violence typically involves a pattern of physical, sexual and emotional abuse and intimidation. It can best be understood as the misuse of power and the exercise of control (Pence and Paymar, 1988), most commonly by a man over a woman who is, or has been, his partner. Occasionally women are abusers, though without the same pattern of societal collusion to reinforce their power. Women may experience abuse, not only from their husband, but also from his relatives, both male and female (Hendessai, 1999; Bhatti-Sinclair, 1994).

Violence may also occur between same sex couples. Throughout this chapter, however, offenders are referred to as male and the victims or survivors of abuse as female. This reflects the dominant pattern and has the advantage of naming this as a predominantly gendered form of violence. However, it does bring with it the attendant problem of marginalising women and men whose experiences lie outside this form of abuse and this should be borne in mind by the reader.

Both the prevalence and the seriousness of domestic violence are beginning to make an impact in the public consciousness. Using the most conservative estimates research suggests that one in four women experience some form of domestic violence over their lifetime, while between one in eight and one in ten women will have experienced assault in the past year (Mayhew et al., 1993; Mooney, 1994; Stanko, 1998). The Home Office figures on homicide show a persistent rate over 10 years of on average almost two women a week dying at the hands of their male partners and ex-partners. However, it is not just the fatalities that highlight the seriousness of the problem.

Studies of women and mental health illustrate the serious impact of domestic violence. Jacobson and Richardson (1987) showed that 60-70 per cent of women in one mental health unit had been abused. Stark (1984) revealed that a quarter of women admitted for emergency psychiatric care had experienced domestic violence. Similarly, 24 per cent of 184 patients screened over a five-month period in an adult psychiatric service were victims of domestic violence (Tham et al., 1995). A marked correlation has also been found between women's suicide attempts and their experience of assault from their partner or ex-partner (Stark and Flitcraft, 1996). Sixty-five per cent had been assaulted in the six months preceding their first suicide attempt.

Child protection, too, is now the focus of an established link with domestic violence, with a range of manifestations. Children themselves may be killed by men who are also violent towards their mothers (O'Hara, 1994). Many men who abuse women also physically abuse children, with an overlap in the range of 45-70 per cent depending on the study (Bowker et al., 1988; Stark and Flitcraft, 1988). There is also evidence to suggest increased prevalence of child sexual abuse in cases of domestic violence (Forman, 1995). The incidence of domestic violence is notably high for children on the child protection register, and the figure may double when active monitoring and screening occurs (Farmer and Owen, 1995; Hester and Pearson, 1998). Women experiencing violence themselves may punish their children more harshly, either to prevent a worse beating from the abusive man or because they themselves are at the 'end of their tether' (Mullender et al., 1998). Women are particularly vulnerable during pregnancy when violence may commence or escalate (Mezey, 1997). Two per cent of women surveyed in GP waiting rooms in Hackney reported a miscarriage as a result of violence (Stanko et al., 1998).

Children may also suffer indirectly. They are usually aware of the abuse towards their mothers (Hughes, 1988; Abrahams, 1994). While there is no recognisable syndrome, with each child reacting differently depending upon their age, support networks, gender, personal resilience and other protective factors in their lives, there are heightened levels of distress. One study showed 2.5 times the rate of behavioural and psychological problems of other children. Children may recover once they feel safe (Wolfe et al., 1989; Mertin, 1995) and when their mothers are in a less debilitating situation where they are more able to meet the children's physical and emotional needs. However, being forced to flee violence creates disruption to family networks, schools, and friendship networks (Mullender et al., 1998). There may be additional issues for black and ethnic minority children who move away from a local community which offers protection against racism (Imam, 1994) or when there are increased risks of abduction and deportation (Patel, 1997).

In short, the risks posed to women and children through male violence are too great to be ignored by social workers who will encounter the issue in whichever organisation and setting they are employed.

The Legislative Context – Swings and Roundabouts

Change and contradiction have characterised the law on domestic violence over the past decade with improvements in some areas, both for women and children, matched by regression or continuing unevenness in others. (Hester et al., 1998, offer a more detailed discussion for interested practitioners.)

Legislation affecting adult survivors of woman abuse

The Family Law Act (1996) Part IV

The Family Law Act (1996) Part IV (FLA) was designed to overcome the complications and inadequacies involved in gaining effective civil injunctions. Non-molestation orders are intended to protect against all forms of violence and abuse, while occupation orders regulate the occupation of the family home. Improvements over previous legislation include: a power of arrest attached to most of these orders; potentially unspecified time limits; comparatively broad definitions of potential applicants; rights to occupation of the family home on the balance of harm; and short term exclusion orders available where children have been abused. For disabled women, being able to stay safely in a house that may have been specially adapted can be a major advantage, though, if the abuser is also a carer, excluding him may not always be a realistic option.

Some limitations remain in the new law. The 'associated persons' referred to in the Act do not cover those people in a close relationship who have not lived together and where there is no child for whom they both have parental responsibility. Black women's groups have argued that this discriminates against a significant group of black women with 'visiting relationships' who fall outside the parameters of the legislation. Legal aid thresholds have also increased so that the accessibility of the orders is undermined by the lack of eligibility for the legal support needed to obtain one.

Providing active support in pursuing these orders can be a significant role for social workers where the woman herself concludes that this is a step towards safety for herself and her children. Certainly, if social workers are considering the safe negotiation of contact arrangements for children, then underpinning these arrangements with a non-molestation order may be important and needs discussion with the woman.

Unfortunately, one section of the FLA which would make a significant difference to social workers in the child protection arena, s.60, has yet to be enacted. This would allow the police or other professionals to take out a non-molestation or occupation order on behalf of the woman or children (so-called 'third party applications') and would markedly assist in shifting the focus of responsibility from the woman to the man (Humphreys and Kaye, 1997). For example, it would be easy to envisage a child protection conference recommending, with the woman's permission, that the police should take out an application for a non-molestation order. This strategy would name the man's violence and its cessation as the pivotal issue in protecting the children from harm, while not forcing the woman into precipitate action if she were not ready at this point either to take her partner to court, or to separate from him.

Protection from Harassment Act 1997

The UK situation is made more complex and interesting, by the passage into law of the Protection from Harassment Act 1997 (PFHA). Whilst this act was not drafted to focus on domestic violence, it did seek to address the problem of 'stalking' which was defined broadly as 'a course of conduct amounting to harassment of another'. Two or more recorded acts of harassment constitute a course of conduct. The use of the PFHA appears to vary across the country. Much of the early training suggested that it would fill the gap for abused women who did not fit the criteria of 'associated persons' under the FLA (Gold, 1997). However, in some areas, the police, the Crown Prosecution Service and solicitors appear to be using it as the legislation of preference for women escaping situations of domestic violence. Its particular advantages are that the police take the action (not the woman) and that a restraining order is given by the judge at the completion of the criminal case, again saving the woman from taking out a non-molestation order herself. The legislation is particularly useful where post-separation violence is occurring.

Housing Act 1996

While the legislation reviewed thus far offers progressive avenues for women escaping domestic violence, the Housing Act 1996 represents a comparatively regressive step in the legislative framework. This is particularly unfortunate, given that there will always be limitations to the effectiveness of occupation and non-molestation orders in creating enough safety and security for women and children to live without fear. Many women will therefore continue to be dependent upon social rehousing as their primary option. In the past, women and children leaving situations of violence were categorised as unintentionally homeless and the local authority had a duty (albeit after some waiting) to provide permanent housing. The Housing Act 1996 Part VII gives local authorities responsibility for housing families only on a temporary basis, though this may be renewable after two years for some applicants. A particular group of women and children who fall outside Part VI of the Act are asylum seekers and women with no recourse to public funds, whose position is not helped by the new legislation and guidance on asylum seekers. Local authorities are expected to provide in limited ways for the children (Children Act 1989 s.17); however, the support is discretionary and does not include the needs of the mother.

The Code of Guidance which accompanies the Act is reasonably sympathetic to women and children in situations of domestic violence. However, there is no duty for a local authority to comply with it in total, and practice throughout the UK is extremely varied. For example, the Guidance states that there is no obligation on applicants to return to their homes with an injunction if they believe it will be ineffective. However, there is increasing evidence of many local authorities demanding this step, rather than providing alternative accommodation. Other housing departments (for example, Leeds) have developed good practice guidance which goes beyond that recommended under the Act and which makes a very positive contribution to the options available for women in situations of domestic violence.

Support Services – Mental Health Act 1983, sections 8, 11, 115, 127 and 135

The developments of sources of support, prevention and therapy for adults are not the primary focus of either the Mental Health Act 1983 or the NHS and Community Care Act 1991. Some councils are, however, drawing up procedures and policies to cover vulnerable adults, including women who have been abused. For example, Calderdale Metropolitan Council (1995) has developed detailed guidelines for the use of relevant sections of the Mental Health Act 1983 to access assessment and resources for persons with mental health problems who are victims of abuse. Again, this is an area that requires further development and resourcing. Other local authorities (for example, Hammersmith and Fulham; Lewisham) are asking practitioners carefully to consider sections of the mental health legislation, which nominate the woman's closest relative. The inappropriateness of an abusive husband in that role needs to be considered and argued for strongly by Approved Social Workers and other mental health advocates.

Legislation relevant to children living with woman abuse

Children Act 1989 – Exclusion Order

An amendment to the Children Act 1989 now allows for the temporary exclusion of an offender from the family home (s.38A [2]). The legislation is only useful for a very particular group of children; those who have an interim care order or emergency protection order in place. The Department of Health Guidance is also very clear that this measure can only be used where the mother's informed consent has been gained and that the safety of the child's carer (usually the mother) can only be considered alongside that of the child. As yet, there appears to have been little use of this new power, though it is unclear whether this is because social workers and guardians ad litem lack confidence in advocating it, or because of the limited eligibility criteria.

Children Act 1989 – Child Contact (s. 8), Family Support (s.17) and the Investigation of Significant Harm (s. 47)

There are critical dilemmas that underpin the use of the Children Act 1989 by social services departments. Since 1995, when *Messages from Research* was published, there has been a concerted campaign by the Department of Health and others to re-focus work with children and families from the investigation of incidents of abuse which may cause significant harm (s. 47) to support for children and their families under s. 17 of the Children Act 1989 (see Chapter 8 for more detail). This latter section of the Act gives local authorities a 'General duty to safeguard and promote the welfare of children in need by providing a range and level of services appropriate to their needs'. The definition of need is then defined broadly, and the Guidance emphasises that local authorities may develop preventative and support services for families through firstly ascertaining the extent of need and then making decisions about the priority for service provision (Tunstill, 1997).

Whilst, in principle, children in situations of domestic violence should be recognised as children in need, the contracting resource base of most social services departments in the UK has made it difficult to prioritise this group of children in their own right. Section 17 budgets are generally small, though there has been some success in accessing modest amounts of direct funding for example in providing taxis to take women and their children to a refuge, to help some (though not all) women and children who lack recourse to public funds, and to provide limited support services such as part-time refuge children's workers. Programme funding is more readily available through partnership initiatives with Sure Start or the Children's Fund

As the connections between child abuse and domestic violence have become clearer, there has been an increase in s. 47 investigations of child abuse, which name domestic violence as significantly harmful to children. Social workers in children and families teams struggle with assessing the thresholds for significant harm in such cases, particularly when witnessing violence is the issue rather than a direct assault on the child (Parkinson and Humphreys, 1998; Brandon and Lewis, 1996), and practice across the UK is varied.

Women's attempts to separate and to move away from violence are often confounded by child contact arrangements which presume in favour of contact to the non-resident parent (usually father), regardless of his behaviour (Parker and Eaton, 1994). Changes may now be afoot with four judgements in the Court of Appeal (June 2000) which upheld no contact in four cases where domestic violence had been a central issue. The LCD has now issued *Good Practice Guidelines for Judges in Cases of Parental Contact Where There is Domestic Violence* following these judgements. A new amendment to the definition of harm in The Children Act (1989) to include 'any impairment of the child's health or development as a result of witnessing the ill-treatment of another person'. The situation has been developing whereby statutory children and families' social workers are urging women to separate and move away from violence, while court welfare officers and judges are just as quickly bringing women back in touch with their ex-partners through unsafe child contact arrangements (Humphreys, 1999b). Both stances can be dangerous. Abuse typically does not cease with separation but may well escalate, and, then, a woman who is trying to escape from this intensifying danger is likely to find that child contact is a particularly common context for post-separation violence (Hester and Radford, 1996). This highlights the need for professionals to work in partnership with the non-abusive parent and to plan actively for both her and her children's safety.

There is clear scope for an advocacy role for social workers in assisting women and children to develop safe post-separation arrangements. High vigilance, supervised contact, indirect contact, or no contact at all can be argued for in situations of grave risk. This could involve writing a report to feed into the court welfare report preparation process, or even suggesting that child protection conference minutes be available to the Family Proceedings Court – particularly in situations where the woman is being told that the children will be accommodated unless she separates, or maintains her separation from, an abusive man and where contact would cut across this. Such a role would involve bridging some of the barriers between specialists in public law (statutory child and family social workers) and specialists in private law (court welfare officers).

In summary, the legislative framework for work in the area of domestic violence has been subjected to change in the last decade. This change has brought with it both progress and problems for women and children escaping situations of domestic violence. In 2003, it is proposed to draft a domestic violence bill to overcome some of the problems with both civil and criminal justice for survivors.

Moving Domestic Violence onto the Social Work Agenda

Since 1994, when the Social Services Inspectorate (SSI) held national conferences on its relationship with child abuse, domestic violence has been officially recognised as a child welfare issue. Inter-agency co-ordination in child protection now names domestic violence as a key issue for consideration (Working Together, 1999). We also have a growing awareness of the seriousness of domestic violence as a social problem and the damaging effect it can have on the health and development of children who are exposed to it. This is a mark of progress since the Children Act (1989) and associated guidance, including the child welfare checklist, had previously failed to mention domestic violence as an issue for consideration in assessing risk factors for children.

The connections between mental health and domestic violence, which were quantified above, are now also being recognised. Some mental health social workers are alert to issues of domestic violence as evidenced by an increase in their presence at domestic violence inter-agency forums and by comprehensive sections for mental health workers in inter-agency guidelines (Calderdale, 1995). *The Mental Health Strategy for Women* (Department of Health, 2002) now recognises women experiencing domestic violence as a high risk group in need of mental health services.

In the field of health, the British Medical Association has issued comprehensive guidelines for health workers, including doctors, and a number of influential organisations have produced reports which highlight domestic violence as a health issue (SNAP, 1997; BMA, 1998) and primary health care as a key service accessed by women in situations of violence (see for example, Stanko et al., 1998), including Asian women if confidentiality can be guaranteed (Hendessai, 1999). However, the potential opportunity is often limited by the narrow medical focus of health professionals and by doctors' reluctance to ask women more probing questions about their injuries (Modood and Berthoud, 1997; BMA, 1998). Health social workers could provide a key interface between 'medical' and the 'social' aspects of health care, if their potential for constructive front line intervention with women and children in situations of domestic violence were more effectively utilised.

Care managers, too, could play an essential role in identifying and responding to domestic violence if levels of awareness were higher. In fact, there are very high levels of abuse of disabled women (Nosek et al., 1998) and amongst women with learning difficulties (McCarthy, 1999). It is also likely to be the case that some 'elder abuse' is actually domestic violence that has continued on into old age (McGibbon et al., 1989). In none of these spheres has social work been at the forefront of revealing the problem but this need not prevent the profession from making a concerted response.

Probation officers are amongst the most active in establishing and running men's projects designed to tackle domestic violence. Such groups typically follow a re-educational model that seeks to change men's attitudes towards women as well as their behaviour. Men may be court mandated to attend or may do so voluntarily, depending on the scheme. Although it is clearly desirable to tackle men's violence at source, there are pitfalls in running such groups. These include high drop-out rates, variable success rates (particularly when based on female partner reports and when measured over time), a risk of competing for funding with emergency services for women and children, and a danger of collusion with men's agendas unless accountability to women is structured into the programme (Mullender, 1996).

In summary, social workers and related professional groupings have always worked with women, children and men where domestic violence is an issue, though they have not always recognised the fact or moved beyond traditional shortcomings to develop best practice.

Barriers to Safe and Effective Social Work Practice

Within statutory social work, both in the children and families arena and in adult services, a range of practices and policies may be found which consistently undermine good practice and maintain the invisibility of domestic violence as a key issue threatening the lives and well being of women and children. Research in the statutory child welfare sector highlights some of the typical 'traps' in this process. These can also be found in other sectors of practice, epitomising as they do the avoidance or minimisation of perpetrator's behaviour (Milner, 1993; Farmer and Owen, 1995; Humphreys, 1999a), notably when professionals consistently redefine the problem to suit the standpoint of their agency (McWilliams and McKiernan, 1993).

Concentration on violent assault

While the dominant pattern of social work practice involves minimising domestic violence, there are exceptions to this practice: a) when children are directly abused or sometimes when women are seriously injured in attacks. These cases, the 'atrocity stories' come to signify domestic violence. It is, of course, entirely appropriate that the plight of women is acknowledged and that the assessment process should recognise that the more violent the actions towards the woman, the greater the likelihood of significant violence and abuse towards children (Ross, 1996). Nevertheless, this response becomes problematic if other forms of abuse, which reinforce the subjugation of the woman, go unnoticed. Physical and sexual violence need only be used intermittently to establish a disabling atmosphere of threat and tension. Other tactics such as enforced pregnancy, economic control, belittling, threats of deportation, threats through the children are equally significant (Pense and Paymar, 1988), yet are consistently overlooked or minimised in much social work practice.

Micro-practices which maintain invisibility

A number of micro-practices have developed which consistently hide the abuse of the woman.

For example, social workers are often aware of domestic violence, mention the issue in case notes, but then fail to mention it in reports, file summaries, and inter-agency forums such as child protection conferences and strategy meetings. Similarly, domestic violence becomes invisible through the 'non-naming' of a significant pattern of abuse and violence against the woman. Instead, gender neutral terms such as 'marital conflict', 'fighting', and a 'conflictual relationship' are used. A case file analysis in two children and families' teams by one of the authors showed that, in some situations, this neutralising effect might be quite extreme (Humphreys, 1999). There were examples in the case files of a stabbing identified as 'an argument between parents', or of an Asian woman leaving her home being described as 'marital disruption'. A closer reading of the file showed that the second woman had been assaulted, that she and the children had been forced to sit in the dark for lengthy periods of time, that her husband had prevented her taking her medication, and that he kept an iron bar on top of the television to threaten his wife and children against failure to comply with his demands.

Frequently, other issues became named as the problem and the focus moved from the father's violence to his alcohol abuse, or to the woman's mental health problems, neglect of the children, or alcohol abuse. While these issues may all be of significance to the children's well being, the man's violence, as potentially the causal factor, becomes invisible. Stanley and Penhale (1999) point out that all thirteen women in their study of children at risk of significant harm whose mothers were suffering from severe mental health problems were also all the subject of domestic violence. However, the children's problems were raised in relation to the mother's mental health, not the father's violence.

This highlights particular 'traps' in the assessment process for social workers who are untrained in assessment of violent offenders. For example, men who are abusive and violent towards their partners often appear the more plausible partner, and present themselves as 'the cornerstone of the family' – the rational voice, the protector of the children in the midst of the mother's depression and neglect. His violence towards the mother and its effects, are minimised or ignored in these cases unless he directly physically or sexually abuses the children. Social workers may name the mother's violence as more significant, or as equally significant as the man's. While occasionally this may be appropriate, research has demonstrated that social workers often inadvertently collude with the man's definition of the situation in which he construes himself as the victim and any resistance on the woman's part as provocation (Stanley and Goddard, 1997). While cases in which there are allegations of child sexual abuse may be less prone to minimising the focus on the offender's abuse of the child/ren, his abuse of the child's mother may again be ignored. There is often little connection either in practice or the literature between workers specialising in domestic violence and those specialising in child sexual abuse. In this process, the debilitating effects of violence towards the mother and the effect on the mother-child relationship may be overlooked.

There are also problems where men are uninvolved in assessments, even when a key issue is their violence in the family. Too easily, in these circumstances, the professionals' attention shifts to the mother and her shortcomings and ignores the man's contribution to the problems in the family (Farmer and Owen, 1995; Milner, 1993). A particular problem lies in gaining appropriate assessments for Asian men, women and children. Here, unacceptably long delays may result in a second class service to each of the family members (Humphreys, 1999a).

Linking Across Specialisms

The problems of delays in referral to other agencies or other teams highlight some particular issues about linking workers across specialisms, particularly where mental health or alcohol problems arise in the context of domestic violence. While linking workers from different teams appears to be an obvious way forward, the barriers and limitations to be overcome if such work is to be enhancing for all members of the family need to be recognised. Firstly, even when joint working across adult and children's teams takes place, there may still be no worker with expertise in domestic violence. Hence, the tendency towards minimisation, and the assessment 'traps' in this area may remain undetected.

Secondly, there may be different thresholds for referral, assessment and intervention between teams. Children may be on the verge of being accommodated with a significant factor being the mother's experience of depression. This would fit into a high priority category for resources and a designated worker on the children and families' team. However, the mental health team may only be prioritising cases where there is acute psychosis or danger of harm to self or others. A woman with a low level, yet debilitating depression may not meet the adult team priorities. A recent SSI report on family support (Hunter, 1999) indicates that, while relationships between children and family teams and agencies working with drug and alcohol misuse showed good co-operation, there were much more significant difficulties with adult mental health services. These are clearly issues that need attention at management level to facilitate joint working.

The problems with adult mental health services may point to some more significant underlying issues. White (1996) cautions against routing women towards mental health teams where they may become inappropriately labelled and subject to monitoring, but not necessarily offered increased support. Stanley and Penhale (1999) also make the point that all 13 women in their study who were labelled with serious mental health problems were subject to domestic violence and six of the women were labelled 'personality disordered'. This category, they suggest, along with others (Grounds, 1995), are often used to preclude people from services, and identify them as 'management problems', placing the responsibility back onto the service user and away from the professionals. A further issue for women caught in situations of domestic violence is that they are constantly told by their abusers that they are 'mad', so that referral to mental health services may inappropriately confirm their worst fears. Post-traumatic stress may be inappropriately diagnosed as psychosis and medication may be substituted for supportive counselling, information and safety planning (Stark and Flitcraft, 1996). Overall, the understanding of domestic violence as a crime has yet to permeate much of psychiatric thinking, which leaves both perpetrators and survivors inappropriately labelled as having

psychological problems and perpetrators seen as influenced by family background rather than responsible for their own choices and behaviour (Mullender, 1996).

Looking at the link from the other end on, women with mental health problems may have great fears of losing their children, particularly if this has been regularly threatened by the abuser. Hence, a referral through to the statutory child care team for joint work may be very frightening. Certainly, there needs to be the greatest care and sensitivity in embarking upon joint work and in telling each family member what is happening.

A further thorny issue lies in the budget for the work to be undertaken. In some areas, 'interface budgets' or 'family budgets' between adult and children's teams have been successfully negotiated at management level to facilitate work. In other areas, 'passing the buck', so that neither team is prepared to fund the 'care package' which would progress work for the family becomes a distressing reality as arguments occur over which team 'owns' the case. This can be particularly problematic when there are expensive residential costs associated with alcohol rehabilitation, specialist offender assessments, or on-going family support work for vulnerable adults. The training package, *Crossing Bridges* (Diggins and Mazey, 1998), written by a mental health worker and a child protection worker and commissioned and distributed by the Department of Health, is particularly strong in recognising that the first step needs to be a workshop for managers to tackle the barriers that impede front line practitioners.

Finally, there are problems for certain groups of women in accessing appropriate services at all. Those who are not abusing drugs or alcohol, who do not have disabilities or mental health problems, and/or who do not have children do not feature in social services' priorities. Women's Aid provides all abused women equally with refuge accommodation and/or with support and information. However, only proportions of women in situations of domestic violence use safe houses or access this specialist provision. Small-scale, flexible services, close to the community, have been established in some localities, though the voluntary sector is perennially under funded. Drop-in centres and general women's advice services can be developed to meet the needs of diverse groups of women (Pryke and Thomas, 1998), including those who have not yet been able to name what is happening to them. There is also no reason why any abused woman, if she happens to contact social services, could not be given basic information about local domestic violence provision or why such work could not be categorised as part of a community care service (Mullender, 1996).

Directions and Examples of Good Practice

A number of good practice suggestions for both assessment and on-going work can be gleaned from exploring the issues of avoidance, assessment traps and the problems of joint working. However, there is also a need to look more broadly across the spectrum of services.

The inter-agency context

Social work responses to domestic violence are most effective in the context of strong inter-agency working, so that housing, policing (see example below), health and on-going support needs can be considered together in the light of the two key principles of increasing offender responsibility and protecting both the children and their mother. Local authority areas such as Leeds, Newham, Hammersmith and Fulham, Bradford and Croydon have been able to offer a greater range of choice, including attention to the diverse needs of women from different ethnic backgrounds, because their inter-agency links have been clearly defined and their resources well developed.

The Department of Health (1998) has urged that social services departments designate an appropriate liaison person to domestic violence inter-agency forums. Similarly, those inter-agency forums have a representative on the local Area Child Protection Committee (ACPC). In England and Wales, this has been an issue, with numerous forums having little consistent representation from statutory social workers (Hague, Malos and Dear, 1996), and

frequently entirely lacking representation from the community care, adult sector. This is less of a problem in Northern Ireland where health and social service trusts are combined, and where the chair of the domestic violence forum frequently holds a senior position in the trust.

The links across agencies also need to be clarified. Scottish research (Henderson, 1997) has shown that both other agencies and women referred to social work services in the statutory sector expected accurate information and assistance from this source. However, most duty teams did not see domestic violence as falling within their remit unless it was in the context of child abuse. Doing nothing, referring on inappropriately, and refocussing the referral onto the children were all reported as particularly unhelpful social work responses. This problem is not unique to Scotland.

The initial response to referrals of domestic violence is also extremely important. There is currently a range from poor to good practice developing in this area in social work departments across the UK. The worst practice occurs where confidentiality and safety are not ensured, and where referral (typically when the police have been called to the home), not only does not result in any help being offered, but triggers a letter to both parents stating that their children may be at risk because they are living with domestic violence. This may feed into an already dangerous situation, giving the man further excuses for abusing the woman, adding to the negative messages the woman is already receiving from her abuser, and closing down her avenues of help-seeking because she now may fear a punitive child protection response if she confides in professionals about the violence. Such a response, lacking any sense of partnership with the woman or awareness of her safety needs, may actively increase the power and control of the abuser. It is a distortion of the link which has properly been established between woman abuse and child abuse, which fails to think through what impact the social services' response can have, both for good and for bad.

Birmingham Social Services has developed a less intrusive model of cross-agency

---

Case vignette: Child Protection

Three children are registered following a child protection conference under the category of physical abuse. The father's violence towards the children's mother has also escalated. The names of the registered children are recorded on the police computers through a process that flags the addresses of this very specific group of children whose parents are already the subject of inter-agency concern and monitoring. In this way, the police when they are next called to an incident at this address have an up to date and immediately accessible record that these children were already at significant risk of harm. A high level response from police towards the offender can occur, and the police know that a relevant professional can be contacted in relation to organising safety planning and support for the women and children involved.

(see Douch and Ross, 1998 for further information.)

---

information sharing, though it still does not necessarily involve active assistance to women.

Moving from investigative to family support models, Cheshire Social Services is an example of a department which has in place assessment procedures specifically for children in need and where children living with domestic violence meet the criteria; this means that a limited number of children who have themselves been physically or sexually abused, or where there are grounds for concern because of repeated calls to the police, can be referred for family support in consultation with the non-abusing parent. A small number of other areas, such as Newham and Leeds, have specialist domestic violence workers within social services whose remit is to give information and support to the woman and consultancy to the child protection worker. Newham is also piloting the use of a single referral form across all agencies in the area, so that the woman does not have to repeat, continually, her story to each new agency she visits. A related innovation has been the secondment of a children and families worker to the police domestic violence or child protection unit (for example in Fife). The effectiveness of these practices is yet to be evaluated (see example below).

Case vignette: Assessment

Two children and their mother are referred to a centre that provides assessment and counselling for children and their carers where child abuse has occurred. During the referral process domestic violence is identified through the screening questions asked by all social workers at the agency during the initial assessment.

The social worker asks the woman:

If your partner or someone in your family were hurting you, do you have someone to talk to?

Have you been hurt or threatened by a partner or family member? Or does your partner ever make you feel afraid?

If the answer is yes to either of the above questions – have any of the children seen or heard someone hurting you or making you afraid? Please give details.

This information then informs safety planning with the woman and children, or is further developed to talk with them about the continuing effects of any of these experiences.

Monitoring and screening

Across all areas of social work practice, proactive monitoring and screening for domestic violence are needed. The links between domestic violence, on the one hand, and child abuse, mental health and/or substance abuse, on the other, are now so well documented that, where one is identified, active exploration of the other needs to occur. Hester and Pearson (1998) found that, by introducing a simple monitoring form into an NSPCC service, the number of cases identified as involving domestic violence increased from one-third to two-thirds of the total workload. Sensitivity to the issue of child abuse occurring in the context of the abuse of the child's mother increased, and intervention changed accordingly, as this widespread prevalence was uncovered. Currently, only a minority of statutory agencies specifically screen for domestic violence; hence, it remains obscured or minimised until major harm occurs to the woman, the child, or both.

As was illustrated above, effective monitoring also needs to take place in adult services, where a proportion of disabled women, women with learning disabilities and older women will be suffering abuse and where awareness of sexual violence has traditionally been low.

Assessment

There are a number of 'traps' in the assessment process that suggest potential for improved practice. Top of the list would be the need specifically to identify domestic violence, rather than allowing its effects on either women or children to be minimised or overridden by other considerations. Wherever possible, this means focussing attention on the man and his violence and including him in the assessment procedures; only in this way is it possible to name who is doing what to whom. Specialist training for the professionals involved needs to take into account all the ways in which the offender's violence can be obscured or minimised by prevailing discourses. Assessment can also become a substitute for action, with support and intervention not offered at the end of it. Throughout all this work, extra vigilance may be needed where black service users are involved so as to avoid both inappropriate responses (for example where there is no interpreting service),

and the unnecessary delays involved in accessing such provision where it is inadequately funded.

A specific complexity in assessing families in which there is violence towards the woman lies in recognising the abusive and controlling dynamic in which the perpetrator demands that his victim accept responsibility for the violence (Jenkins, 1989). Social workers are invited to collude with these definitions by plausible and often socially assured abusers. Good practice in assessment requires triangulation of information from a range of different sources, including careful analysis of the documentary evidence on case files, obtaining information from other professionals who work with the woman or the children, and listening carefully to what both will feel able to tell the assessor if they feel safe.

Particular issues arise for black and other minority ethnic women in the assessment process. Interviews with Asian women survivors suggest that abuse not uncommonly involves not only their husband but also a number of his relatives, for example, his mother, brother and/or sisters (Hendessai, 1999). Any one of these may come to light first, so that domestic violence is not necessarily easily named as the problem by a professional unaccustomed to this kind of dynamic. Interviewing women alone and finding interpreters who they feel able to trust are particularly necessary. The problems of abuse may take longer to identify, too, because the consequences for a woman in naming her abuse may be more drastic in a family and community setting where it is seen as her responsibility to uphold her family's honour and where her range of alternatives may be more circumscribed (Rai and Tiara, 1997).

Particular difficulties may arise in accessing mental health assessments that are sensitive to cross-cultural issues. Lack of psychiatric expertise in domestic violence can lead to unacceptably long delays, lack of intervention and an overuse of drugs (Humphreys, 1999). Innovative work is now being undertaken in areas such as Newham, where a mental health project runs alongside the Asian Women's Support Service, while, elsewhere, black psychiatrists have consistently pushed for more appropriate assessments and services for minority ethnic populations (Sashidaran, 1989).

In adult services, the 'trap' is typically that no one is looking for domestic violence. Yet it is important to be alert to the fact that proportions of women with physical and learning disabilities that have experienced abuse (in childhood, adulthood or both) are likely to be particularly high because physical restrictions in movement or communication or understanding can heighten the risks from staff, other service users and intruders in social and health care settings. With formal or informal carers, too, the need for physical contact to perform caring tasks can pose a threat. If the partner is also a carer, the woman may be stuck in the relationship and in the abuse; her disability may also be used against her if the abuser restricts her mobility, her access to information, and so on (London Borough of Hounslow, 1994). Options may be fewer and harder to access than for other women if the disabled woman is not mobile or is reliant on a complex care package. For example (Cross, 1999) common themes are that economic dependence, social isolation, and the disability are turned against the woman so that she may feel trapped and her self-esteem may be destroyed (Nosek et al., 1998). Similar limitations apply to mothers of disabled children, creating a need for workers in this field of practice to raise their awareness – even when assessing for something apparently routine, like respite care services.

Joint working

Assessment and on-going work with families where there is domestic violence lend themselves to joint work between adult teams (mental health workers, drug and alcohol specialists and workers with vulnerable adults), practitioners from perpetrators' programmes, and social workers from children and families' teams. Clearly, joint working, in spite of the pitfalls mentioned above, can overcome a number of important problems. For instance, while all work needs to recognise that protection of the child's carer (usually the mother) is frequently the most effective form of child protection, this principle should not suggest that the children's needs and the mother's needs are conflated. Moreover, the tendency of children and family social workers to be interested only in the children, and in the woman solely in her role as a mother, can lead to a significant alienation of women through the assessment process. The deployment of one worker focussed on the woman's needs and another on the children's can be one way of

bridging the gap (see case vignette, Neglect), as can working in partnership with an advocacy, refuge or outreach worker from a women's organisation. It can also be very helpful to operate in a context where 'partnership with parents' is disaggregated between one worker involved with the mother and another with the father, thus allowing a differentiation to be made between an abusing and a non-abusing parent; for example, where there is a perpetrators' programme involved with the man. Increasingly, the benefits of experienced assessment teams (as opposed to individual workers with experience of domestic violence) are being recognised, particularly noting the potential therapeutic progress which can be made when the needs of the primary adult carer are given attention (Dale and Fellows, 1999).

However, the most obvious benefit of joint working is the pooling of expertise from different workers' specialist backgrounds. These are not just about domestic violence, but about the range of other problems to which it tends to give rise. Well planned, joint assessments and interventions can overcome the present separation of the assessment of adults' and children's needs with the consequent unhelpful fragmentation and incomplete information. Stanley and Penhale (1999) point out, for example, that adult psychiatrists who do not observe the mother or father with their children are not in a good position to comment on their parenting capabilities, though their expertise in this area is often inappropriately called upon. Involvement of a child care professional in such an assessment would be helpful. Similarly, children and families' social workers lack expertise in assessing the mental health needs of parents. Sheppard (1994) found that they underestimated by more than a third the level of depression in women on their caseloads (which testing placed at 36 per cent), and misdiagnosed half of those they did think were depressed.

Where other personal and social needs co-exist with domestic violence, specialist expertise may be essential to an effective response. For example, a woman with a severely physically disabled four year old daughter was able to access refuge services because a disability project worker had worked on an adapted flat within a purpose built local refuge (Mullender et al. 1998). There would have been still greater complexities if the girl had already started school.

Case vignette: Neglect

Mrs K has one two year-old child who was recently the subject of a child protection conference and registered under the category of neglect. Mrs K is a woman with moderate learning difficulties who is also the subject of domestic violence from her boyfriend. A comprehensive assessment was recommended to assess the potential for Mrs K to parent her child more effectively. Initially, progress was poor, the violence towards the mother continued and the work in relation to the children floundered.

However, a social worker specialised in working with people with learning disabilities was bought in to work with Mrs K. Clearer, more understandable goals were agreed. The children and family social worker concentrated on implementing the safety plan developed with the specialist worker and Mrs K. In particular, this involved co-ordinating a more effective multi-agency response to the offender, ensuring the resources and support required for the mother to pursue a non-molestation order, alternative housing and day-care provision. Within twelve months, Mrs K's child was no longer on the child protection register, though following the recommendation of the specialist worker a package of family support continued.

(Humphreys, 2000.)

Inter-agency training

Arrangements for joint training across intra- and inter-agency divides can increase knowledge and facilitate skill sharing across specialisms. Courses may need to draw from more than one training source; for example, while *Crossing Bridges* (Diggins and Mazey 1998) brings together childcare and mental health, exercises from *Making an Impact* (Hester et al., 2000) would add in domestic violence. Multi-agency events are being organised in many areas through Area Child Protection Committees, and sometimes through domestic violence forums. This often starts with awareness raising and can usefully move on into detailed consideration of domestic violence as it impinges on specialist areas of work, for example at the interface between health visitors and children and families workers, or between the latter and the police (Hammersmith and Fulham Interagency Working, undated).

Concluding Comments

The recent surge of interest in the seriousness of domestic violence, and particularly its impact on children has seen the proliferation of more than 200 domestic violence forums throughout England and Wales and new structures developing in Northern Ireland and Scotland. There are particular ramifications for social workers in attempting to take domestic violence seriously in agencies that have traditionally marginalised the issue. The translation of the rhetoric of concern about domestic violence into the practices of front line social workers and into the policies of the agencies which employ them is still in its early stages.

At times, the barriers to the development of good practice seem insurmountable. However, the inroads which have been made, both by individual workers and by their employing organisations, into the tradition of neglect have started to move domestic violence from an issue which is everywhere yet nowhere, to one which is visible, acknowledged and tackled. In particular, it is encouraging to see more responsibility placed on offenders and appropriate support increasingly being provided for survivors and their children. Social work has a fundamental role to play in intervention in both these areas. This can only be brought to fruition, however, if domestic violence is named in monitoring, assessment, intervention and training, if specialist domestic violence expertise is made available, and if effective inter-agency links are established across historical divides. There will then be every reason to hope that policy rhetoric can be translated into practice achievements.

Further Reading

Davies, J., Lyon, L. and Monti-Catania, D. (1998). *Safety Planning with Battered Women: Couples Lives/Difficult Choices*. London: Sage.

Hester, M., Pearson, C. and Harwin, N. (2000). *Making an Impact: A Reader*. London: Jessica Kingsley.

Humphreys, C., Hester, M., Hague, G., Mullender, A., Abrahams, H. and Lowe, P. (2000). *From Good Intentions to Good Practice: Mapping Services With Families Where There is Domestic Violence*. Bristol: Policy Press.

Mullender, A. (1996). *Re-thinking Domestic Violence: The Social Work and Probation Response*. London: Routledge.

Mullender, A. and Morley, R. (1994). *Children Living With Domestic Violence: Putting Men's Abuse of Women on the Child Care Agenda*. London: Whiting and Birch.

Mullender, A., Hague, G. Imam, V., Kelly, L., Malos, E. and Regan, L. (2002). *Children's Perspectives on Domestic Violence*. London: Sage.

Chapter 7

The Protection of Vulnerable Adults: The Role of Social Work

Bridget Penhale and Jonathan Parker

Introduction

In recent years there has been an increased emphasis on violence and abuse within society. Following a focus in the UK on child abuse in the 1970s and domestic violence in the 1980s, in the 1990s the abuse and neglect of older people and other vulnerable adults has moved towards centre stage. Increasingly, social workers are required to assist individuals who have experienced abuse or who have a history of abuse, so it is relevant to consider this type of work as an area of specialism.

Initially, the concept of protection will be introduced, together with consideration of some of the implications for health and social care practice. The dual role of social work and social care in seeking to promote change and self-determination whilst also being responsible for controlling and regulating social life will be discussed. It will be suggested that these roles are not mutually exclusive but are both important to an understanding of health and social care work in the UK today and to practice, which protects rights and reduces risks.

This chapter aims to provide a brief overview of the status of current knowledge concerning the abuse and neglect of vulnerable adults and to include consideration of the legal and practice contexts. Recent and potential changes in legislation and policy will also be covered. This will be followed by an examination of current practice and potential developments in this area of work, together with issues and dilemmas raised by such practice. The framework of prevention, provision, protection and empowerment of vulnerable adults will be critical within this. The chapter will conclude with a section on good practice in work with vulnerable adults who have experienced abuse, or who are at risk of abuse. Brief case examples will be included throughout.

What is protection?

Everyone has some basic notion of the concept of protection. The immediate picture that springs to mind may be of a vulnerable person, most often, perhaps a child, who is in some kind of danger of harm. The concept generally carries with it an implicit assumption that the protector has the right, responsibility or power to protect an individual. There is also, perhaps a sense that the protected individual is in need of this protection. The concept of protection assists our understanding of the rules on which society operates and in which individuals interact.

Protection can be both preventive and reactive. Prevention aims to ensure that individuals are not harmed, whereas reactive measures may be necessary to ensure that no further harm takes place after an initial act warranting protection. Protective actions may include the formation of rules and laws to protect from injury and harm or the promotion of policies and procedures aimed at increasing health and safety in the workplace. It may also relate to taking actions to remove dangers and, at times, removing people from situations perceived to be a danger to them.

Sometimes actions may also be preventive in reducing the risks of future harm as shown in the following case study.

Case vignette: Enid

Enid, who is in her 80s, has rheumatoid arthritis, which particularly affects her hands and feet. She has been finding it increasingly difficult to use cooking equipment, such as the cooker, tin opener, and to lift pots, pans and the kettle. Recently, she dropped a pan of soup, which narrowly missed hitting her. Enid was so shocked by this that she asked her GP for advice about this matter. She referred Enid to the local social services team for adults who assessed her needs for support and assistance with daily living tasks.

In order to protect Enid from the risk of injury and harm the social worker and occupational therapist provided a range of equipment such as a kettle-tipper, special tin opener, and jar and pan grips. As Enid was also beginning to have difficulty in turning on her gas cooker, special adaptations were made to the cooker.

These actions helped to protect Enid by allowing her to use her kitchen safely and to remain in her own chosen environment without outside help from others who might take over these tasks and not allow Enid to be independent.

Social work: care and control

In social work, protection is popularly associated with children and families. However, protection in social work is much more than simply working to ensure the safety of vulnerable children. It refers also to the protection of adults who are vulnerable because of a physical disability, mental health problem or a learning disability. It may be that individuals are placed in a vulnerable position because of the actions of other people towards them. Protection concerns the maltreatment and neglect of older people too. The term also relates to people who may by their own actions or neglect of themselves put themselves at some degree of risk of harm or injury.

Work in adult protection has developed from the confluence of a number of different areas, and is seen as separate from other areas such as violence against young women or abuse resulting from racism. In general terms, adult protection relates to those individuals where social care agencies might have some involvement or 'duty of care'. In the UK there has been consistent work on elder abuse since the late 1980s. Initially this concerned abuse occurring in the domestic setting, but more recently the focus has shifted to emphasise abuse occurring in institutional settings (Bright, 1997; Glendenning, 1999; Parker, 2001). For adults with learning disabilities, sexual abuse was initially highlighted as a major concern in the early 1990s (Brown and Turk, 1992). However, physical abuse has emerged more recently as the most dominant form of abuse for adults with learning disabilities (Cambridge, 1998). Within the area of mental health there has been much more attention by service users to issues concerning abuse within treatment settings (McLeod, 1999; Williams and Keating, 1999; Stanley and Manthorpe, 2001) (see Chapter 10), whereas for disabled people (as described in Chapter 2) there appears to have been more focus on issues of access, discrimination and exclusion (Oliver, 1990; Shakespeare, 2000).

Social workers practice in ways that can be seen as both caring and controlling when seeking to protect people. A social worker or care manager may seek to provide services and help to a person, which allows them to make choices in a safe and enabling way and to maintain a life style of their choosing. It may also refer to the controlling actions, which regulate and, at times, prevent a person living in the way they would choose. Examples of this are contained in the case study below.

Case vignette: Janet

Janet lived in a hostel for people with learning disabilities. She had lived in a long-stay hospital for forty years, from childhood, and spent twelve years living in the hostel. She developed a life-threatening physical illness that needed surgery. Janet refused to go into hospital because of her past experiences. Without surgery she would die but she did not appear to understand this fully. Discussions took place, however, concerning the possibility of Janet being admitted to hospital against her will. Her keyworker went to the hospital with Janet for a visit in order to show her that it was not the same one she had lived in for forty years.

Fortunately the hospital was quite new and modern and did not resemble the long-stay hospital that she had lived in before. Following her visit to the hospital, Janet agreed to go in to hospital if her keyworker could stay with her throughout her stay. In addition, negotiations were held with the hospital, which then provided a single room for Janet and her key worker to stay in throughout the period of Janet's stay. It was fortunately not necessary to have to use legislation to enforce an admission to hospital in this instance.

Social workers are authorised by legislation to take certain actions to ensure that people do not put others at risk and to protect people from danger, injury and harm. Many people enter qualifying training because they want to help people learn or recover the skills to live independently. They may not, however, wish to be involved in taking actions, which might limit choice and freedom of individuals. Despite this common situation, it must be emphasised that care and control are essential elements of the social work task. In fact, they are like two sides of the same coin. One can enter a career in the helping professions because of a deep commitment to the care of vulnerable, disadvantaged and excluded people. This may demand a protective role in working to prevent exploitation at an individual, group or social level. However, such a commitment can also imply a degree of control in using relevant legislation to ensure that people are granted their rights, are protected from abuse and harm, and receive the care to which they are entitled.

In many respects, social work gains its meaning from its role within protection, and this role may partially define both health and social care work. The social work task implies that social workers have a responsibility to take action to protect people from harm and injury whether this is from themselves, others or from society itself. It also implies that individuals within that society have a right to be protected. This raises a number of ethical questions for the practitioner. These include:

- the rights people have not to be protected
- the right to take risks
- the right to privacy and self-determination
- questions about professionals' rights to limit the rights of others and control actions

As professionals, social workers are bound by codes of practice concerning standards and ethics. These are designed to ensure that basic principles concerning values are adhered to and that control, when necessary, is legitimate and warranted. Such values and principles include a need for commitment by the social worker to the dignity of individuals and the 'right to respect, privacy and confidentiality' (CCETSW, 1996). There is also, however, a need for social workers to be committed to enabling individuals to live their lives free from abuse, neglect and exploitation.

Prevention in social work

Prevention is much talked about in social work and allied professions as a way of working with people deemed to be in need of protection.

Browne and Herbert (1997) identify three levels of prevention:

- *Primary prevention* refers to policy and actions taken before a situation becomes a problem. It reduces the need before the potential for harm and danger is apparent.

- *Secondary prevention* relates to people who might be identified as potentially in need of protection. A practitioner offering secondary preventive measures might suggest certain services and assistance to reduce levels of need, such as stress, before an abusive act occurs, which demands further action. This could include, for example, periods of respite care as a secondary preventive measure, or attendance at a carers' support group. Such services would be likely to be targeted towards both parties involved in the situation.

- *Tertiary prevention* refers to providing services and intervention after an actual protection issue has been identified, e.g. an act of physical violence or emotional abuse has already occurred. The objectives of acting at this stage are to reduce the risk of harm or danger occurring again. It may also be the result of a need to act when caring is no longer possible. Unfortunately, the majority of actions undertaken by social workers and other helping professionals in relation to protection are of this tertiary type. This may include removal of the person from their environment on a long-term or permanent basis. It may, in other situations, relate to the provision of temporary safe shelters, counselling support or on-going monitoring.

Using the tripartite prevention typology created by Browne and Herbert, we can explore the links between contemporary practice and legislation. This is perhaps best demonstrated in table 7.1.

A Framework for Protection

There are many different pieces of legislation used by social workers, social care staff and allied professionals. There is no substitute to experience in using the legislation but a basic knowledge is fundamental for all practitioners.

Social workers protect individuals from others, from themselves, from circumstances and from disadvantages in life. In some ways they also protect society from danger and harm, by regulating individuals' lives. As will become apparent, in order to do this, a wide range of law and policy is needed.

Legislation to protect

Older people and adults with impairments, (physical and/or cognitive) may be vulnerable and at risk of abuse from others, and may also put others at risk of harm by their actions. There is no single piece of legislation that concerns the protection of vulnerable adults. What we find, rather, is that there are a number of different pieces of legislation, which may be used by individuals who are in need of protection. At times another person, for example a practitioner, can use legislation on behalf of an individual.

There is legislation designed to protect people with mental illness from harm or harming others (Mental Health Act 1983, Supervised Discharge Procedures, 1995). The legislation concerning mental health also extends to adults with severe learning disabilities, and includes such provision as guardianship and arrangements for the Court of Protection to assist in the management of a person's finances (see Chapter 11). A review of the Mental Health Act has taken place, although a clear view of changes is not yet in place. Additionally, an announcement has been made concerning revision of the Court of Protection to include personal and welfare decisions as well as finances (Lord Chancellor's Department, 1999). The modernising agenda for Social Services Departments also includes explicit recognition of the need to both promote independence and to increase measures of protection for vulnerable individuals (Department of Health, 1998). These changes are likely to be occurring over the period 2002–2005.

Adults with a range of needs are to an extent protected from life's difficulties by entitlement to an assessment and provision of services to meet identified need (National Health Service and Community Care Act 1990). A more co-ordinated approach to assessment , including health and social care, can be expected with the

Table 7.1 Levels of Prevention: The Tripartite Prevention Typology (after Browne and Herbert)

Level of prevention	Primary prevention	Secondary prevention	Tertiary prevention
Legislative base	Policy frameworks at national and local levels including joint planning and practice initiatives	Care planning and care management to reduce risk of harm/ danger and account for identified need by service planning	Direct use of legislative powers to determine action and protect/ restrain individuals
Examples of legislation/ policy	Department of Health guidance, for example No Longer Afraid (DoH, 1993); It could Never Happen Here (NAPSAC, 1993)	National Health Service and Community Care Act 1990; Social Services Inspectorate guidance on Assessment and Care Management (1991a; b)	Mental Health Act 1983; Theft Act 1968; Family Law Act 1996 (Part IV); Protection from Harassment Act 1997
Practice example	Development of multi-agency guidelines for the protection of vulnerable people at local levels (see Kingston upon Hull and East Yorkshire, 1999)	Assessment of safety needs and risks. Establishing safety plan for individuals as part of care planning process	Compulsory admission to hospital of person with a mental health problem in an effort to protect the individual and others
Value dimensions	Social attitudes, social problem construction (Blumer, 1971)	Professional attitudes and value bases conjoin to determine action, see confluence of respect for persons versus best interests	The interface of professional and personal values. For example, individual, family, agency/ organisation and societal attitudes and values

development and implementation of a single assessment process, which forms a key part of the *National Service Framework for Older People* (Department of Health, 2001).The Sexual Offences Act 1957 offers protection to people from unwanted sexual advances, and the Protection from Harassment Act 1997 may offer protection from bullying and stalking. Additionally, Part IV of the Family Law Act 1996 offers some protection from violence which occurs within the domestic setting. This provides a range of measures that might be used, including non-molestation and ouster orders (concerning perpetrators) in certain situations. The scope of this legislation was widened to include a greater range of individuals living together, not just spouses or cohabitees. There is also the possibility of a third party taking action on behalf of an individual, so it is therefore worth further consideration within situations concerning the safety and protection of vulnerable adults.

The modernising agenda for Social Services Departments included plans to improve systems of protection for individuals receiving assistance from Social Services (Department of Health, 1998). To this end, the Care Standards

Act, 2000 provided for the establishment of the National Care Standards Commission in relation to regulatory and inspection functions for residential , nursing, day and domiciliary care, private and voluntary hospitals as well as agencies in relation to children. The General Social Care Council, established at the same time, will cover the registration and in effect licensing of individual practitioners. Additionally the Act introduced the Protection of Vulnerable Adults List (POVA List) concerning a register of individuals considered unsuitable to work with vulnerable adults. This is similar to the Protection of Children Act List (POCA List) in relation to people working with children, which had been established by the Protection of Children Act, 1999. The Care Standards Act also mandated the introduction of the Care Standards Tribunal from April 2002, part of whose remit includes appeals by individuals whose names have been entered onto either the POCA or POVA Lists. These measures were designed in order improve what might perhaps be considered as the more institutional systems of protection for individuals.

However, as we have also noted, there is no comparable legislation to the Children Act 1989, which concerns the abuse of adults. At present, legal remedies to abuse and harm of a vulnerable adult include use of the above-mentioned laws and even, at times, the removal of the person in need of protection (see also the National Assistance Act 1948, section 47). Of course, general legal measures, using both criminal and civil law may also be used to protect individuals. These would concern such situations as assault or theft. It is incumbent on social work practitioners to be well versed in what is possible in relation to existing legislation.

Protection and risk: the importance of professional training

The previous section concerning the appropriate use of legislation is important to the development of good management systems. Health and social care are not simply about the provision of direct care and protection to individuals. The delivery of such care is based upon clear policies and

procedures designed to ensure that the services and care provided are the most appropriate, use resources effectively and represent good value for money.

Thus there is a need above all for health and social care practitioners to have a good working knowledge of the policies and procedures of their agency and the legislation that underpins these. In any policy there should be clear lines of responsibility and accountability so that decisions made are checked and authorised by those persons with the training and experience necessary to make them.

It is essential that social workers and others in the helping professions begin to learn protective practice during qualifying training. This should include training in the assessment and management of risk and 'risky' situations. This has been emphasised for social workers by CCETSW in their revised Paper 30 (CCETSW, 1996). At the present time, social workers need to be competent in six key areas, each of which has a number of practice requirements attached. These requirements include competence in protective practice. In addition, traditional social work values, such as those espoused by Biestek (1961) need to be explored to ascertain their coherence in relation to present-day practice, and account needs to be taken of the effects on social work practice of political correctness (Philpot, 1999). Education for social workers is changing, and a new qualifying degree commences in 2003. With the development of National Occupational Standards and subject benchmarking criteria for social work, it is important that there is still sufficient emphasis on risk assessment, protection and practice within qualifying education.

Education and developing knowledge and skills does not stop once social and health care workers become qualified. There is a need to continue learning and increasing skills throughout professional careers. One important way of achieving this has been through the development of post-qualifying training and awards. This can include establishing links within practice settings between different areas of specialism and provide knowledge and skills to increase the ability and competence of individual practitioners to protect vulnerable adults.

Accountability – professional /public measures

Accountability operates at different levels: public; agency; professional and personal. These levels overlap but can act as a framework to help us to understand our individual responsibilities in connection with work. Social work is at present predominantly a statutory endeavour. It is commissioned by the state to help regulate and improve social life for its citizens. The state passes laws and publishes guidelines to mark out the ways in which social care is operated. Agency policies, procedures and the actions of individual practitioners working for the agency all contribute to the responsibility for carrying out these requirements.

The measures set by individual agencies also reflect its particular mission and field of operations. Thus there will be different procedures to follow in different agencies. The practitioner should be fully aware of these in order to work as an accountable and effective employee. For example, social workers cannot simply work according to their own preferred methods or towards their own desired ends. The responsibility of individual practitioners is to carry out ethically the requirements of state and the agency for which they work.

Working across specialisms: multi-disciplinary approaches

Within the difficult, complex and sensitive situations that arise, and across the range of different types of abuse that can occur, it will be necessary for there to be effective collaboration between agencies. Multi-disciplinary working is essential within situations of adult protection; no single profession or specialism holds sufficient expertise to deal with all potential situations, particularly when we consider that adult protection covers a wide range of different adult service users (see Department of Health, 2000). There is likely to be a need, therefore, for participation and collaboration between

different specialisms from within social work and also on an interdisciplinary basis. So, for example, when considering a situation of potential sexual abuse of an older adult, it may be highly appropriate for a practitioner to seek guidance and assistance from colleagues from the field of child protection, as well as from professionals from health, police, housing, victim support and other voluntary agencies. This emphasis on joined-up approaches to systems and to service delivery has also been apparent in the National Service Frameworks that have been developed by the Department of Health.

This is where a co-ordinated approach to adult protection, including a post similar to the ACPC (Area Child Protection Committee) co-ordinator, can be of particular value. This role would include the provision of consultancy in relation to specific cases. The co-ordinator, can of course, put practitioners in contact with each other or suggest other avenues or options to explore as well as assisting in the overall co-ordination and direction of a situation. This is likely to be in addition to the involvement of the practitioner's normal processes of line management. Adult protection units are a fairly recent development in the UK, but some local authorities, such as Sheffield, Leeds and Gloucestershire have well established and experienced units and may provide advice and guidance to other authorities in how to create and promote such approaches. The co-ordinator may come from any disciplinary background in the helping professions. Thus the need for awareness, understanding and clear communication skills in dealing with professionals from the range of professions is essential.

Specialist input from different disciplines is likely to be valuable throughout the process of assessment and investigation of a situation; this may be in the form of a specialist contribution to an assessment or an assessment conducted jointly between agencies. For example, a younger adult with Huntington's disease will benefit from specialist nursing and social care involvement in community care assessment and subsequent care management. In other situations, involvement of police, housing and voluntary organisations is likely to be useful in addition to contributions from health care professions. Within the single assessment process for older people, at more complex, comprehensive levels of assessment, issues concerning safety and protection are also likely to be addressed (Department of Health, 2001).

Multi-disciplinary input at the stage of a case conference can also be very important. The contributions from as many of the disciplines involved with a person as possible helps to ensure that all aspects of an individual's care are properly taken into account. The case conference is likely to be the culmination of events and risks and will not be used in all situations. However, the majority of situations will benefit from regular and systematic meetings between those professionals involved in assessment, service delivery, monitoring and review. Strategy, network and safety planning meetings may all be used to good effect within adult protection, albeit at different points in the process. We need only look at the number of inquiry reports into failures of care to confirm the importance of interdisciplinary communication in effective case management.

Again, drawing on the experience of child care case conferences, the issue of service user involvement and participation in the process is also an essential component here. Much useful work has been undertaken within child protection concerning parental involvement (Thoburn et al., 1995). There are clearly lessons to be learnt relating to increasing engagement with and participation in the processes that can be transferred between specialisms. In addition, the steady growth in information and knowledge relating to sexual abuse of young women and children means that useful information concerning, for example, how to handle disclosure interviews can be used with vulnerable adults who have been sexually abused (Drauckner, 1992).

The involvement of colleagues from the police is likely to be of particular importance in situations of alleged abuse. Many Domestic Violence Units (DVUs) within police forces have widened their remit in recent years and are now concerned with children and a range of adults who experience violence and exploitation. Some units have been renamed as Family Protection units, whilst others retain the title DVU. A large number of such units,

whatever they are called, will, however, consider the needs of vulnerable individuals beyond a narrow interpretation of either family or domestic setting. Involvement of the police from an early stage is generally beneficial. This would include the provision of advice and guidance, if not direct involvement, and attendance at case conferences. It is therefore increasingly a necessary part of the process.

Of course, obtaining clear legal advice concerning situations is also likely to be needed. This may be achieved through access to local authority legal sections, or through the involvement of independent legal advice for an individual. Professionals working with vulnerable adults need to have a basic understanding of legal frameworks in relation to protection and ready access to expert assistance where necessary. Individuals may require help to gain access to appropriate legal support. This can add unnecessary stress to an already difficult situation, which can easily be ameliorated by timely professional advice.

National guidance, local approaches

Guidance from government in relation to adult protection does not generally appear to have been a priority area of concern. Indeed, it was not until 1993 that any guidance concerning elder abuse was forthcoming from the Department of Health, initially from the Social Services Inspectorate. Guidance in connection with adults with learning disabilities was also first issued in 1993 (ARC/NAPSAC, 1993). Both of these documents were limited, however, in their approaches. The document concerning elder abuse did not consider situations occurring beyond the domestic setting, whilst that relating to learning disabled adults focused solely on situations of sexual abuse. The provision of guidance in these areas, albeit limited, is, of course, preferable to the complete lack of official guidance concerning adults with physical disability, sensory impairment or mental health difficulties who might also have needs relating to vulnerability and protection. Practitioners do not operate in a vacuum and need the direction of national government and employing bodies to ensure clearer standards of practice.

The Social Services Inspectorate began work in 1998 to rectify this situation and to produce guidance on adult protection for authorities and organisations to adopt in their work. The process of working party participation and development of guidance has been understandably lengthy, given the need for involvement across the spectrum of adult protection. In late 1999, a draft guidance document was produced for consultation purposes (Department of Health, 1999), with a final document appearing during the year 2000 (Department of Health, 2000). The guidance document *No Secrets* concerned the roles and responsibilities of differing organisations and disciplines and the processes that should take place in relation to abuse. Social services departments were designated lead agency within adult protection, and the guidance itself had Section 7 status, so that it was a requirement for the guidance to be implemented by authorities. This guidance was implemented at the end of October 2001.

Many local authorities began work in the area of adult protection some time ago and have not waited on national initiatives to improve practice in this area. Successive surveys throughout the 1990s have indicated that an increasing number of health and social care organisations have implemented policies and procedures in adult protection. It is also now generally agreed that the frameworks developed should be inter-agency in approach and perspective (Pritchard, 1999). Policies and procedures may be shared across agencies, or separate procedures developed by agencies but working to a shared over-arching policy which is multi-agency in nature and scope. It is important to acknowledge that policies and procedures are important to inform practitioners of the actions that should be taken at particular points in the process. However, policies and procedures alone cannot ensure good practice. How they are operationalised in practice is very important. And of course, strategies of intervention and how these are used are unlikely to be entirely prescribed by procedures. Good practice in this area must evolve beyond the development of documentation designed to guide practitioners through a sequence of processes.

Practice Dilemmas

Social workers often work in situations that are complex and fraught with difficulty. They need to keep clearly in mind aspects and dichotomies of care and control, protection and self-determination. The right of service users, generally, to accept or to reject assistance must also be considered. At times, such aspects can result in dilemmas for the practitioner, either ethically, or in practice, or both arenas. Some of these dilemmas will be explored in the following sections.

Care and control: rights versus risks

It is necessary to recognise that an element of control may be necessary within professional practice. As we have seen, in order to protect an individual, some control over their actions may be required. Protection concerns the reduction of the risks and dangers of harm and injury to self or others. It also concerns the protection of people in danger of harm or injury from challenges of life such as discrimination because of race, gender, disability, age or creed. The essential point is that respect for the person is fundamental either because they need protection from others or from their own actions. This value runs throughout social work thinking and action. In a utilitarian sense, it is possible to maintain respect for the individual even when some control over their actions is needed. Actions here are judged by their consequences. This echoes 'protective responsibility', which we will deal with more fully later.

It is important to remember that health and social care work are undertaken by a diverse range of individuals in a wide range of contexts and with different individuals and cultures. No two situations are exactly the same. To navigate a pathway through this and find appropriate responses to individual needs requires an understanding and acceptance of the value base of health and social care work.

Decisions about intervention are based not only on what we think as individuals or what society at large suggests is a right and proper course to take. In health and social care work, it is essential that actions are taken that respect the rights of individuals as far as possible whilst recognising that some risks cannot be taken and that control may be necessary. There is a delicate balance and tension between rights and risks in all cases worked with by social workers.

Protection or self-determination?

One of the most crucial difficulties for professionals to deal with is that of achieving and maintaining a balance between the protection of the individual and the right to self-determination. Vulnerable adults have the right in most cases to be autonomous and should be enabled to be so. It is quite possible for professionals to work hard with an individual to determine both their needs and appropriate treatment options and for the person to then refuse such offers. There may of course, be issues of capacity that affect the autonomy of the vulnerable adult, and recent work by the Law Commission and the Lord Chancellor's Department is likely to assist with this area (Law Commission, 1995; Lord Chancellor's Department, 1998, 1999).

Vulnerable people can and do say no to offers of assistance. In general terms, and many instances, they have the right to do so and they frequently exercise that right. This right to self-determination should remain one of the central tenets of practice: it should not be ignored. Fulmer et al. (1987), for example, found that older people preferred independence to safety and protection whenever possible. Risk taking was seen very much as part of daily life for elders; the ability to take risks was seen as an essential and necessary part of growing older. It can be a critical factor in the preservation of independence and autonomy for a significant number of people.

Such findings should not be surprising; particularly when considering our own lives and wishes about how we should be treated and how we might react if faced with issues of safety and protection. Practitioners have to learn to feel comfortable with such facts; these issues must be acknowledged and worked with when they occur. In particular it is necessary to be mindful of our own likely needs, wishes and expectations as practitioners and how these may impact on practice. Respect

for the person (service user) and the right to self-determination are evidently critical factors in this area of work.

Protective responsibility

Practitioners do, however, need to know when it is necessary for them to act in terms of 'protective responsibility' towards a vulnerable adult or their carer (Stevenson and Parsloe, 1993). There are a number of distinct aspects to this concept: the practitioner must act, sometimes, in a way that is protective towards and of the person. Such actions must be carefully considered and considerate of individuals. They should assist and empower the person rather than demeaning and disempowering them through the creation of unnecessary dependency.

Furthermore, the concept confers on practitioners a moral duty to act in ways that are protectively responsible towards their clients. The fact that vulnerable people do sometimes refuse offers of help and express their rights to be self-determining should not mean that offers of assistance are not made principally on the basis that they will be rejected by the person anyway and are therefore not worth making. Practitioners need to be aware of this need to act protectively at times and may need guidance in recognising such circumstances and what actions to take when they occur.

Guidance may be provided by those with management and/or supervisory responsibility for practitioners or be in written form as procedures and guidelines for practitioners to follow. Once such situations have been identified, practitioners must act in a wholly professional and responsible manner. In this regard, it is important that attention is also paid to the role of external forces that may affect how practitioners react. This may relate to the views and wishes of relatives, or even neighbours within a situation. It may also, however relate to the role (actual or potential) of the media in the attention given in recent years to the concept of dangerousness. This has been particularly apparent in relation to mental health and community care. The dilemmas between self-determination and protective responsibility may be exemplified within such situations, as the following case study illustrates.

Case vignette: Edward

Edward was in his mid 70s and was experiencing the early stages of dementia. He was also, however, quite depressed and uncertain about what the future might hold. He was very clear that he wished to remain living at home, and his wife, Doris, who indicated that she wished to continue caring for Edward, shared this view. Over a period of time, Edward's mood swings, which included an aggressive component, developed into physical violence directed towards his wife, and on occasion other members of the family who attempted to intervene. Doris contacted social services for assistance and support, recognising that this change was too great for her to deal with on her own. Edward, however, refused all help, failing to recognise the effect that his behaviour was having. His refusal was at times aggressive, which served to worsen the situation, and at one point he was compulsorily admitted to hospital in order to ensure the safety of his wife.

Issues concerning acceptance and rejection of help

It can be very difficult, if not impossible, for an individual at the time of the initial contact with a health or welfare professional to be able to take in all the information and then to act on the advice given, especially if they are distressed. Therefore it is essential for the person to be given a clear message that even if unable to pursue actions at that particular time they can return in future and gain appropriate levels of support and further assistance as necessary.

It is possible that people may refuse offers of assistance and support initially but then return at some later point for further information and/or assistance. It is crucial therefore that enough groundwork is achieved during that first contact to enable the individual to come back in future. Aspects of this might include information about the following:

● abusive situations (in general terms)

● what systems for assistance and support might be available

● identification of support networks for the person that might be utilised in future (safe people; safe houses; safety routes)

● how to summon help and assistance

The amount of information given to the person is likely to depend of course on the ability of the individual to absorb amounts of information at one time. In such instances, the practitioner needs to take care in terms of the amount of information that is given during the initial contact. One of the most important pieces of information to convey to the individual, however, is likely to be how to renew contact with the practitioner in future when (if) this is considered to be necessary in order to obtain enough assistance to resolve their situation.

The person needs to know who to contact, where they can be contacted and when they are available and how to go about this. It may be that a letter or leaflet containing all this information would be an advantage. It is likely to be necessary, however, to bear in mind any issues concerning the safety of the individual if they have information in written form about how to access help. In addition, if the person has a sensory disability, it may be necessary to be creative and consider other ways in which information can be given, e.g. using cassette recordings or Braille leaflets. If the person has a learning disability, they may not be able to read and understand a leaflet unless special attention has been paid to make it accessible. Again, issues of safety need to be considered in relation to this.

Within such situations there is of course a strong educational component: it is very important for vulnerable people to have an understanding that abusive situations rarely consist of single acts but that generally the abuse becomes more severe and more frequent over time (Breckman and Adelman, 1988). It is also desirable for individuals to know that many other people experience abusive situations and that the majority of them survive, some of them (although as yet an unknown number) managing to alter their situations so that they can live lives free from abuse or neglect. Additionally, the person should gain enough knowledge and understanding of their particular situation to be able to obtain the necessary support and assistance if required in future.

Good Practice Issues

The development of appropriate responses to situations of adult abuse appears to be at an early stage of formation. Most work seems, so far, to have been done in relation to the establishment of procedural systems for professionals to follow. This is particularly in relation to the assessment and investigation of situations that are held to be abusive. There is some agreement that Social Services Departments should have a lead role within this area and that assessment should take place within the context of overall systems for assessment and care management (Department of Health, 1993). Assessment must therefore be holistic, but should also be 'abuse-focussed' (Bennett et al., 1997) where necessary as a part of this process. The development of the single assessment process, which at comprehensive levels includes consideration of safety and protection issues, is helpful in relation to this (Department of Health, 2001).

Good practice within adult protection should include such elements as a distinction between initial referral (or report) and subsequent investigation; the careful co-ordination of the investigation; separate, sensitive and suitable arrangements for interviews. The use of case conferences in order to determine a protection plan for an individual, where necessary and as an effective means to promote shared decision making is also suggested as indicative of good practice. Clearly a balance between the needs of the service user for support and protection and the need for sanction for the abuser is necessary here. The protection plan is likely to include attention to the needs of the service user for safety, support and service provision (or treatment), together with issues relating to the ongoing management of risk. Multi-disciplinary working with individuals and with abusers, is an essential part of the equation here as discussed above.

The modernising agenda for Social Services as outlined in 1998 (Department of Health, 1998) appeared to relate more to institutional and service settings as key areas where attention was needed in order to protect vulnerable service users. As seen earlier, this is apparent within the provisions of the Care Standards Act, 2000. Notwithstanding such subsequent developments, however, the emphasis in the White Paper on partnership and working to improve protection for individuals is an essential pre-requisite to the development of effective responses (Penhale et al., 2000). Even prior to this publication, however, the Department of Health was working to produce guidance on developing a co-ordinated approach to adult protection as a whole (Department of Health, 1993), and regulation of the situation remains a possibility. Effective inter-agency working is likely to be required within many situations; this may be achieved in future through the development of inter-agency fora similar to those already found in relation to domestic violence, or the development of Adult Protection Committees similar to those established for child protection, as advocated in the *No Secrets* document (Department of Health, 2000).

Conclusions: Promoting Good Practice Through Making Links

As already suggested, the whole field of adult protection is one in which there has been a conjunction of work from a number of discrete areas. It is also one that arguably can contribute much to other fields of work. There are linkages across a range of specialisms; some of these may be more obvious and apparent than others. So for example, it may be more likely that the similarities and differences in relation to child protection are more likely to be recognised, perhaps, than the developing area concerning victims within criminology.

There are also, however, lessons to be learned from some other areas of specialism. This would include the potential for increased risk of abuse for some individuals with dementia, for example (Penhale and Kingston, 1997; Parker and Penhale, 1998). Additionally, the risk for a person with a history of substance misuse or long-term mental health difficulties of finding caring responsibilities problematic may exacerbate any risk of abuse (Pillemer and Finkelhor, 1988). Those additional risk factors for abuse that have been identified, such as a history of a poor long-term relationship (Homer and Gilleard, 1990), of the dependency of the abuser (Pillemer, 1986) or of living together with poor systems of social support and/or social isolation (Grafstrom et al., 1992) also need to be taken into account. And of course, although there is no proven direct causal link between the stress of caring and the development of abusive situations, it is also apparent that there is some linkage. So that, for example, additional stressors, either internal (due, perhaps to relationship, personality factors or other dependent individuals requiring care) or external (due to inadequate accommodation or poverty) may exacerbate a difficult situation to a point where the situation fractures and abuse results.

What is being promoted here is of much more interaction between areas of specialism, with much needed interchange of ideas, information and knowledge. For as Brown et al. astutely recognise:

Adult protection is an agenda which requires practitioners, managers and researchers to look outwards and to learn from colleagues in allied fields such as domestic violence, racial harassment, child protection, criminal justice, probation, crime reduction, victim support, and related user movements. We have much to learn from each other. (Brown et al., 1999, p. 15)

As we move forward into this new century and the next hundred years of the profession that is social work, we must widen the debates and move forward together, learning from each other indeed.

Further Reading

ARC/NAPSAC (Eds.) (1993). *It Could Never Happen Here: The prevention and treatment of sexual abuse of adults with learning disabilities in residential settings.* Bradford: Thornton and Pearson.

Department of Health (2000). *No Secrets: Guidance on developing and implementing multi-agency policies and procedure to protect vulnerable adults from abuse.* London: Department of Health.

Kingston, P. and Penhale, B. (Eds.) (1995). *Family Violence and the Caring Professions.* Basingstoke: Macmillan.

Pritchard, J. (Ed.) (1999). *Elder Abuse Work: Best practice in Britain and Canada.* London: Jessica Kingsley Publishers.

Stanley, N., Manthorpe, J. and Penhale, B. (Eds.) (1999). *Institutional Abuse: Perspectives across the life course.* London: Routledge.

Chapter 8

Meeting the Needs of Children and Families Through Working Together

Jan Horwath

Introduction

We cannot begin to improve the lives of disadvantaged and vulnerable children unless we identify their needs and understand what is happening to them in order to take appropriate action.

(Department of Health et al., 2000: pvii.)

The statement made in this quotation may appear obvious. Yet, how do professionals understand what is happening to a child? A brief reflection upon social work practice over the last forty or so years indicates that different factors have influenced professional understandings of the experience of the vulnerable child during that period. There is a different emphasis upon particular aspects of that experience at different times that is dependent on shifts in government policy, research and practice developments. For example, in the early 1960s, Winnicot highlighted that the needs of a child cannot be addressed, unless one considers the child within the context of their family situation and the wider community in which the child lives. The very title of his book written in 1964, *The Child, The Family and The Outside World* emphasises these links. This book encapsulates a systematic or what would now be termed an ecological approach to child welfare. Taking this approach, the experience of a child is determined by cultural context, social values, traditions and expectations. The cultural context is described by Bronfenbrenner (1979) as the macrosystem. Communities create institutions that incorporate the cultural values (exosystems). Within the community, families operate as small communities (microsystems) with their own standards and values that may or may not reflect those of the main or majority culture. Advocates of such an ecological approach argue that professionals can only begin to understand and intervene effectively in cases of maltreatment if, 'the systematic interconnectedness of experience from cultural to individual levels' is recognised (Crittenden, 1991: p165). Social policy in the UK, during the

early 1960s, made some of these connections. For example, the Children and Young Persons Act 1963 addressed concerns regarding the effects of poverty and lone parenting upon children, by enabling the payments of small sums of money to families in crisis (Jordan with Jordan, 2000). However, the 1970s and 1980s witnessed a different approach to the identification of the needs of vulnerable children. This change in emphasis resulted in a narrowing of the scope of child welfare policy to provision targeted at protecting children from abuse. Whereby legislation and guidance focussed on child protection and meeting the needs of abused children through reception into the care of the local authority or the provision of services to prevent the reception into care (Adcock and White, 1998). This change in emphasis had two causes. First, public and media attention was drawn to issues of child abuse as a result of the plethora of public inquires into child deaths that occurred throughout the late 1970s and 1980s. Demands were made on government by the public through the press, to meet the needs of children at risk or those suffering from maltreatment. In addition, the government of the day placed emphasis on issues of order, social discipline and family responsibility (Jordan with Jordan, 2000). The result of these changes was a narrowing of perception of the needs of the child to issues related to child safety, i.e. child protection (Parton, 1996; Stevenson, 1998). In addition, assessing the experience of the child centred on family assessment. The developmental needs of the child, parenting issues and the parenting environment were marginalised in terms of social work practice. Field social work with children and families became synonymous with child protection.

By the late 1990s, the emphasis changed again. Research studies commissioned by the Department of Health highlighted that a 'child protection' focus was too narrow. These research studies indicated that in order to meet the needs of children, assessment and interventions should focus on both safeguarding and promoting the welfare of children (Department of Health, 1995). Current policies and accompanying guidance therefore seek to broaden the child welfare system to safeguard children from maltreatment and simultaneously promote the welfare of children whose health and development may be impaired if their needs are not met (Department of Health, 1999).

The changing emphasis in terms of both assessing the needs of children and identifying their experience has had a considerable impact on the current role of social workers and other professionals engaged in working with children and families. This chapter explores this impact and considers the contribution that social workers from adult services can make to meeting the needs of children and their families. The focus of the chapter is on assessment and intervention in relation to children living in the community with their parents or permanent carers.

The Inheritance of the 1970s and 1980s and the Impact on Practice in the 1990s

The legislative framework

The Children Act (1989) provides the current legislative framework for child welfare. As described above, child welfare legislation in the 1970s and 1980s centred on child protection. By comparison, the Children Act 1989 takes a broad view of child welfare provision, emphasising the need to both safeguard and promote the welfare of children.

As is stated in the Act:

> *It shall be the general duty of every local authority to safeguard and promote the welfare of children within their area who are in need and so far as is consistent with that duty, to promote the upbringing of such children by their families, by providing a range of services appropriate to those children's needs.*

> (Children Act 1989, s.17 (1).)

The Children Act (1989) gives recognition to the principle that for the majority of children the family is the most appropriate place for a child to be brought up, and that parents should have responsibility for their children. Local authorities, as a result of this legislation, are expected to balance supporting and working in partnership with parents with a need to protect children from harm.

The Children Act (1989) cannot be considered in isolation. It marks a significant change when the spirit of legislation shifted from an over reliance on statutory intervention to a more negotiated, partnership and voluntaristic approach towards work with families (Jordan with Jordan, 2000). However, the spirit of the Act was diluted when implemented in the early 1990s. This occurred for two reasons. The Act was introduced at a time when there was still a need for an ordered protection service for children (Department of Health, 1995). This ordered approach was reflected in the government guidance that was produced around the late 1980s and early 1990s, which focussed particularly on assessment and interventions in relation to child abuse. For example, in 1988 the government produced *Protecting Children: A Guide For Social Workers Undertaking a Comprehensive Assessment* (Department of Health, 1988). This guidance became known as *The Orange Book*. It explored and defined expectations for long-term planning in child protection cases. In 1991, further child protection guidance was issued *Working Together under the Children Act 1991* (Department of Health, 1991). The guidance outlined the roles and responsibilities of professionals working with suspected cases of child abuse. While practitioners and managers welcomed guidance for managing cases of child maltreatment, accompanying guidance regarding assessment or working together for children identified as being in need, under section 17 of the Children Act 1989, was not produced. In addition, the guidance, *Working Together*, was targeted at professionals working with children, such as teachers and paediatricians. No consideration was given to the roles and responsibilities of professionals working with parents or carers in situations where parenting issues could influence parenting capacity. This was particularly significant in terms of social work practice, as the introduction of the National Health Service and Community Care Act 1991 entailed the development of an organisational and practice split, at a local level, between community care services for adults and services for children. Social workers redirected their attention from generic responsibilities for all client groups to more discrete and specialist remits. An opportunity was missed at this juncture to provide national guidance regarding ways those social workers might work together across specialisms to meet the needs of children and families. This failure has had a detrimental effect on practice and resulted in the development of 'boundaries separating adults' from children's services, a process which inevitably increases the difficulty of securing a holistic approach to the needs of the family' (Cleaver et al., 1999: p6).

The impact on practice

The implementation of the Children Act (1989), at a local level, has been influenced by public inquires into both child deaths and child sexual abuse that occurred during the 1970s and 1980s (Stevenson, 1998). A number of inquiry reports raised issues regarding the way professionals and agencies responded to or failed to respond to potential cases of child abuse (Reder et al., 1993). This led to both practitioners and managers developing a 'watch your back' approach to practice. They followed incident driven procedures and targeted their practice at the potentially high profile child protection cases. A climate of fear developed in which social workers and other professionals were afraid that a mistake might result in their names being on the front page of the national papers. By 1995, the situation was such that the Department of Health concluded that, 'real benefits may arise if there is a focus on the needs of children and families rather than a narrow concentration on the alleged incident of abuse' (Department of Health, 1995: foreword).

The government reached this conclusion after commissioning 20 research studies designed to explore the management of child protection cases. A summary of the findings was published (Department of Health, 1995). The findings of these studies highlighted a lack of recognition concerning the impact of a range of issues upon parenting capacity. For example, Farmer and Owen (1995) studied the outcomes for 44 children during the period of twenty

months after registration. They found that 70 per cent of children were protected from further abuse and the welfare of 68 per cent of children had been enhanced. However, in only 30 per cent of cases had the needs of the parent or carer been reasonably met. Farmer and Owen note that there are limits to the ability of professionals to enhance the welfare of the child who remain with their parents, where the parents' needs are not addressed. Farmer and Owen summarised the reasons why the needs of parents were not addressed as being that:

- Child care workers had a narrow perception of their role believing their task was to protect children from further abuse.

- Parental needs were often not recognised.

- Parents' experiences of the child protection inquiry resulted in them feeling negative about social work intervention and were therefore reluctant to engage in further social work activity. (1995)

Farmer and Owen concluded that a child protection system had developed that was fairly effective at keeping children safe in the short term. However, this system did not meet the wider developmental needs of children or the welfare needs of families. Yet, where these broader needs are ignored, the longer-term protection of children from abuse cannot be assured. Farmer and Owen completed their data gathering between 1989-91. Thoburn et al. began a further study in 1993, two years after the implementation of the Children Act 1989. Their findings were similar to those of Farmer and Owen. They noted that of the 105 parents involved in this study, there were concerns regarding the parents' ability to fulfil the main parenting role in 98 per cent of cases. They also noted a high incidence of violence between adults in households where children were in need of protection. In only 17 per cent of cases were the problems of the parents eased, while in 29 per cent of cases parents still had serious debilitating problems and unmet need after social work intervention (Thotum et al., 1995). In addition, there is clear evidence that parenting issues such as alcohol and drug misuse, domestic violence and mental health issues can impact on the well being of children (Becker et al., 1998; Cleaver et al., 2000). Crittenden (2000) emphasises that meeting the needs of parents as individuals is crucial in order to promote better outcomes for children who are subject to neglect. She notes that parents often have long-standing problems that result in neglectful behaviour. In order to effect change these parenting issues need to be identified and addressed.

One of the consequences of a narrow focus on child safety within the family is that social workers do not take into account the social context in which child maltreatment occurs (Stevenson, 1998). The social context or the 'parenting environment' (Burke et al., 1998) can have a significant impact on meeting the developmental needs of a child (Jack, 1997). For example, racial abuse against children from minority ethnic groups can impact on both their sense of identity and their emotional and educational needs (Department of Health, 2000). Children growing up in poverty are at a greater risk than other children, both from chronic illnesses and also failure to reach their full educational potential (Jack, 1997; Macdonald, 2001). Polanski et al., (1985) found that isolation from social and family networks impacts on the ability of parents to meet the needs of their children. Two types of parents or carers are particularly vulnerable to social isolation: parents of disabled children (Middleton, 1999) and lone parents (Dubowitz, 2000; Jack, 2000; Macdonald, 2001).

The Framework for the Assessment of Children in Need and Their Families

Concerned that the principles of the Children Act 1989 were being marginalised, the government introduced guidance designed to make the principles of the Act more explicit in practice. This guidance, *A Framework for the Assessment of Children in Need and their Families* (Department of Health et al., 2000) became effective in April 2001. The framework is intended to:

> *...provide a systematic way of analysing, understanding and recording what is happening to children and young people within their families and the wider context of the community in which they live.*
> (Preface, Department of Health et al., 2000.)

The assessment of the child and their family should form the basis for making decisions regarding the needs of the child and the family.

Moreover it should assist in identifying which services would best meet these needs. The framework therefore is designed to enable practitioners to make explicit links between the needs of the child, parenting capacity and the parenting environment.

The framework itself is represented as a triangle with three interrelated *domains* . These domains refer to the:

- Developmental needs of children.
- Capacity of parents or caregivers to respond to those needs.
- Impact of wider family and environmental factors on parenting capacity and children.

Each domain is further divided into critical *dimensions*. The dimensions are derived from both research findings and practice knowledge regarding factors that influence the developmental needs of children. For example, the dimensions concerning the child's developmental needs draws upon the work of Parker et al. (1991), regarding the developmental needs of children 'looked after' by the local authority. For the dimensions concerning parenting capacity materials used effectively for the assessment of potential foster carers and adopters have been adapted and applied to parenting more generally (Rose, 2001).

The framework is designed to be used for *all* assessments of children in need – including those where there are concerns regarding child abuse and neglect. Moreover, the guidance promotes a multidisciplinary approach to assessment involving, social workers and other practitioners from both children's and community care services. The completed assessment is designed to make explicit ways in which the child and family's needs can be met through a multidisciplinary plan for service provision.

Contributing to the child in need assessment: the role of the social worker from adult services

Working with parenting issues

As indicated previously, social workers from adult services should engage in the assessment of children's needs, by assessing the impact of

---

Figure 8.1. Dimensions used in Assessment Framework

Childs developmental needs	Parenting capacity	Family and environmental factors
Health	Basic care	Family history and functioning
Education	Ensuring safety	Wider family
Emotional and behavioural development	Emotional warmth	Housing
Identity	Stimulation	Employment
Family and social relationships	Guidance and boundaries	Income
Social presentation	Stability	Family's social integration
Selfcare skills		Community resources

---

particular parenting issues on parenting capacity. But, what are the issues that are likely to impact on parenting capacity? Cleaver and Freeman (1995) developed a typology linking families suspected of child abuse with identifiable parental problems. They suggest the following categories:

- **Multi-problem families:** these families have usually had long term on-going contact with welfare agencies as a result of chronic problems. The parents' problems are likely to include poor health, inadequate housing, long term unemployment, domestic violence, alcohol and drug misuse, and financial problems.

- **Specific problem families:** these families rarely have on-going contact with welfare agencies but come to their attention as a result of a specific concern. Parental problems may include mental health, acute physical or terminal illness.

- **Acutely distressed families:** these families manage, until an accumulation of problems or a crisis overwhelms them. The parents' issues may include learning or physical disability, lone or unsupported parents.

The key parenting issues identified by Cleaver and Freeman include: domestic violence; mental health; alcohol and drug misuse; disability. Each

of these is considered below; in terms of the influence the issues can have on the capacity of the parent to meet the needs of the child.

Domestic violence

Living in a situation of violence has an impact on children, as described by Humphreys and Mullender (Chapter 6). First, children may be injured if they physically come between violent carers. Second, studies completed in both the USA and the UK, indicate that witnessing domestic violence impacts on the child's development (see for example, Hester et al., 1999). Studies from the USA highlight the impact in terms of conduct disorders upon children, who live with domestic violence (Jouriles, 1998), in particular the development of aggressive, antisocial and confrontational behaviours in children. Studies from the UK, suggest a far broader range of responses amongst children, ranging from increased aggression to withdrawal and anxiety (Mullender, 1996). Children will respond differently to the impact of domestic violence depending on their age. For example, Sinclair cited in Mullender (1996) notes that children of pre-school age are likely to demonstrate their fears and anxieties physically, through symptoms such as headaches and sleeping disturbances. Whilst, Jaffe, Wolfe and Wilson

(1990) note that both pre-schoolers and young children witnessing domestic violence tend to show signs of terror. Adolescents may try to remove themselves from the situation physically, for example by running away, suicidal acts or by emotionally 'cutting off' from the situation through the use of drugs (Karr-Morse and Wiley, 2000). The impact on children will to some extent be determined by the supports available to the child, within both the family and the community. For example, Levendosky and Graham-Bermann (1998) found children's responses to witnessing domestic violence towards their mother varied depending on the quality of maternal parenting. Cleaver et al., (1999) identified that the existence of a safe environment, where the child can go if there is a threat of violence, may increase the protective factors for the child living in a situation of domestic violence.

Mental health

As discussed by Mello-Baron, Moore and Moore (Chapter 10), various studies have highlighted a link between parents who have mental health problems and the health and development of their children. For example, Gibbons, Conroy and Bell (1995) identified that 13 per cent of their sample of children, who had their names placed on the child protection register had a parent or carer who had been treated for a mental health issue. Thoburn, Lewis and Shemmings (1995) in their study noted that 20 per cent of child protection cases involved a parent or carer with a mental health history. A study by Falkov (1996) of Part Eight Reviews indicated that there is a link between mental illness and serious child abuse. Falkov studied 100 cases, and found that in 32 cases, there was some link to mental illness and 25 perpetrators of the abuse (19 women and 6 men) suffered from a psychiatric disorder. It is not only the extreme cases of mental disorder that cause concern. A child living with a carer who has mental health problems may have their health and development affected in a number of ways. For example, a parent in a depressed condition may neglect their child as they are unable to meet the physical and emotional needs of a child (Cassell and Coleman, 1995; Dubowitz, 2000). The delusions and hallucinations suffered by parents with

schizophrenia may result in a preoccupation with their own private world and consequently the needs of the child being ignored (Cleaver et al., 2000).

Alcohol and drug misuse

Alcohol and drug misuse amongst carers of children has become an issue of growing concern for those working with both carers and their children. Concerns centre around two main areas: first children exposed to alcohol and drugs in utero; second the lifestyle of the carers and the impact on their ability to meet the child's developmental needs (Hogan, 1998; Cleaver et al., 1999). Research, primarily from the USA, indicates that infants exposed to substances, in utero, such as opiates, stimulants and benzodiazepines may suffer withdrawal symptoms often referred to as Neonatal Abstinence Syndrome (Mounteney, 1998). Infants suffering from this syndrome can exhibit distressed behaviour which in turn parents find difficult to manage. American studies into parental cocaine exposure report divided results. Some indicate that substance use can result in major peri-natal difficulties, including changes in the nervous system and growth deficits; others suggest that the effects on the infant are more likely to be related to poor ante-natal care and a disadvantaged lifestyle (Mounteney, 1998). While, Karre-Morse and Wiley (2000) conclude that most crack/cocaine babies placed in nurturing and stimulating environments do go on to perform normally. They go on to argue that alcohol use amongst pregnant women appears to cause damage that is far more enduring to children than cocaine use. Cleaver et al., (1999) note that mothers who use alcohol excessively during pregnancy can cause foetal alcohol syndrome, which may damage the baby's central nervous system and result in a range of anatomical abnormalities and behaviour problems for the child.

Living with drug and alcohol abusing parents can also have an impact on a child. The Local Government Drugs Forum (1997) stress that most parents who use drugs are able to respond to the needs of their children. Yet there are a minority of parents who allow their substance or alcohol use to impact on their ability to meet the developmental needs of their children. Klee, cited in Mounteney (1998) identifies factors existing amongst drug using parents that may be indicators of risk of significant harm, while other factors can act as protectors. Although she considers these factors in terms of parents who use drugs, they are as relevant to parents who misuse alcohol.

The risk factors include the:

- Behaviour and mental state of the parent for example depression, aggression and lethargy.
- Social environment such as the home being used for drug dealing or drinking binges.
- The physical environment, such as leaving bottles of spirits or tablets lying around.

The protective factors include:

- Strategies used by the parents to safeguard the welfare of the child; for example, ensuring drug supplies are kept in a safe place.
- Sources of support and positive influence for the child such as extended family and professionals (for example, teachers).
- Treatment and abstinence.

These findings would indicate that one cannot automatically equate parental use of alcohol or drugs with inadequate parenting. Rather, an assessment is required of both the factors that have a negative impact on parenting capacity and the protective strategies designed to ensure the child's needs are met. These assessments can be influenced by the attitudes of workers. Forrester (2000) found for example, that social workers gave very different ratings of concern to alcohol compared to heroin using parents. Both were heavily related to child neglect in his study, but social workers were more concerned about heroin misuse than alcohol misuse.

Disabled parents

'Disabled parents' is a wide ranging term. In this section, consideration will be given first to parents with learning disabilities and second to issues for young carers caring for parents with physical disabilities or illness.

Learning disabilities

When assessing the impact of learning disabilities on parenting capacity, one needs to consider a number of factors. Cotson et al. (2001) identify three essential areas that need to be considered: the parents' cognitive functioning; psychological factors; and the parents' relationships with partners and family. Each is considered in turn. Actual levels of IQ are not necessarily good indicators of parenting ability. What is important is cognitive functioning, that is the ability of the parent to learn and make use of support services. For example, a parent with a learning disability may not realise that a bath that is at an acceptable temperature for an adult will be too hot for a young baby. However, they may have the ability to understand the importance of bathing a baby at the right temperature and once shown how to measure the right temperatures are able to do this. A significant area of concern when assessing the parenting capacity of parents with learning disabilities is their ability to meet the emotional needs of the child. As Cotson et al., (2001) note, while practical and concrete parenting skills can be taught, issues in terms of meeting a child's emotional needs are much harder to address. Consideration also needs to be given as with any parent, to psychological factors such as the parents' own experience of being a child and the impact this can have on their parenting skills. For example, people with learning disabilities are vulnerable to abuse (Westcott, 1993), which can affect their ability to protect themselves and their children from future abuse. The majority of parents with learning disabilities appear to be mothers. Jackson (1998) notes that mothers who have a learning disability are particularly vulnerable to having liaisons or developing relationships with sexual offenders, which can be a major child protection problem. In these situations, mothers need to understand how to keep themselves and their children safe. Cotson et al. (2001) note that the success of parenting by parents with learning disabilities depends on their support network. Such networks, if effective, can meet the developmental needs of the child that are not met by the parent. In addition, the network may provide guidance and support to the parent, thus ensuring that they are able to offer quality care to their children. Yet, such a network is often lacking or the support may be inconsistent or undermine the role of the parent (Booth and Booth, 1994). In addition, Feldman et al., (1997) note that adverse social circumstances increase levels of stress and depression amongst learning disabled parents, which in turn contributes to their parenting difficulties.

Young Carers: *Caring for a parent with an illness or disability*

In 1996, the Office for National Statistics suggested that 51,000 young people were caring and taking some responsibility for another person, usually an adult. Other researchers indicate this figure is significantly higher (Becker et al., 1998). These young people are generally carers because their parent has an illness, disability or the parent has substance, alcohol or mental health issues. Becker et al. (1998) in their study of 641 young carers found that young carers caring for a parent with a disability or illness were involved in providing a wide range of caring tasks such as health care, emotional support, intimate care and household tasks. Alderidge and Becker (1993) note it is the *impact* rather than the *number* of tasks that affects the child. They identified some common problems that children may experience:

- impaired intellectual development
- isolation from peers and extended family
- lack of time for age related activities
- conflict between caring role and child's own needs
- feeling isolated
- lack of positive feedback
- feeling stigmatised
- lost opportunities

(Alderidge and Becker cited in NSPCC Turning Points, 1997: p174.)

Social workers working with adult service users are frequently in a position to identify the impact of parenting issues on parenting capacity. Despite a growing awareness, during the late 1990s, of the benefits of including community care professionals in assessments of children in need, there is a low involvement of workers from adult services in these types of assessment. Therefore, methods for closer collaboration between professionals need to be identified. The rest of this chapter considers guidance and systems designed to promote collaborative practice when assessing and intervening to meet the needs of children.

Frameworks for Working Together to Safeguard Children

The Framework for the Assessment of Children in Need and their Families (Department of Health et al., 2000) includes guidance regarding ways in which professionals should gather information, make decisions, plan and intervene in order to meet the needs of children. Further specific guidance has been produced by the government about ways in which professionals should work together for a small group of children in need – that is the group of children who may be suffering, or are at risk of suffering significant harm and need to have their welfare both safeguarded and promoted. This guidance *Working Together to Safeguard Children, A guide to inter-agency working to safeguard and promote the welfare of children* (Department of Health et al., 1999) recognises the need to 'work across boundaries' and to 'pool expertise to strengthen parents' capacity to respond to their children's needs, where this is in the best interests of the child' (p23 2.26). The guidance states that this work across boundaries should take place through; referral; assessment; planning and intervention. Each of these stages will be considered in turn.

Referral

Working Together (Department of Health et al., 1999) states clearly that all professionals have a role to play in promoting and safeguarding the welfare of children. For example, any professional who is made aware of a situation of domestic violence should consider the safety and well-being of any children in the home. Then, if concerned about the children, refer any concerns to the local authority social services department, police or NSPCC. When making the referral, the referrer should be as clear as possible about the nature of their concerns, how and why these concerns have arisen and the apparent needs of the child and family.

One of the most significant barriers to making referrals can be the existence of different interpretations about the nature and extent of confidentiality amongst professionals. It is clearly stated within *Working Together* and the Assessment Framework, the Common Law Duty of Confidence allows for confidential information to be shared if it is necessary to safeguard a child or children (7.32). None the less, every effort should be made to obtain the consent of the individual involved before sharing information. The Data Protection Act 1998 introduced controls on the processing of 'sensitive data' (including information as to the commission or alleged commission of any offence), and stated that there should be a 'legitimate basis' for sharing this information (Department of Health et al., 2000). At the time of writing, it would seem that information regarding the developmental needs of the child or parents' capacity to meet these needs, where the safety of the child is not a concern or a suspected offence against the child is not being investigated, can only be shared with the consent of the individual concerned (Hendry and Horwath, 2000). This raises issues for professionals who need to think carefully about the consequences before sharing information without consent. Organisationally, practitioners would benefit from protocols that provide them with guidance regarding information sharing. What is clear is that all professionals will need to develop and use skills in working with families in order to facilitate the sharing of information in situations where parents or carers may be reluctant to disclose information.

Assessment

Once a referral has been made, an *initial assessment* should be completed within seven working days (Department of Health et al., 2000). This assessment will normally be co-ordinated by a children and family social worker employed by a local authority social services department. The assessment should address the following questions:

> *What are the needs of the child?*

> *Are the parents able to respond to the child's needs?*

> *Is action required to safeguard and promote the child's welfare?*
>
> (Department of Health et al., 1999: 5.12.)

Collaborative practice between professionals from adult and children's services is crucial. Each professional and family member holds a piece of the jigsaw. It is only when the pieces are connected together that professionals can begin to understand the child's experience. Social workers from adult services have an important contribution to make during the initial assessment in terms of identifying both issues affecting parents' or carers' capacities to respond appropriately to their child and also family and environmental factors which impact on the child and family. The Assessment Framework guidance clearly states that attention should be paid to parents' strengths as well as any difficulties they are experiencing (Department of Health et al., 2000).

The outcome of an initial assessment may be a need for further information and a more detailed assessment – *a core assessment* – this should be completed in a further 35 working days. If however, the referral or initial assessment indicates the child has suffered or is likely to suffer significant harm and is therefore subject to s.47 Children Act 1989 inquiry, then a core assessment should begin immediately. The purpose of the core assessment is to:

> *Address the central or most important aspects of the needs of a child and the capacity of their parents or caregivers to respond appropriately to these needs within the wider family and community context.*
>
> (Department of Health et al., 2000: para 3.11.)

It is often at this stage that tensions in terms of working together across specialisms can manifest themselves. This is illustrated using mental health concerns as an example. As identified above, mental health workers can focus on mental health issues, with the consequence that the service user, as a parent, becomes marginalised. Likewise, childcare workers can focus on the immediate safety and well being of the child either by ignoring or overemphasising the impact of mental health issues on the parent's capacity to respond to the needs of the child. Cassell and Coleman (1995) argue this approach is the result of two distinctive pieces of legislation. The Mental Health Act 1983 is concerned with psychiatric diagnosis and the rights of adults with mental health issues. The Children Act 1989 balances children's needs with parental responsibility.

Although the paramount principle of the welfare of the child should set the agenda, professionals working with parents with mental health issues, may experience a conflict of interests. Cassell and Coleman suggest that there are a range of ways in which the situation can be managed effectively between child and adult psychiatrists. Their recommendations apply equally to social workers from children's and adult services. Social workers should be clear about their responsibilities and roles. For example, who has the primary responsibility for the child and who is attempting to meet the needs of the parent? The worker with the adult should contribute to the assessment by providing information about the diagnosis and prognosis of the parent, in terms of the impact of their issue on parenting capacity, such as the impact of medication on general functioning. The worker for the child should assess the needs of the child and the impact upon the child of the parenting issue. The adult worker should not only be aware that they are providing a care plan for the parent but also that they have a responsibility to recognise and work with the child welfare issues. Cassell and Coleman conclude:

> We believe that clear enough distinctions between roles are both necessary and possible and, if combined with appreciation of the respective needs of the parent and the child, will allow complementary assessments to be made to the benefit of both.
>
> (Cassell and Coleman, 1995: p179.)

However, specialist workers can be uncertain of their role or may feel that they do not have the knowledge and skills to identify, and work with the needs of both children and carers (McKellar and Coggans, 1997). If this is the case, guidance such as *The Local Government Drugs Forum and Standing Conference on Drug Using Parents: Guidelines for Inter-agency Working* can be useful in terms of clarifying roles and responsibilities. One of the issues highlighted by Forrester (2000) is that workers are often unaware that such guidance exists. The guidance should therefore be accessible to all practitioners and their managers. Training and supervision can be useful vehicles for disseminating and familiarising staff with available guidance. Training, as described in Chapter 13 can promote effective work across specialisms. Cleaver et al., (1999) recommend that joint training involving both adult and children's services should focus on information regarding the link between parenting issues and the needs of children, as well as exploring ways that professionals can work together by using such mechanisms as a common language. Hendry (2000) goes further, stating that any training should ensure relevance, currency and pitch and place emphasis on the shared nature of responsibilities.

Planning

Part of the assessment includes analysing and making sense of the information gathered in order to plan interventions that promote effective outcomes for children (Adcock, 2001). Experience from inter-agency child protection practice indicates that professionals are prepared to share information, but are not as engaged in the on-going process of analysis and planning (Calder and Horwath, 1999). As one of the aims of current childcare policy is, *to ensure a holistic approach to both assessment and intervention*, practitioners from adult and children's services should be involved in analysis and planning. Decision making, left to child and family social workers, can result in the development of a distorted plan that seeks to meet children's needs without paying attention to carer and environmental factors that could impinge on meeting those needs.

The vehicle for planning interventions for children and families is determined by the degree of concern regarding both safeguarding and promoting the welfare of the child. This means if professionals have concerns, supported by evidence, that the child is suffering or likely to suffer from significant harm, then the planning process is likely to commence with an initial child protection conference. The purpose of this meeting is to decide whether the child's name should be placed on the child protection register and whether the most effective way to meet the needs of the child is through an inter-agency child protection plan (Department of Health et al., 1999). If this is agreed by conference members, an outline child protection plan, with clear objectives will be drawn up by those present at the conference, including the parents and where appropriate the child. A 'core group' of professionals will then be identified.

Subsequently this group will be expected to work with the family to translate the outline child protection plan into a *working plan* with a view to achieving identified objectives. The plan may include the need for a further core assessment, as well as recommendations regarding the provision of services.

Alternatively, situations may arise where the concerns of professionals are not as severe as those described above. In these situations, the concerns are more likely to centre upon the health and development of the child being impaired, if services are not provided. When this occurs, planning takes place in a more informal forum such as a network meeting, 'family group conference' or a case planning meeting. The aims are the same, i.e. to produce a multidisciplinary plan, designed to meet the needs of the child and family. This plan may include further assessment of the needs of the child and their family. Social workers from adult services are more likely to be familiar with the formal child protection system than informal case planning. This informal planning requires the same level of involvement from social workers in adult services as does formal planning to ensure that issues related to parenting capacity are analysed and addressed.

Intervention

Macdonald, in an overview of evidence based approaches to helping children who have been abused or neglected concludes:

> At their most successful, interventions are multi-faceted and pay careful attention to process factors, such as the careful engagement of families, particularly parents….Work with abused children is most successful when the sequelae of abuse are specifically targeted.
>
> (Macdonald, 2001: p197.)

Cleaver et al., (1999) highlight a number of factors that are likely to result in effective intervention in cases where both child and carers' needs are to be addressed.

●   Service provision, wherever possible, should be non-stigmatising and provided under both community care and childcare legislation. Integrated service provision should be the aim: this can be achieved

through a co-ordinated care plan involving all professionals who work with the family.

●   If stress for carers is reduced this indirectly benefits children. Interventions should therefore take into account stress factors for carers, such as lack of family and social support and lack of social integration. Services such as Home Start and other community resources should be utilised.

●   The role of the key worker is crucial. The worker should be able to work effectively with both the family and the professionals who contribute to the care plan. Their role is very much that of co-ordinator, ensuring that both professionals and family members are contributing to the plan as agreed.

Intervention strategies should consider not only the needs of the child but also the needs of the parents (Department of Health, 2000). An example of an effective approach to addressing issues of domestic violence has been described by Skyner and Waters (1999). They established an anger management programme for male perpetrators of domestic violence who were completing probation orders. The programme is run in partnership with the NSPCC and offers a package of support to children and women. The aim of this multidisciplinary approach is to ensure that there is a victim/survivor focus to the programme and that the needs of the non-abusing partner and children are considered throughout. Jackson (1998) also emphasises the importance of considering both the needs of the child and the parent. In describing a project operating in South Devon for mothers with learning disabilities, she stresses the importance of thinking both 'learning disabilities' and 'children's needs' arguing that it is only when both are recognised and addressed by the workers that the family can survive together.

In many situations, it is important to take a family centred approach to assessment and intervention. An example of this approach is to be found in the intervention strategies used to meet the needs of young carers. The Department of Health, in a summary of four SSI workshops that focussed on young carers, emphasised that both social workers working with parents and also social workers concerned with the child should take an approach that:

- Recognises the needs of the family.

- Assesses the child as part of the family unit.

- Acknowledges the rights of the child.

- Recognises the impact of the environment for example poverty, attitudes towards disability.

- Acknowledges a difference between parenting and parenting activity.

- Takes a long term approach to intervention rather than crisis management.

- Focuses on young carers as children in need rather than at risk from significant harm.

- Works with child's fears regarding professional interventions.

- Works in partnership with families.

(Department of Health, 1995.)

Conclusion

The Department of Health has provided a framework to promote making links across specialisms when working with children and families. The intention being to safeguard children, promote their well-being and address the parenting issues that affect parenting capacity. This means that practitioners in both adult and children's services should work together to consider not only the needs of the child but also the needs of parents. It is only through this co-ordinated approach that a holistic assessment and strategy for intervention can be completed. This creates a new challenge for social workers. As Stanley and Penhale have noted:

> *The needs of the parent and child…in most cases intertwine in a manner which can be likened to a complex spiral. This image allows us to see these needs as commensurate at some points, complementary at others and conflicting in places.*

(Stanley and Penhale, 1999: p42)

If workers are to manage these challenges, an organisational framework is required that promotes effective practice. This can be achieved if managers, both within and between services, develop organisational structures, protocols, practice guidance and systems that enable professionals to work together. An organisational environment is required that recognises and addresses the tensions and issues for workers seeking to safeguard and promote the welfare of the child while respecting the rights of adults and children. Managers need to consider the following:

- What systems are in place within the organisation and between organisations to ensure that relevant information can be shared, assessments made and interventions co-ordinated in cases where both parents and children have needs requiring social work intervention?

- Are systems in place that enable joint commissioning and planning of services?

- Are polices and procedures in place, which enable issues relating to conflicts of interest between the child and the carer to be addressed?

- Do local service level agreements encourage and facilitate joint work across specialisms, particularly between community care and children's services?

- Are joint training strategies in place for both practitioners and managers?

At a practice level, child care practitioners should ask themselves the following questions:

- Do I recognise the needs of the parents when preparing children in need assessments?

- What assumptions do I make about the impact of parenting issues on parenting capacity?

- Do I know whom to contact within my own or other agencies if I have concerns regarding particular parenting issues?

- How do I attempt to work with professionals from adult services when identifying and meeting the needs of children?

- How would I manage conflicting views and opinions between myself and social workers from adult services?

Adult service social workers should consider:

- Am I familiar with local child protection and children in need procedures?

- Do I recognise that the adult service user is also a parent? How do I reflect this in my practice?

- Do I know whom to contact if I have concerns about children within a family?

- How do I attempt to work with professionals from children's services when identifying and meeting the needs of children?

- What views do I have about child care services? How does this impact on my practice?

- What are the tensions regarding the service user's rights to confidentiality? How do I manage this?

Identifying and meeting the needs of children is everybody's business, according to new government guidance. If this guidance is to be implemented effectively to both safeguard and promote the welfare of children, professionals need to recognise the importance of making links across specialisms. It is only through building these links that social workers can ensure a sharp focus on the child in the context of the family and the outside world.

Further Reading

Cleaver, H., Unell, I. and Aldgate, J. (1999). *Children's Needs Parenting Capacity. The Impact of Parenting Mental Illness, Problem Alcohol and Drug Use and Domestic Violence on Children's Development.* London: The Stationery Office.

Department of Health, Department for Education and Employment and the Home Office (2000). *The Framework for the Assessment of Children in Need and Their Families.* London: The Stationery Office.

Horwath, J. (Ed.) (2001). *The Child's World Assessing Children in Need.* London: Jessica Kingsley.

Chapter 9

The Assessment Process in Work with Offenders

Charlotte Knight

Work with Offenders – Background and Context

The National Probation Service in England and Wales (Home Office, 2000a) has prime responsibility for the assessment and supervision of offenders in the community and for through-care with offenders both in prison and on license post-release. In England and Wales, work with young offenders has, historically, been shared between social services departments and the probation service with responsibility changing according to age of the young person or adult, as different legislation has been introduced. Currently, young offenders up to the age of eighteen years of age, are the responsibility of the multi-agency youth offending teams (YOTs) introduced by The Crime and Disorder Act (1998). This development is part of a wider governmental move towards developing inter-disciplinary and multi-agency working across a range of social and health issues. In particular this is a central focus of work with high risk and dangerous offenders. In Scotland, work with offenders is undertaken by criminal justice service teams within social work departments

From the early beginnings of the probation service until the late 1960s, the predominant ideology in work with offenders had been that of rehabilitation. This approach was initially challenged in a number of different ways during the 1970s and early 1980s. Martinson (1974) argued, based on his review of criminal rehabilitation literature and a broad survey of research on correctional treatments, that in respect of the rehabilitation of offenders almost nothing works. Although Martinson was later to modify some of his earlier views, nevertheless his work had a profound impact on probation practice in the 1970s and undermined confidence in much of the rehabilitative work of the service. This period is sometimes referred to as the 'Nothing Works' era.

The late 1980s and early 1990s also saw the probation service grappling with an unprecedented level of government attention and saw the move towards a more managerial and evidenced based approach to work with offenders. This was partly as a response to the negative legacy of the 'Nothing Works' era. Research by a number of different authors (such as, Ross, Fabiano and Ewles, 1988; Raynor, 1988; Roberts and Camasso, 1991; Raynor and Vanstone, 1994; and McIvor, 1990), began to form a substantial body of knowledge that proved that the *best* of probation practice can substantially reduce reconviction rates. This research also highlighted the fact that the *average* probation intervention yielded no better results than custodial sentences (Chapman and Hough, 1998). Thus began the drive to encourage probation services to evaluate programmes of intervention thoroughly. Moreover, to systematically introduce management structures and practice developments based upon what became known as the 'What Works' principles. The publication by HM Inspectorate of Probation (HMIP) of two reports in 1998, *Strategies for Effective Offender Supervision and Evidence Based Practice: A Guide to Effective Practice*, laid down important markers for the probation service in these developments.

In addition to the move towards targeting effective methods of reducing offending, the Home Office instruction to chief probation officers to set up and maintain registers of Potentially Dangerous Offenders (Home Office, 1988a) began the process of placing the assessment and management of offender *risk* at the centre of the work of the probation service. This development was enshrined in the legislative changes of the Criminal Justice Act 1991 and the introduction of National Standards (Home Office, 1992; 1995; and 2000).

The shift in emphasis to address risk has generally been welcomed as an appropriate and constructive response to increasing concerns about rising crime and particularly violent crime. However, Kemshall argues that:

> Social workers and probation officers have struggled to formulate and consistently use operational definitions of risk.
>
> (Kemshall, 1996: p3.)

In addition, concern has been expressed that risk assessment, as a central purpose, takes the probation service away from its traditional role of providing help and advice to offenders. Instead, it moves the service towards an emphasis on managing, controlling and punishing offenders. The substantive shift of philosophy is a marked feature of *The New Choreography* for the service (National Probation Service and Home Office, 2001), written by Eithne Wallis the first Director of the newly established National Probation Service. Until 2000 there was a series of regional probation services.

Assessment is central to the purpose of these new approaches within probation. The practice and management of assessment is, however, substantially different to that of the social work ethos of the service in previous years. For example, less attention is given to 'needs' in a welfare context and there is a greatly enhanced emphasis on risk and public protection. The removal of probation training from the Diploma in Social Work courses in 1996 effectively ended twenty years of association with social work principles and values, although undoubtedly many of the current skills and processes in probation assessment call on similar methods, theories and values.

The Role of Assessment

An overview of current practice in the field with offenders and their families; the primacy of assessment

The need for careful and structured assessments with clear identification of appropriate 'programmes' of intervention to address offending is highlighted in all the current literature that falls within the 'What Works' framework (McGuire, 1995; Underdown, 1995 and 1998; Chapman and Hough, 1998). Historically, the notion of 'programmes' referred to a few specialist group work programmes generally available within probation centres, either as voluntary additions to individual work with offenders (such as anger management, or social skills training), or as mandatory requirements within probation orders (such as, sex offender programmes). However, the concept of 'programme' now includes any group work, one-to-one work and family work that follows a planned and structured programme of intervention to address offending behaviour. The range and types of programmes have grown rapidly in recent years and have moved from primarily a voluntary, educative and social skills focus to a mandatory, cognitive-behavioural approach to addressing offending behaviour. Probation areas are now required to refer the majority of offenders to core offending behaviour programmes (Think First, Reasoning and Rehabilitation, Priestley One to One) that have been accredited by a central accreditation panel. Other, more specialist programmes; for sex offenders, drink drivers, aggressive offending, domestic violence etc, are in the process of becoming accredited and implemented nationally (Criminal Justice Conference, 2001).

The role of the assessment process is, therefore, to identify the *risks* that the offender poses in relation to reoffending and harm to the public, and their *criminogenic needs* (also referred to as dynamic risk factors): i.e. needs that are seen to have a direct causal link to offending and that could be addressed by means of targeted intervention. This is set out in the new assessment tool, OASys (Criminal Justice Conference, 2001) explained in more detail later in this chapter. Probation officers are reminded, in the course of undertaking assessments that effectiveness research indicates that:

- *The higher the risk of reoffending the more intensive and extended the supervision programmes (the risk principle).*

- *Programmes which target need related to offending (criminogenic needs) are likely to be more effective (the need principle).*

- *Programmes which match staff and offenders' learning styles and engage the active participation of offenders are likely to be more effective (the responsivity principle).*

(Chapman and Hough, 1998: p6.)

Assessment work with offenders is expected to focus on these three elements of risk, need and responsivity; in order to determine which programme of intervention is likely to be the most effective in reducing or eliminating offending behaviour.

Assessment of risk and need

Kemshall identifies two elements of risk assessment: actuarial and clinical. The clinical assessment method derives primarily from mental health risk assessment; probation staff may refer to this as their 'professional judgement'. This is the traditional method by which probation officers collect and analyse information in order to formulate a judgement about the level of risk. Kemshall highlights the fact that clinical assessment has a poor record of accuracy (Gondolf et al., 1990; Monahan, 1981; Steadman and Morrisey, 1982; and cited in Kemshall, 1997), not least because it is highly dependent upon the relationship between the offender and the risk assessor, and the self-report of the offender. However, Kemshall argues that this does not discredit clinical assessment but highlights the need for workers to combine this with actuarial data and adopt a holistic assessment process. Actuarial assessment is based upon predicting an individual's likely behaviour from the behaviours of others in similar circumstances or with similar profiles (Farrington and Tarling; 1985 cited in Kemshall, 1997). Whilst actuarial assessment is more accurate than

clinical assessment, prediction is only in terms of probabilities, and the transferability of information about group behaviour to the individual remains a matter for judgement. Kemshall makes the case for the 'defensible decision' (Carson, 1996 cited in Kemshall, 1997), a decision on risk that will stand up to scrutiny in the light of 'hindsight bias'; i.e. in the light of a negative outcome having occurred.

Alazcewski defines risk as having two components:

> ...the chance or probability that an undesired event, behaviour or action will result and that this undesired event will be negative resulting in harm, loss or damage...
>
> (Alaszewski et al., cited in Kemshall, 1994: p102.)

While the Effective Practice Guide describes a continuum of risk from:

> ...too dangerous to be supervised with a reasonable degree of safety in the community to of no real risk to the public.
>
> (Home Office, 1998: p30.)

The guide states that assessment on this continuum will determine the level of restriction of liberty and surveillance required. Kemshall offers the following format for an initial record of risk assessment:

Table 9.1 Kemshall's Format for an Initial Record of Risk Assessment

	Estimation of risk				
Probability of reoffending	very high	high	average	low	very low
Risk of harm to public	very high	high	average	low	very low
Risk of harm to staff	very high	high	average	low	very low
Risk of self-harm	very high	high	average	low	very low

Table 9.2 Other Risk Factors

Other Risk Factors		
Registered as Schedule 1 Offender?	yes	no
Are there child protection register Issues?	yes	no
Registered as dangerous offender?	yes	no

(Kemshall (1997a) Management and Assessment of Risk, Home Office.)

Probation officers are also required to assess *dangerousness* and be able to predict the risk of violence. This has as its focus the potential harm to the public that an individual offender poses which is different from the *likelihood* of an offence occurring. Indicators of harm will include previous behaviour, availability of weapons, proximity to victims, gender, age, socio-economic status, behavioural traits and situational triggers (Kemshall, 1997: p184).

> *The historical welfare focus of the service meant that offenders' needs were often assessed independently of their propensity for recidivism. This has now changed and probation officers are required to ensure that the assessment of need should focus on identifying the factors which, if changed, would lower the chances of future offending behaviour. Needs are identified as either criminogenic or non-criminogenic. Criminogenic need might include factors such as anti-social attitudes and thinking, reducing criminal dependencies and associations and increasing identification with anti-criminal role models. Non-criminogenic might include matters related to finances, relationships, accommodation, employment and education and are likely to be referred on to other resources either within the service, or externally through partnership agencies or community based networks. Intensive programmes of intervention are targeted at those offenders assessed as being high risk and the focus is on targeting criminogenic need and community reintegration.*
>
> (Chapman and Hough, 1998: p30.)

Offenders with a lower risk assessment are monitored within National Standards (National Standards for the Supervision of Offenders in the Community, 2000), and may be referred to service and external service resources.

Working with Different Offenders: A Multi-disciplinary Approach

Young offenders

Many of the issues of risk assessment for all offenders apply to young offenders, although with some notable difference. Youth crime tends to be more visible and naïve than that committed by older offenders – therefore more easily detected. Young offenders are frequently demonised in the press, most notably the boys responsible for the death of James Bulger, which triggered widespread moral outrage. In the early 1990s, a range of youth behaviour, including truancy, drug taking, disturbances on housing estates, joy-riding and the idea of 'one-boy crime waves' raised levels of public concern and fuelled this negative image of youth. Interestingly, this is set against a relatively sharp decline in recorded juvenile crime during the 1980s and early 1990s (Haggell and Newburn, 1994). There is a 'risk' therefore, that the assessment of the risk of young people reoffending may be disproportionately inflated by stereotypical concerns about youth. This highlights the importance of the use of evidence related to actual offending rates.

The evidence suggests that those convicted at an early age (10-13) tend to become the most persistent offenders (Farrington, 1994 cited in McLauglin, 2001). They found that if children had a convicted parent by the time they were 10 then that was the 'best predictor' of them becoming criminal and antisocial themselves. However, to use this 'actuarial' form of assessment also runs the risk of false positives, and of wrongly labelling a young person as potentially delinquent. The importance of inter-agency work through the youth offending teams cannot be overemphasised in work with young people, where risk to the young person of harm to themselves may be strongly equated with a risk of harm to others. The offending behaviour may be addressed primarily through a cognitive-behavioural programme of intervention, but if the welfare needs of the young person are not addressed in tandem by social workers and youth workers then it is unlikely that the risk of reoffending and harm to the public will be reduced.

Mentally disordered offenders

In work with offenders who may be assessed as having a mental disorder (as defined by the Mental Health Act 1983), or where the worker considers there may be some mental health concerns, the risk assessment needs to take account of a number of additional factors. The legal definitions of mental disorder are generally held to be inadequate to identify all those who may have mental health concerns and some definitions include sex offenders, substance misusers and those with neuroses, behavioural and/or personality disorders as well as those with learning disabilities (NACRO, 1993; Drewett and Shepperdson, 1995). The probation officer's assessment would need to consider issues of *culpability*, *compliance* and *liaison* with other workers. For example, assessment of culpability relates to how or if the mental disorder bears upon the offender's personal responsibility for their conduct and whether the disorder makes further offending more likely. Assessment should include a consideration of whether the disorder makes it unlikely that the offender would be able to comply with the requirements of community supervision, and the potential implications of a custodial sentence. *Liaison* with the psychiatric and social services would be a core factor in addressing these issues.

Some of these practice issues are addressed in the Learning and Development Programme for work with Mentally Disordered Offenders (Home Office, 1999: p176). These can additionally include the factors that lead to the belief that the defendant may be mentally disturbed and a consideration of how this

perception should be tested and shared with the person. Practitioners need to reflect on the advantages and disadvantages of raising this possibility with the person concerned and also when and how should this be dealt with in a court report. For example, they need to decide when and how the court might be asked to adjourn further for formal psychiatric assessment and how this could be invoked without raising inappropriate anxieties about risk and other kinds of adverse labelling. There are important issues here related to the potential for discrimination against people who are mentally disturbed. Inter-agency work involving, in particular, the community mental health team and the community psychiatric nurse, needs to recognise that different agencies, working with the same person, may well perceive, and assess risk in different ways. For example, taking into account the potential tensions that can occur between a primarily *offending* focus of assessment and a primarily *health/welfare* focus. Workers need clarity about their respective roles and a willingness to share differences of perception in a constructive rather than competitive manner, if the best outcomes are to be reached for the person concerned and the protection of the public.

Another important assessment stage for risk and mental health, is the point of discharge from prison or special hospital. Mental Health Service providers must maintain Supervision Registers of people with severe mental illness, who pose a significant risk to themselves or to others (Stone, 1995). Risk in this context, at the time of registration should consider: significant risk of suicide, significant risk of serious violence to others and significant risk of severe self-neglect. In some probation areas probation officers may be responsible for the supervision of patients discharged conditionally from hospital, who are subject to a Restriction Direction (Mental Health Act 1959, s. 41 or s. 49). In other areas, this responsibility is undertaken by social workers, often those who are members of forensic community mental health teams. Systematic risk assessment is crucial at this stage, as is vigilant supervision, including management of risk that gives priority to the safety of the community. Some of the risk factors associated with mental ill-health and offending include: being a survivor of abuse, the denial of problems, being known to several agencies, having a poor social network, being resistant to medication, the misuse of drugs and alcohol, previous convictions for offences of violence and previous convictions for criminal damage (Home Office, 1999).

Multi-Agency Public Protection Panels, (Criminal Justice and Court Services Act 2000, s.67 and 68) are convened in all cases where risk to the public is considered to be high and where joint decisions need to be taken about the management of the risk posed. These panels bring together the key agencies, notably the police, local councils, mental health NHS trusts, probation, health, social services etc. to consider the risk to the public and to plan strategies of surveillance, monitoring and intervention to manage the risk identified. Ideally, these panels are constituted with an awareness of the process of multi-agency decision making as well as the substantive matters in hand.

Offenders with learning disability

The number of offenders with a learning disability is a matter for speculation. NACRO (1994) cite studies that suggest that less than 1 per cent of the prison population have a learning disability (perhaps 400 nationally). The numbers on community caseloads may be higher. However, research undertaken as preparation for the *Learning and Development Programme for Work with Mentally Disordered Offenders* (Home Office, 1999: p13) found probation officers expressing general concerns about this group. Yet, the Reed Report (Department of Health, 1992) suggested that people with learning disabilities, while under-represented in most violent offences, might be over-represented as sex offenders and in offences of fire-raising. Faulk (1994 cited in Home Office, 1999) cautions against this interpretation, but the Learning and Development Programme suggests that it may well be true that lack of foresight, lack of restraint and/or social naiveté may lead to an increased incidence of offending of certain kinds. In addition, there is the potential that policies of community care may make visible behaviour that had previously been 'hidden' in institutions. Close liaison between social

workers, who may be involved with the person, and the probation officer undertaking an assessment for court, for example, would need to pay particular attention to the extent of their understanding of what may be taking place and of what is expected of their respective roles. Issues of culpability for the offence should be jointly assessed, and proposals agreed for the most suitable court disposal. Some forms of cognitive-behavioural intervention might be appropriate but the impact of group dynamics and association with a potentially more sophisticated offender group would need careful consideration.

Sex offenders

Sex offences occur at a rate far in excess of the official figure, and in the assessment of sex offenders the question of whether their offences are sexually motivated or primarily crimes of aggression is a key factor (Hollin and Howells, 1992). Risk factors associated with sexual offending are somewhat different from other forms of offending behaviour and can include: a developmental history of abuse, impaired relationships with adults, lack of empathy for the victim, a willingness to use extreme force to gain victim compliance and cognitive distortions. These are identified as 'irrational ideas, thoughts and attitudes that serve to perpetuate denial around sexually aggressive behaviour, and foster the minimisation and trivialisation of the impact of sexually aggressive behaviour on victims, and justify and sustain further sexually aggressive behaviour' (McGuire, 1995: p163).

The whole area of sexual offending is fraught with fear, prejudice, and stereotypical assumptions. Agencies working with the *offender*, predominantly the probation, prison and psychiatric services are likely to take a different focus and form differential assessments from those working with the *victims* of sexual offending, who may include social workers working with children as victims, and a range of voluntary sector organisations working with women as victims/survivors. The increasing focus on inter-agency working has reduced some of the most common misunderstandings and interpretations, but there is still considerable room for these to occur. The most fruitful work addresses the risk of harm to the particular victims and other potential victims in a way that does not collude with the offender's own levels of denial and minimisation of harm. However, there are particular tensions, for example when the Children and Family Court Advisory Service (CAFCAS) prepares reports for the court, when there are allegations of abuse by one parent against the other in the case of disputed residence of, and contact with, their children. The CAFCAS worker can be faced with very considerable dilemmas about whose interests are being considered. Significantly, the risk to the child has to be paramount but where abuse is alleged but not proven, that child also has a right to on-going contact with both parents. Multi-agency conferences convened to address all these perspectives and agree a procedure are the most obvious process for resolving these tensions. CAFCAS was formerly the Court Welfare Service but was re-formed by the Criminal Justice and Court Services Act 2000.

Assessment Tools

Probation services have, for some time, been developing a range of assessment tools to identify both risk and need principles. However, these have developed in a piecemeal fashion, and with no centralised co-ordination. Research has indicated that not only have the methods used been very varied, but also that individual probation officers continued to exert considerably autonomy in the way that they assessed and referred their clients. The increasing complexity of the assessment process and in particular the concerns in relation to the assessment of risk, has led to calls for a unified and universal assessment tool, to be used within the probation service, but also to be common across other criminal justice agencies. For example, the consultative document Joining Forces to Protect the Public: Prisons-Probation Review (August 1998) proposed the adoption of common approaches and techniques to risk assessment and risk management based on agreed principles. The Home Office, working with the prison and probation services has developed a new assessment tool, OASys (Offender Assessment Systems) to assess both

criminogenic need and risk. The purpose of the joint work was to ensure the use of a common approach and tool in risk assessment work, and to enable the facilitation of information sharing. This now constitutes the key tool, with additional specialised assessment tools used to cover particular groups such as mentally disordered offenders, sex offenders, violent offenders, young offenders and women. OASys is designed to achieve the following:

- Assess how likely an offender is to re-offend.
- Identify and classify offending related needs (social and personal).
- Assess risk of serious harm.
- Assist with management of risk of harm.
- Link the assessment to the supervision or sentence plan.
- Indicate if further, specialist assessments are required.
- Measure change during the period of supervision or sentence.

(National Probation Service, Bedfordshire – Training Programme.)

This development has built on work undertaken on a range of assessment tools currently in use. These include: the *Offender Group Reconviction Scale* (OGRS, Copas, 1994), the *Level of Service Inventory – Revised* (LSI-R, Andrews and Bonta, 1995), the *Assessment, Case Management and Evaluation Tool* (ACE, Oxford University and Warwickshire Probation Service, 1997) and *Aubrey and Hough's Scale* (1997). OGRS was intended for use as an assessment tool in the preparation of Pre-Sentence Reports and is purely an actuarial assessment tool. It is described by Colombo and Neary as:

> ...a highly standardised measure designed to statistically predict a convicted offender's chances of being reconvicted at least once within the next two years.

(Colombo and Neary, 1998: p214.)

They suggest that as an assessment tool it is limited in the sense that it can only make prediction estimates about the likelihood of reconviction in terms of groups of offenders with similar characteristics – not for the specific individual concerned.

Probation services have, historically, been keen to develop their own approaches to work with offenders that reflect the needs and characteristics of their locality. This has been true of the development of assessment tools, and has led to some resistance to the imposition of a national assessment tool. However, OASys is now being implemented nationally, with a compulsory training programme for all staff engaged in all forms of assessment.

Anti-discriminatory Assessment Practice

The nature of the inequality of treatment of different groups within the criminal justice system is well documented: see for example, Dominelli et al., 1995; Denney, 1992; Worrall, 1990; Smart, 1989; Cook and Hudson, 1993; Heidensohn, 1985; and Bridges and Steen, 1998. Section 95 of the Criminal Justice Act 1991 imposed a duty not to discriminate and established a need for monitoring to ensure equality of treatment and outcome between groups. Probation services have attempted to deal with this through a range of equal opportunity policies and strategies for developing anti-discriminatory practice. These current initiatives about effective practice highlight the need to work in a way that does not discriminate. However, the ability to conduct assessments in a manner that is anti-discriminatory and values diversity, depends on a complex range of interpersonal skills, knowledge and awareness of individual workers and an organisational culture that recognises and values diversity and difference in its many forms. Many of the good intentions of individual workers to address discrimination in offender groups are inhibited by some of the structures currently in place. For example, anti-discriminatory practice would seek to place service user choice and empowerment as central themes but in a climate that requires assessment of risk and correction of offending behaviour to be central, 'consumer' choice can be offered only within a limited range of options. Issues of offender consent to orders, removed by the Crime (Sentences) Act 1997, have been further eroded by pressure to place offenders on programmes and prove success by monitoring attendance, rather than seeking to empower and enhance the quality of life of individual offenders. The traditional continuum of care and control within which the service has always operated has shifted considerably in the last few years towards a greater emphasis upon control.

On the positive side, the introduction of National Standards (Home Office, 1992; 1995; and 2000) has gone some way to ensuring a much greater consistency of practice with offenders, when previously the quality of intervention depended very much on the idiosyncratic preferences of individual workers. Also, the move to be more responsive to victims' rights within the practice of the service can only have helped to address some of the imbalance of justice within the system (Home Office, 2000c).

The challenge to probation officers is to take account of the differential experiences of offenders within the criminal justice system and to ensure that their assessments are as free of prejudicial assumptions and outcomes as possible. Within the specified frameworks of assessing risk and need, probation officers should listen carefully to the experiences of the offender, and check their mutual understanding of the context and reasons for that person's offending behaviour. Some probation services operate a policy of offering choice to black and female service users of a black or female worker. This is based on the understanding that the criminal justice system predominantly reflects a white male hierarchy and that black and female offenders can feel further disempowered if they have no choice of worker. A Home Office research study by Mair and May (1997) found that over half the male offenders on probation orders in the sample were supervised by a female probation officer and three quarters of the women offenders were supervised by a female officer, which suggests that services are endeavouring to meet the particular needs of women offenders. Interestingly, most offenders both male and female, when questioned, indicated a preference for a female officer.

There is a tendency, within the context of offending behaviour, to concentrate on problems and risks rather than strengths and opportunities. Also, risk is now conceptualised entirely in negative terms as, 'the possibility of adversity which in turn should be reduced, controlled and avoided,' (Kemshall, 1998: p 6) and moreover a keenness to apportion blame. Anti-discriminatory practice within assessment processes should ensure that individual strengths are identified together with family and community resources that can contribute to reducing the risk of reoffending. Workers have been criticised for failing to acknowledge the strengths and coping strategies of minority groups and for presenting assessments of them in a negative way (Dominelli et al., 1995). Practice should include collaborative working, affirmation of the experience of service users when describing their experience of discrimination, the seeking of diverse solutions to complex situations and the use of a range of formal and informal networks. Liaison with voluntary sector projects that have strong links with the community can be essential to good practice in this area.

Programmes of intervention should address diversity by offering separate groups to black and women offenders when possible and when not possible avoiding the isolation of one person within a group because of their different identity. There is clearly a need for research into this area of practice. Reconviction rates are lower for women than men on community rehabilitation orders (formerly probation orders, renamed by the Criminal Justice and Court Services Act 2000): 48 per cent for women as opposed to 58 per cent for men. Also age plays a significant role in reconviction rates, with offenders under 21 years the reconviction rate is 74 per cent, whereas for offenders over 30 years the reconviction rate is 53 per cent, for those commencing orders in 1993 (Kershaw, 1997).

Case vignette: the Pre Sentence Report (PSR)

Mike is an eighteen year old white man whose parents separated when he was young, and who spent periods in local authority care and, more recently, in a series of lodgings. He is currently living in a probation hostel, having been made subject, by the Crown Court, to a community rehabilitation order for two years with a requirement to reside initially in an approved probation hostel, and thereafter as directed by the probation officer. The community rehabilitation order was made for six offences of taking without consent, two offences of driving whilst disqualified and two offences of criminal damage, one of which related to damage caused to a police car as a result of a chase. Mike has previously been subject to a community service order (renamed community punishment order: Criminal Justice and Court Services Act 2000) made by the Crown Court which was revoked at an earlier date, when he received three months youth custody for similar offences of taking without consent. Since his early teens, his main interest has been cars – his own and other people's – for pleasure and gain. He has a large number of previous offences all related to cars and in addition to the above sentences he has received fines, an attendance centre order and a supervision order. He has also had a number of jobs when he has made a good impression on his employers. His behaviour at the hostel is problematic, as is his reporting to his probation officer. He has been arrested and charged with three offences of aggravated car theft and is due to appear before the Crown Court for sentencing shortly.

The PSR represents the most highly developed assessment process in work with offenders. Probation Officers are given detailed guidance and training on this area of work which is seen as high profile and influential in the sentencing arena (Home Office, 1997b). PSRs are:

> *...reports submitted in writing to assist magistrates and judges in determining the most suitable method of dealing with an offender.*
>
> (Criminal Justice Act, 1991: s. 3 (5) (a).)

They are required to take into account the sentencer's perspective, the victim's perspective and the offender's perspective. The following section comments on how the process might unfold in relation to Mike whose situation is described in the case vignette.

The sentencer's perspective requires the writer to have knowledge of the sentencing framework and to consider the seriousness of the offence in order to formulate an assessment of the appropriateness of a range of sentencing options and to make a proposal for the most suitable disposal. For less serious offences, a discharge or fine might be appropriate. If the offence is sufficiently serious for some restriction of liberty to be imposed, then the writer has to decide which community sentence might meet this requirement as well as addressing any concerns about reoffending. If the offence is so serious that only a custodial sentence can be justified then the writer has to assess the likely impact on the offender and their family and make this known to the court. If the offence is of a sexual or violent nature issues of public safety should be at the fore of the writer's thinking and knowledge of the particular sentencing implications known to them. In Mike's case the offence is likely to be deemed 'so serious' as to make a custodial sentence almost inevitable, given the nature and number of the present offences and the link to his previous pattern of offending, although it would not fall into the sexual or violence category.

The victim's perspective requires that the report writer seeks information from the prosecution case about the victim and, where known, the impact on the victim of the offence. The writer also needs to assess any specific features of the crimes, for example the targeting of particular victims or the vulnerability of particular victims. PSR writers are not expected to make contact with victims in this process and neither is it their responsibility to assess the degree of loss or harm suffered by specific victims. In Mike's case the victim is the general public who are at risk from Mike's driving when he is uninsured and driving at high speed.

The writer has to consider the offender's perspective and assess their attitude to the offence, their awareness of the consequences to the victim, the degree of premeditation involved, the degree of culpability (which may be effected for example in the case of potential mental disorder) and the degree of remorse. The writer would need to assess the extent to which Mike is aware of the danger he poses to the public in general and the impact on people whose cars have been stolen. He may have been able to distance himself from recognising any direct victim in his offending. The writer would have to have a range of knowledge and skills in order to assess criminogenic need and risk. They also need awareness, and effective use of, a range of techniques and programmes in confronting offending behaviour, and of the range of resources available to the offender (Chapman and Hough, 1998: pp 32-33).

In Mike's case the report writer, in completing the OASys form, would need to complete an *actuarial* assessment using the information about Mike's age, gender, previous offending history, including type and number of convictions and his custodial history. This would place him at high risk of reoffending. A *clinical* assessment would then examine the above patterns in the context of present circumstances and opportunities, which might include disaffection with his present circumstances, criminal associates, high rewards from offending linked to excitement, peer status, and financial gain, and low motivation to address his offending behaviour.

The holistic risk assessment would assess him at high risk of reoffending. It would also have to consider the risk to the public of harm from his offending, which would be linked to the potential for car accidents while driving for excitement and without insurance. The assessment would draw on the positives in relation to Mike's employment and consider a range of interventions that might begin to address both elements of risk, namely continual car theft and 'joy-riding' via, for example, a core offending behaviour programme such as *Think First* (Criminal Justice Conference, 2001) followed by a 'responsible road user programme' and victim awareness work in relation to the risk to the public of irresponsible road use.

If mental ill-health appears to be a factor in the offending, then the report writer would need to be aware of the implications of the Mental Health Act (1983: s. 35 as amended by Crime (Sentence) Act, 1997) and the fact that the court must, before passing a custodial sentence (other than one fixed by law) obtain a medical report and consider the effect of the sentence on the offender's mental condition. This does not appear to apply in Mike's case although detailed questioning might reveal mental health and/or drug misuse issues that required intervention. (Module 2A of the Learning and Development Programme for Work with Mentally Disordered Offenders, Home Office, 1999, provides detailed guidance on this aspect.)

Report writers are no longer encouraged to write detailed social histories, as was often the case in the previous Social Inquiry Report. Information contained in PSRs should be relevant to an understanding of the current offence or offences, an understanding of the pattern of previous offending, to decisions about possible sentences and to the risk of further offending. Thus, report writers have to examine patterns of offending in the light of personal and social factors. They should refer to the outcomes from previous court sentences including community supervision orders and in particular the response of the offender to these orders, both positive and negative. Where breaches or further offending occurred during previous community sentences, there should be an assessment of any partial successes, and indeed failures, upon which future work might build. Information about the offender's domestic and social circumstances are included if they pass the relevance test, but writers are cautioned to be careful about material which may reinforce negative stereotypes. In Mike's case his response to his present order is highly relevant and will give some indication of his level of motivation to work with the service to address his offending.

Where a community sentence is being considered the report writer should assess the suitability of the offender for the community sentences that might be available and propose the most suitable one, taking into account:

- The seriousness of the offence as indicated by the court.
- The offender's personality, needs, ability and responsivity.
- The prospect of successful completion.
- The risk to the public, especially the likely risk of reoffending.

Within a proposal for a community sentence, the report writer has to draw up a supervision and risk management plan that identifies the intensity of supervision and the objectives and type of programme to be followed. The level of motivation of the offender to address their offending behaviour is very relevant to the likely success of such an order, and where appropriate, a report writer would address the need for motivational interviewing as part of the process of engaging the offender in plans for change. On the presenting evidence Mike does not appear well motivated, but during the course of the PSR preparation and with the threat of custody hanging over him, Mike might prove more willing to consider ways of tackling his behaviour within the community. The judge is unlikely to impose a further community order in this case, unless there are very persuasive arguments about how the report writer thought that the risk of reoffending and harm to the public could be reduced by intensive intervention (Chapman and Hough, 1998: p32).

Other forms of assessment

Whilst the PSR is the predominant and most public form of assessment within the probation service, probation officers undertake a wide range of other forms of assessment including:

- home detention curfew assessment
- sentence planning within prisons
- pre-release reports
- parole assessment
- on-going reviews

Issues Raised from Current Practice in Assessment and its Impact Across Other Specialisms

Issues of consent/voluntarism/coercion

Offenders are no longer required to consent to community supervision, (Crime (Sentences) Act, 1997). Although, all the current literature stresses the importance of engaging the motivation of the offender to participate in a programme of change. Despite its authoritarian image, the probation service has not traditionally been involved in much active coercion of offenders. Its recent history has demonstrated a reluctance by probation officers to propose community supervision for unmotivated offenders. However, the current focus on public protection and risk assessment now requires that offenders should be placed on programmes that will tackle their behaviour, whether or not they are themselves persuaded of the need. Group workers have expressed concern at working with group members who have not fully accepted the need for intervention and the impact this can have on other members. However, there is also evidence, particularly in group work with male perpetrators of domestic violence, that listening to men acknowledging their abuse of their partners can have a significant impact on levels of denial in other participants. This needs to be handled carefully by group workers, in order to maintain an overall positive interaction within the group. Where other public sector workers are involved with the offender and their family, then a detailed sharing of information about the programme would be crucial in helping to sustain the commitment of the offender to the programme and maintaining change after its completion.

There are clear links here with workers who need to exercise control in child protection and mental health situations or work with service users considering change as described in Chapter 3. There are transferable skills in relation to motivational interviewing, for example in working with parents to improve their parenting skills or substance users wishing to change their life style. Motivation is, of course, the key to any successful intervention. Miller and Rollnick argue that:

> *Motivation should not be thought of as a personality problem, or as a trait that a person carries through the counsellor's doorway. Rather, motivation is a state of readiness or eagerness to change, which may fluctuate from one time or situation to another. This state is one that can be influenced.*
>
> (1991: p14.)

Millner and Rollnick describe the 'wheel of change' and the different approaches a counsellor needs to take with the client:

Table 9.3 Millner and Rollnick's 'Wheel of Change'	
Client stage	**Therapist's motivational task**
Pre-contemplation	Raise doubt – increase the client's perception of risks and problems with current behaviour
Contemplation	Tip the balance – evoke reasons to change, risks of not changing: strengthen the client's self-efficacy for change of current behaviour
Determination	Help the client to determine the best course of action to take in seeking change
Action	Help the client take steps towards change
Maintenance	Help the client to identify and use strategies to prevent relapse
Relapse	Help the client to renew the process of contemplation, determination, and action without becoming stuck or demoralised because of the relapse
	(Miller and Rollnick, 1991: p18.)

There are also common issues in relation to denial of responsibility for behaviour and how workers might begin to tackle this denial in order to move the person on towards changing elements of problematic behaviour. Whilst the concept of social control can be problematic for individual social workers, there are many examples of behaviour within the criminal, mental health and childcare fields which is dangerous to others and needs intervention to curb or reduce. Social workers cannot shy away from this responsibility and should, instead, be making the links across professional boundaries to maximise best practice that respects people's rights but aims to minimise harm.

A standardised assessment tool across agencies

The increasing use of actuarial methods of assessment offers a baseline against which individual assessments (clinical) can take place. In many respects this approach offers a much more structured and 'scientific' approach to risk assessment which most would welcome, and which all agencies involved in the assessment of risk are using with increasing regularity. A common approach and a common language in the assessment of risk have to be seen as crucial in the development of multi-agency risk panels and closer working relationships between agencies.

Some view this change to more scientific assessments positively as they believe discretion is arbitrary and introduces bias based on race, class, gender and so on into decisions. However, others contend that it detracts from professionalism and personal discretion. They are fearful of the reduction of 'professional' judgement to a bureaucratic decision in risk assessment (Beaumont and Mistry, 1996).

Kemshall et al. (1997b) suggest that there is very little literature that focuses on risk across the spectrum of personal social services, despite the increasing focus on issues of risk. Risk analysis is most developed in the criminal justice and child protection fields (see Chapter 8). However, the mental health literature, being centrally preoccupied with notions of

dangerousness, is quickly adopting risk terminology. Apart from work on elder abuse (see Chapter 7), literature on child welfare and community care has been framed in terms of *need*, issues of *risk* only coming to the fore around potential admission to residential care. The writers contend that as issues of rationing and accountability become more dominant, so do concerns with risk. They predict the extension of notions of risk as central organising principles throughout the social services and probation (Tidmarsh, 1998; Smith, 1997 cited in Kemshall et al., 1997b).

A cautionary note needs to be struck in relation to the universal application of actuarial scores, most of which are currently based on samples of white men, who constitute the largest group of offenders. Care needs to be taken in using them indiscriminately with other groups of offenders such as women and black people. Kemshall makes a good case for the use of both methods in undertaking holistic assessments.

A challenge would be to see the development of a universal assessment tool, applicable across all the agencies involved in the care and management of problematic and difficult behaviour within communities. This would require an unprecedented level of co-operation and negotiation across boundaries, and would require very careful attention to issues of civil liberties and anti-discriminatory practice. It might, of course, also run the risk, mentioned earlier, of becoming too unwieldy to be managed in practice.

Ethical and moral issues in risk assessment

Kemshall (1996) highlights the risks of errors and bias in risk assessment, in relation to both false positives and false negatives. The Home Secretary's proposals, as part of the Review of the Mental Health Act, (Department of Health, 1998) to detain those people identified as a high risk to the public but who may not have committed an actual crime, raises alarms about erosion of civil liberties, and requires very careful debate. Issues of creating stigmatising labels for certain people, and wrongful detention of those who may never be harmful, have to be weighed against the risks of overlooking the warning signs and exposing the public to unacceptable levels of risk. The recent conviction of Roy Whiting, for the murder of Sarah Payne, has refuelled this debate. Unfortunately, the current climate is one where no risk is seen as acceptable, and workers feel the need to 'protect their backs' by over-estimating rather than underestimating the level of risk a particular offender might pose. Good probation practice has traditionally involved *positive* risk taking with offenders. For example, locating an offender on an individual placement, as part of a community punishment order, in the belief that they can learn from the experience as much as the beneficiary might benefit. Trusting offenders in the context of good working relationships has always involved an element of risk, i.e. they may breach this trust. However, the absence of trust creates a corrosive and negative atmosphere in which to expect that someone might change and develop in positive ways. This has close associations with other areas of 'risk work' such as child protection, where trusting a parent to care for their child might be a crucial factor in their ability to safeguard the child's interests.

The focus on criminogenic need

Traditionally, a probation officer working with an offender and their family might be expected to meet the majority of welfare need identified within the family, with the exception of child protection issues. The current focus on assessment of criminogenic need by probation officers challenges this assumption. The positive implications are that identifying non-criminogenic need increasingly involves probation officers in liaison and negotiation with a wide range of other community agencies and resources for referral on to other agencies. This requires a good understanding of these resources and the roles of different workers, and a high level of partnership working, to ensure a planned service is offered. Negative implications could include the failure to address welfare need adequately, which might have a developmental impact on the potential for reoffending.

The impact of a particular theoretical perspective

Recent research undertaken to consider the most effective methods of addressing offending behaviour, suggested that the most promising outcomes are based on a 'cognitive-behavioural' approach (see for example McGuire, 1995: p16; and McGuire, 2000: p13). This is a form of intervention based on a synthesis of methods drawn from behavioural and cognitive psychology (Hollin, 1990 and 1992; Meichenbaum, 1977). The role of assessment, using this approach, is to collect relevant information about the behaviour and thinking of the person under scrutiny. In general, the term cognition refers to concepts such as memory, imagery, intelligence and reasoning, although most widely used as a synonym of thinking (Hollin, 1992: p10).

The A B C model is the essential building block for work with offenders and can be of relevance to a range of other forms of behavioural assessment. This framework enables the practitioner to consider, with the offender:

A. The antecedents to the behaviour.

B. The actual behaviour.

C. The consequences of the behaviour.

The theoretical premise for this approach is that the rate or frequency of behaviour is governed by the consequences of that behaviour – or, as Hollin calls it the 'pay-off' (Hollin, 1992: p97). The immediate environment at the time the behaviour occurs – the antecedent or setting conditions, will also play an important part in determining whether a given behaviour will occur.

The cognitive-behavioural position acknowledges the importance of environmental influences, while seeking to incorporate the role of cognition in understanding behaviour. The strong focus on a cognitive-behavioural approach to work with offenders, as identified within the *What Works* framework, has caused concern, particularly amongst experienced probation officers, who regret the demise of the social work ethos of the service and the ability to respond in a wide range of ways to individual offender need. It is clear that a cognitive-behavioural approach cannot meet the needs of all offenders all of the time, and the assessment process needs to address this. There is evidence that some offenders do not respond well to structured programmes, for example those with particular learning difficulties, and people with a recognised mental disorder and/or with strong patterns of drug/alcohol misuse. There is also concern that most of the current work of the service takes an individual focus and pathologises offending within the person, largely ignoring environmental and structural factors as causes of offending.

Nevertheless, the application of assessment theory and methods, over and above the techniques identified within particular assessment tools, should ensure that inappropriate referrals are not made. The attention to research findings, previously lacking in much probation practice, has to be welcomed, and if the continuing evidence is that a cognitive-behavioural approach is the most successful in reducing offending behaviour then, it is appropriate that this should be the major form of intervention (Singh Bhui, 1996; Nutley and Davies, 1999). Evidence of success from research has helped

to bring back a sense of optimism into the probation profession. Research should also be conducted on those groups of offenders whose needs are not addressed by this method and alternative programmes and forms of intervention should continue to thrive within the culture of the service. The wider implications for social workers addressing a range of problematic behaviours include the crucial role of the assessment process and the need to pay careful attention to up-to-date research on effectiveness.

Further Reading

Dominey, J. (2002). Addressing Victim Issues in Pre-sentence Reports. In Williams, B. (Ed.) *Reparation and Victim-focussed Social Work. Research Highlights in Social Work 42*. London: Jessica Kingsley.

Kemshall, H. (2002). *Risk Assessment and Management of Known Sexual and Violent Offenders: A Review of Current Issues*. London: Home Office Police Research Unit 140.

Kemshall, H. (2002). Risk, Public Protection and Justice. In Ward et al. *Probation: Working for Justice*. Oxford University Press.

Tyrer, P. (2000). Improving the Assessment of Personality Disorders. *Criminal Behaviour and Mental Health*, 10: ss 51–65.

Chapter 10

Mental Health:
New World, New Order, New Partnerships?

Sam Mello-Baron, with Aileen Moore and Ian Moore

Introduction

The election of a Labour government in 1997 heralded the arrival of a 'bright new dawn'. The aura of a 'New Jerusalem' hanging in the air that sought to balance economic dynamism and social security based upon a philosophy that emphasised individual rights and responsibilities. Promising change, integrity and greater equality, the government emphasised a need for balance with a desire for greater individual freedom. This chapter provides an example of a sustained analysis of the political and social context of one service area, mental health. (As the editors' note in Chapter 1.) Readers may wish to supply a similar analysis for themselves in respect of other areas.

Rhetoric or reality? A question of interpretation. Whatever the view taken, it is centralised management by legislation coupled with local interpretation of policy, (which has its roots in historical and contemporary discourses) that is key to current mental health policy, procedures and professional practice. Whilst, Allsop (1984) states that the policy process is a combination of a 'statement of intent' and an 'outcome of a process' the development of mental health provision becomes influenced by the key cultural estates of our existence. Reflecting the lack of consensus about mental (ill) health diagnosis, treatment and service provision, we have witnessed the development of a mental health discourse, which is created from the historical and contemporary discourse of health, illness, and social policies through the functions of key institutions such as the media. Consequently, this discourse becomes challenged, frequently misinterpreted and open to individual and organisational legal recourse, leaving families, individuals and carers to 'manage' the consequences.

This chapter aims to examine the contested contexts of mental health policy and practice by critically analysing key thematic debates contained within contemporary government policies. By considering significant historical debates, the chapter begins by addressing the relationship between historical influences, contemporary developments and the shaping of social policies to mental health practice. By describing current issues in practice, it concludes by identifying and analysing implications for practice, in terms of establishing and maintaining links within the context of a 'new world, new order and new partnerships'. This chapter begins with a detailed and extensive political analysis of the context of service provision.

Contested Contexts

The current development of mental health, ill-health, diagnosis, treatment and service provision reflects a range of ideological and material changes in our society. Rogers and Pilgrim (1996) use the notion of 'stakeholders' to describe how individuals and groups have steered the development of policy and practice, to maintain powerful individual positions, a process that has allowed policy and practice to remain contested.

Yet unequivocally, what is often referred to as the 'rise and fall' of the asylum, arguably is now the 'rise, fall and re-invention' of the asylum. Developments in mental health policy and practice can and will be charted via key historical periods. However, the development, fragmentation and re-emphasising of the notion of asylum, subtly objectifies all elements of contested contexts, to such a degree that practice and provision appears to be a reflection of recent government policy, 'appearing' simultaneously objective and independent. The focus on the policy process and outcomes through performance management provides little opportunity to examine, discuss and expose the contested contexts, leaving professionals to deal with inter-agency and inter-professional difficulties.

An analysis of history and contemporary political perspectives will allow an opportunity to expose these contexts for debate, rather than consume them within notions of organisational management.

Through the introduction of 'asylums' in the nineteenth century we witnessed the forerunner not only to community care, but also to the legacy of mental health and society's need to 'identify, label and manage' behaviour considered unacceptable. However, the 'rise and fall' was largely small-scale, dominated by medical practitioners, businessmen and rural aristocrats (Rogers and Pilgrim, 1996) who objected to central interference on what was considered matters for 'local regions'. Combined with prolific economic growth during industrialisation, we begin to understand the shaping of mental health discourse and its relevance today. The era symbolised notions of segregation, industrialisation, medical dominance, private entrepreneurship, central/local tensions and a lack of consensus about the unplanned growth of industrialisation. Debates on causation largely became medically constructed, with a focus on 'separation' of individuals from communities. The period finally concluded with maintenance of asylums, medical and business interests and as Rogers and Pilgrim state (2000) the notion of 'total solution'.

The focus on ' total solution' continues to dominate with containment of supposedly dangerous individuals at the apex, however, interests within mental health continue to reflect this era, which until recently remained unchallenged and separated by compelling interests, leading to interpretation, and contestation by individual, families and professionals. However, subsequent historical eras saw the development of:

- The pharmacological revolution and impact upon medical models of care.

- A refocussing upon the causation of ill-health through the war experience of 'shell shock'.

- The introduction of the NHS and hospital care.

- Financial planning and management.

- Government questioning of care for mental (ill) health.

- Creation of open debate on the care and treatment of individuals with mental health difficulties.

Whilst the twentieth century saw key changes and developments to diagnosis, treatment and provision, the 'asylum period' continues to echo through current professional practice.

Community Care legislation of the 1980s and 1990s, efficiently appeased many stakeholders, noting a departure from consensus politics, yet at the same time a veil of professional consensus appeared. This enabled the political process to gain and gather unprecedented momentum where critiques of professional groups (Walker, 1982) argue that professionals were either 'brought off' by the focus on 'assessment of need' or 'blinkered' by social policy perspectives of the marketisation of welfare. Whilst history clearly demonstrates the importance of private provision within mental health, the introduction of the 70/30 funding arrangements, fundamentally changed the welfare arena with little opportunity for debate or challenge. Consequently, the 1980s, and the early 1990s were characterised by welfare pluralism with a focus on 'cost' 'quality' and pluralistic containment with little regulation. This 'dispersal' to community care enhanced the complexity and diversity of mental health care whilst simultaneously increasing the number of stakeholders. The process of marketisation, rather than policy became the method of achieving change for entrepreneurs, professionals, users and carers, regulated only by the process of managerialism. In focussing upon the mixed and managed economy, little attention was given to causation and diagnosis, assuming the two competing domains would be challenged through the process of privatisation. Concurrently, we witnessed a cultural shift that acknowledged the need for professional co-operation/ inter-agency work. As Beardshaw and Morgan (1990) state the inter-agency collaboration was complex and inefficient largely due to the different ideologies, priorities, organisation and professional cultures. A change, which arose from, increased media pressures, which highlighted the lack of planning and co-operation between agencies. An interface, Tony Blair later referred to as the 'Berlin Wall'.

Clearly, it can be seen that the focus on unified diagnosis, treatment and service provision has never yet been a focus of professional or political change. Consequently, these three arenas became 'socially constructed' through history and stakeholder interest, with little emphasis upon user power, involvement or decision making. Whilst, user involvement generated a powerful lobby during the 1980s, concurrent to the political movement of identity politics, only in small pockets of the country has significant change occurred through user participation as stakeholders in diagnosis, treatment and service provision. This however, is not to undermine developments to date, but rather to suggest that they need further advancement to locate users and carers within Blair's philosophy of the 'Third Way'. This location and emphasis may allow opportunities for continual involvement and changes from user perspectives. How does this philosophy enable this process?

The 'blend' or 'unification' of left and right with an emphasis on the values of equality and freedom, as Powell states, leaves us to conclude that:

> New Labour is defined by, but departs from Thatcherism. It has moved to the right, but with anti-Thatcherite emphasis. In this sense it is post Thatcherite.
>
> (Powell, 1999.)

It implies that the discovery of a 'third way' between old left and new right implies a political philosophy and economy that is distinctive but is defined by its relationship to the alternative models. Blair describes the 'Third Way' as:

> Building a Welfare State for the 21st century: not dismantling welfare, leaving it as low grade safety net for the destitute, nor keeping it unreformed and under performing, but reforming it on the basis of a new contact between citizen and state.
>
> (Powell, 1999.)

Whilst the political arguments ensue (for example, is the 'Third Way' a new political philosophy or a re-shaping of social democratic policies?), it marks a departure from Keynesian economics whereby the state assumed responsibilities for 'management' of the economy and associated social problems. Through the universal provision for sickness, disability, unemployment and old age, there was a 'social contract' between individuals (employees), employers and the state. It is this

contract that has been challenged under the 'Third Way' and therefore the shaping (discourse) of diagnosis, treatment and service provision in mental health.

The work of Etzioni and Giddeons in shaping Blair's notion of community and communitarianism, reasserts the notion of rights with responsibilities, individuals vis-à-vis communities and has the intention, as Jordan states, to 'Establish a new social contract between citizens, and state, based on a change of culture…' (Jordan, 2000). One of which as reported in The Guardian comprises:

> Solidarity, social justice, the belief not the society comes before the individual fulfilment that it is only in a strong society of others that the individual will be fulfilled. That is these bonds of connection that makes us not citizens of one nation but members of one human race… We are putting our values into practice; we are the only political force capable of liberating the potential of our people. Knowing what we have to do and know how to do it.
>
> (The Guardian, 29/9/99: p6.)

Interpretation of key statements and messages leaves us with two areas of analysis. A clear set of values which lend themselves from collective movements fighting oppression (e.g. feminism, anti-racism) and secondly a sense of the process of change.

The values are clear: equality, rights with responsibilities, inclusion in society and a focus on equality of opportunity as opposed to equality of outcome. Whilst it is difficult to understand how such values can be operationalised when detracted from their ideological base, it is yet more arguable how the processes to achieve change will be implemented:

> The Third Way does not stand for riding forms of state ownership or provision. It is pragmatic as to whether public or private means are the best delivery mechanism.
>
> (Jordan, 2000.)

Consequently, the 'Third Way' views such organisational change as central to the delivery of the 'Third Way' irrespective of its history within care and specifically mental health care. The eradication of the 'Berlin Wall' can be seen through numerous pieces of legislation, but specifically, The Health Act 1999 (Department of Health, 1999) and Partnership in Action

(Department of Health, 1998). Organisational restructuring is therefore one element of a process of change within the 'Third Way'. Health Service reconfiguration including the development of Primary Care Trusts and Strategic Health Authorities by means of mergers and promoting partnerships between health and social care, appear to be one aspect of the solution. Secondly, the Third Way focuses on outcomes, referred to as performance management, which is seen as a mechanism for ensuring this level of organisational change. The introduction of *Modernising Social Services* (Department of Health, 1999), *Quality Protects* (Department of Health, 1998) *Modernising Mental Health Services* (Department of Health, 1999) and *Shifting the Balance of Power* (Department of Health, 2000) are examples of instruments of performance management whereby organisational and professional practice is being reshaped.

However, what are the consequences and implications for individuals, families, carers and professionals working in the mental health services? Where Beveridge saw health and social care workers as 'foundations' of the welfare revolution, the 'Third Way' sees individuals as 'necessary' to the cultural revolution. That is, it has an emphasis on 'people' as 'agents of change' whereby health providers and social care workers become agents to transform attitudes, culture and practices for providers and service users, and there the dichotomy is raised. Organisational change may occur to meet the needs of performance management, but structural change is limited. Rather, focus is again placed on individuals to manage and change bad practice and attitudes, whilst concurrently being subject to the regulation, and performance management criteria imposed by government. It can be said, therefore, that the 'solution' has become 'individualised' with pockets of good inter-professional practice based on clear values and the integrated practice of individuals working within agencies. For service users, this individualised response becomes a balance of 'rights and responsibilities' and their construction within a given framework.

The contested context therefore remains unresolved, and to some degree left in the sidelines, avoiding debate. Yet, the powerful forces of the discourse of fragmentation have clear implications for practice and future developments.

The National Service Framework for Mental Health

Over the last five years, we have witnessed a consistent 'tightening' of diagnosis, treatment and service provision for people experiencing mental health distress. Combined with Blair's focus upon centralisation, standardisation and performance management, we also see the implementation of policy and legislation, which is shaping the mental health agenda. The focus is primarily on the National Service Framework (NSF), The Care Programme Approach, The Mental Health Act (1983) and reform of the Mental Health Act.

The NSF applies to people of working age and standards are set in five areas:

- mental health promotion
- primary care and access to services
- effective services for people with severe mental illness
- caring for carers
- preventing suicide

The standards concentrate on services for those with severe and enduring mental health problems. Each standard is supported by evidence based upon a range of systematic reviews of research including expert opinion, and the views and opinions of service users and carers. Evidence reflects current views about which drugs and psychosocial approaches are most effective. For example, research pointing to either the use of the newer atypical anti-psychotic medication used for symptoms of schizophrenia (which has fewer side effects for most people) or the use of cognitive-behavioural approaches and family work (which helps people to manage their delusional voices and to prevent a relapse of symptoms of schizophrenia). Service models and examples of provision from around the country are used as examples of good practice. National milestones have been established. Progress towards these milestones will be measured by systematic service reviews. Additional investment is available through the Modernisation Fund and the Mental Health Grant and the principles of Best Value apply. The priorities for new service development by April 2001 were:

- 170 assertive outreach teams
- 24 hour access to services for all, regardless of location
- almost 500 secure beds

The need for 1,000 secure beds to meet the needs of those who required more security than a local hospital facility could provide but less than a Special Hospital, was identified in the *Review of Services for Mentally Disordered Offenders and Others who Required Similar Services* (Department of Health, 1992).

Assertive outreach

Lack of engagement with services has been found to be a factor in some inquiries into homicides and suicides. Concern for those who have complex needs, but who are not engaged effectively with mental health services, has led to the development of teams with the remit of identifying those most at risk of 'falling through the net' and assertively offering intensive support. The target group includes people who may:

- Have had frequent admissions for inpatient care.
- Have drug and alcohol related problems.
- Have a diagnosis of psychotic illness.
- Have a diagnosis of severe personality disorder.
- Be homeless or have housing problems.
- Be involved with the criminal justice system.
- Have a history of violence, suicidal ideation, significant self-harm or severe self-neglect.

Keys to Engagement (Sainsbury, 1998) identifies that the provision of services to this often high risk group has a wider political significance, since 'public confidence in services is determined partly by the adequacy of services to this group' (Sainsbury, 1998: p1). Estimates of the numbers of people for whom assertive outreach is appropriate produce a national average of 45 per 100,000, with figures for some inner cities as high as 200 per 100,000 (Sainsbury, 1998).

Assertive outreach typically involves small teams of very experienced community mental health nurses and/or social workers with case loads of ten to fifteen clients using a more overt teamwork approach in client work than is found in traditional service provision. Teams have the advantage of being enabled to be persistent in their efforts to engage and remain engaged with individual service users. As a result of specialist expertise and small case loads, staff are enabled to have frequent supervision and to intervene early in a crisis. It has been found that assertive outreach teams can establish a more stable community base and reduce hospital admission rates (Meuser et al., 1998). Recognition of a vulnerable individual's needs and the levels of risk they present need to be balanced against their right to refuse treatment and to privacy.

Crisis services

The need for 24-hour service delivery in the community is being met by the development of Mental Health Crisis Teams. In addition to providing a rapid skilled assessment of the situation, they are generally able to offer a range of interventions including therapy, liaison with other services, practical support, respite care, or admission to hospital. One of the claims of proponents of crisis services is that they can prevent hospital admissions, which would otherwise have occurred. Development of crisis services is one of the priorities for implementation of the NSF. Social work input is crucial in order to ensure social needs are identified and addressed. Managing crises often necessitates work with families, accessing other agencies and demands sound knowledge of resources available. Services are targeted upon those people seen to be at imminent risk of admission to hospital or nursing home care.

Staff involved in crisis services require considerable assessment skills, an ability to rapidly engage with service users and carers often in severe distress, and knowledge of all available services. Social workers working in such services are likely to be service brokers as well as providers. Working with other agencies is made easier when they see a flexible, intensive support system in place to meet the needs of service users and carers.

The Role of the Approved Social Care Programme Approach

The most important and comprehensive policy for delivering mental health care is to be found in the Care Programme Approach (Health Circular 23:90). This approach was revised in April 2000, to comprise two levels of care; 'standard' care for those with less severe problems and 'enhanced' care for those with more severe mental health needs and complex problems. Key features of the Care Programme Approach (CPA) are:

● assessment of health and social care needs

● an agreed, written care plan

● a key worker or care co-ordinator to co-ordinate the plan

● regular review

Integration of Care Management with CPA has been patchy but is essential for accessing and co-ordinating the delivery of appropriate resources (*Still Building Bridges*, 1999). Robust care plans need to be based on evidence from research and to match interventions to needs. For specialists from other areas of social work wishing to understand mental health practice it is essential to develop a good understanding of the Care Programme Approach.

Mental Health Act 1983

Although most hospital in-patients are voluntary patients, having agreed to their admission, the number of compulsory admissions to mental hospital has been rising dramatically since 1984 (Department of Health, 1999). The Mental Health Act (1983) allows for the detention in hospital and forcible treatment of those who will not or cannot accept treatment voluntarily and who are assessed as meeting the required grounds as specified in the Act. To be compulsorily admitted to mental hospital, people have to be suffering from a mental disorder (which can be mental illness, mental impairment, severe mental impairment or psychopathic disorder) and it must be in the interests of their health, or safety, or for the

protection of others, to be so detained. The most important sections of the Mental Health Act, for the non-mental health specialist to have some knowledge of, are:

● **Section 2:** provides for assessment (of their mental state) and/or treatment, which lasts for up to 28 days and is not renewable.

● **Section 3:** provides for treatment, which lasts for up to six months and can be renewed.

● **Section 4:** an emergency power to admit – lasts for up to 72 hours to allow for assessment for Section 2 or 3.

● **Section 7:** guardianship which does not allow for forcible treatment but is a community order which gives the guardian a range of powers designed to meet the needs of the person without hospital in-patient care.

It is important to recognise that patients should not need to deteriorate to a point whereby they pose a danger or significant risk to themselves or others before action can be taken. For people who may be well known to the service the risk assessment might focus on previous patterns of deterioration and the need for early intervention in the interests of the health of the person. This may avoid a major breakdown and require shorter periods of treatment or care under compulsion.

(ADSS, 1998: p1.)

People who are deemed to be at significant risk of suicide, severe self-harm or neglect, or harm to others can be placed on the Supervision Register. On discharge from hospital people who present a significant risk can be made subject to Section 25 (Supervised Discharge). Both systems are designed to ensure assertive follow up and that care is not allowed to cease without proper review.

A range of other powers exists: for example, Part III of the Act gives the court powers to deal with offenders who have mental health problems. The use of Hospital Orders (Section 37) through the court system have slightly decreased but transfers from prison (Sections 47 and 48) have increased (Department of Health, 1999).

With fewer beds available, it might be expected that a higher proportion of those in hospital would be compulsorily detained. However, the figures show that the number of admissions under the civil sections for assessment and treatment has been increasing since 1984; emergency sections have decreased – probably due to stringent criteria being applied to their use.

The reasons for the increase in use of Section 2 and Section 3 appear to be linked to the higher number of people with mental health and substance use issues (dual diagnosis), which increases management difficulties, and affects the attitudes of professionals involved in decisions to manage risk (Department of Health, 1999), hence as Holloway states:

> *Increasingly psychiatry is characterised by a reluctance to take risks.*
>
> (Holloway, 1996.)

Approved Social Workers

Local authority social services departments have a duty to provide specially trained Approved Social Workers (ASWs) who have responsibilities defined by the Mental Health Act 1983. Approved Social Workers, are qualified, experienced social workers who undertake a three month specialist training programme and are assessed in respect of their competence (CCETSW, 2000). An important part of their role in assessment is the exploration of alternatives to hospital admission and to provide a social care perspective. Approved Social Workers are integral to Community Mental Health Teams (CMHTs), Assertive Outreach Teams, Crisis Teams and are sometimes linked to Court Diversion schemes, where their particular expertise is valued. They are a valuable resource to other specialist workers and can offer consultation and advice on mental health issues and management of risk. Mental health social work encompasses what appears to be a conflicting function of advocacy on behalf of mental health service users with legal powers to remove their liberty. Risk assessment and management can then become the focus for decision making.

Mental health services now have formal risk assessment as part of CPA documentation. Most protocols are similar to those developed by the Health of the Nation Outcome Scale (HoNOS) and the 'Risk assessment and training pack' (Aldberg et al., 1998).

A comprehensive assessment of risk should form part of any initial psychiatric assessment by every mental health professional. Thereafter risk assessment is a dynamic process that requires on-going re-evaluation of risk, in the context of the person's changing mental state or social situation. Identification of risk should always lead to planning of how to manage risk within the care planning process, including strategies for intervention should levels of risk escalate.

Risk assessment and management should include the following areas; violence; child neglect and abuse; suicide and self-harm; self neglect; elder abuse; staff safety. Assessment should always include attention to the issue of risk of harm to self or others, and should consider the following five factors:

- Risk factors: stressors/factors in current situation.

- History: mental health, offending, reactions to stress in past – family history.

- Ideation: what are they thinking? What are they experiencing – content of voices.

- Plan: have they decided what to do? Taken steps?

- Intent: justification – determination – relief that they have made decision?

Managing risk requires skills in the identification of clients' strengths and previous coping strategies in conjunction with agency policies, management and procedures that reflect good practice in assessing and managing risk. Good communication intra and inter-agency is essential along with common tools for recording important information linked with CPA and Care Management.

Clear guidelines on the limits to confidentiality, where serious risks are present should be agreed across health, social services, housing, probation and voluntary sector providers. Service users should be informed of their rights to confidentiality and its limits, to be able to plan care effectively and safely. Good practice dictates that service users are consulted and asked permission to pass on information and that managers are consulted when the need to breach confidentiality arises.

Having access to the right information is key to making appropriate decisions. Sources of information should include statutory agencies/professionals with current or previous involvement with the person; family members; friends; other carers; the person themselves. Good risk assessment means actively seeking out information. Components of a good risk assessment are:

- Collecting full information.
- Using actuarial as well as clinical data.
- Awareness of the range of risks presented by the person, to whom, when, and how.
- Awareness of particular risk situational triggers or 'risk factors'.
- Communicating with all interested parties.
- Identifying all potential outcomes and their likelihood.
- Establishing a plan for managing identified risks and dangers.
- Clarifying individual roles and responsibilities.
- Recording rationale for decisions and demonstrating they are 'as good as can be'.

(adapted from Tony Ryan, 1994.)

Good practice should be based on evidence from research, which means updating staff and providing training opportunities.

Violence

Violence usually occurs when high levels of stress are evident. This could be due to internal feelings as experienced in paranoia, agitation, responding to voices, when angry or when feeling cornered. Past history of violence and current substance use increase the risk of violence (Walker, 1996).

Suicide

Mental health professionals need to have skills in identifying suicidal intent and matching services to those at risk (Vaughan, 1995). Guidance on suicide risk interviews and managing suicidal people offers practical advice to professionals (Barker, 1998). Other workers especially in primary care settings, probation and prisons need to be able to access appropriate support and advice.

Suicidal intent is a feature of depression. Older people are the group most likely to commit suicide. Specialist teams working with older people can develop good rapport across professional boundaries but there is a need for staff to recognise mental health problems as appropriate to refer to other specialists. For example, depression should not be accepted as an inevitable part of an older person's life as it can be lifted with sensitive interventions.

The interaction of life events, mental state, illness and isolation all increase risk. There is also a worrying trend of increased suicides amongst young men with suicide being the second most common cause of death in the 15-34 year old age group (Department of Health, 1993). There has also been particular concern for those remanded in custody who are a high suicide risk. Of those who commit suicide: 90 per cent have some form of mental disorder; 66 per cent have consulted their GP in the previous month; 40 per cent have consulted their GP in the previous week; 33 per cent have expressed clear suicidal intent; 25 per cent are psychiatric outpatients (Department of Health, 1993).

Carers

Over recent years, groups like SANE and the National Schizophrenic Fellowship representing informal carers' perspectives have gained prominence. Managing people with high dependency mental health needs in the community means carers and families take on a range of responsibilities and can lead to them having their own needs for support. Families can have knowledge and information about how to help prevent relapse and improve outcomes of intervention as well as how to handle crisis situations should they arise. Educational programmes for carers focussing on psychosocial interventions and evidence from research are available (National Schizophrenia Fellowship and Sainsbury Centre for Mental Health, 2000). As described in Chapter 8 young carers are a group who are particularly vulnerable and whose needs are often neglected. 'Where the person with a mental illness is a parent, health and local authorities should not assume that the child or children could undertake the necessary caring responsibilities. The parent should be supported in their parenting role' and 'The young carers plan should take account of the adverse impact which mental health problems in a parent can have on a child' (Department of Health, 1999: p5). In some areas, NCH Action for Children projects offer emotional and practical support to young carers, many of whom take on caring responsibilities for parents with mental health problems.

Meeting the needs of parents with mental health problems whilst ensuring the safety and well being of dependant children is an area that can generate anxiety in workers. It is important to acknowledge the links between mental health in carers and the impact of this on their children and to respond appropriately (Falkov, 1995; Kaplan, 1998; Philips and Hugman, 1998). In his study of reports into the death of children who had contact with social services, Falkov found that in 32 cases out of 100 studied there was clear evidence of psychiatric disorder in parents. Key findings were that mentally ill perpetrators tended to be older natural mothers with a history of overdose and self-harm. They killed children using a variety of methods and often attempted suicide at the time or shortly after the child's death. The issue was not the absence of agency involvement, but rather the absence of effective inter-and intra-agency co-ordination, collaboration and communication. In general, a parental mental health perspective amongst child agencies was lacking whilst little emphasis was placed on child protection or the nature of children's experiences by adult services involved.

Preventative work is the key to addressing issues before crises occur, although it is clear that the policy of increasing specialisms in social work may not be a productive experience for women caught between child protection and mental health services. As the threshold for offering services is raised and high levels of risk become the criteria for access, coercion and control come to the fore in work with mentally ill people. This focus on control exacerbates the feelings of powerlessness, worthlessness and guilt associated with depression (White, 1996).

Reforming the Mental Health Act

The government's mental health white paper replaces the special role ASWs have played in assessment for compulsory treatment with *sectioning orders* which will be made by two doctors and 'a social worker or another suitably qualified mental health professional.' This is a major move from ensuring a non-medical perspective as a part of an assessment under the Mental Health Act. The guiding principles of the new Act are that:

- Informal care be considered before recourse to compulsion.

- That patients should be involved as far as possible in the development and review of their care.

- The safety of the individual and the public are of key importance in determining whether compulsory powers should be imposed.

- Where compulsory powers are used, care and treatment should be in the least restrictive setting consistent with the patient's best interests and the safety of the public.

Planned legislation will introduce:

- A wide definition of mental disorder covering any disability or disorder of mind or brain, whether permanent or temporary, which results in an impairment or disturbance of mental functioning.

- Compulsory treatment in settings other than in hospital.

- A new independent tribunal (mental health tribunal) to determine all longer-term use of compulsory powers.

- A new right to independent advocacy.

- New safeguards for people with long term incapacity.

- A new commission for mental health.

- A statutory requirement to develop care plans.

The new procedures for use of compulsory powers involves a three stage process. The decision to begin assessment and initial treatment under compulsory powers will be based on preliminary examinations by two doctors and a social worker or another suitably trained mental health professional. Specialist services may provide preliminary examinations; for example, if the person is elderly, a child, has learning difficulties or a history of serious offending. If the preliminary examination concludes that the person requires further assessment or urgent treatment and without this would be at risk of serious harm or the person would pose a serious risk of harm to other people then the process moves on to a second stage. Stage two provides for formal assessment of health and social care needs and initial treatment for a period of up to 28 days. Treatment must be set out in a formal care plan. Stage three provides for further treatment under compulsory powers in the form of a care and treatment order obtained from the Mental Health Tribunal. The first two orders granted in respect of one individual will be for up to six months then for periods up to twelve months. Care and treatment can be provided in the community, although there are no plans for patients to be given medication forcibly except in a clinical setting.

In the case of mentally disordered offenders, the assessment will be ordered by the court, or, in the case of prisoners, by the Home Secretary. In line with the National Service Framework, there will be a duty on health and social services to share information.

The new Mental Health Act will, as at present, apply to children and young people raising particular issues for staff in assessing a child's capacity to consent to treatment and how to administer compulsory treatment other than in hospital (Harbour and Bailey, 2000). In making decisions in respect of children the Mental Health Tribunal shall obtain expert advice on both health and social care aspects of the proposed care plan and give consideration to whether the location of care is appropriate to the young person's needs.

The most contentious proposals are outlined in *Reforming the Mental Health Act Part II – High risk patients*, which reflects thinking in the consultation paper *Managing Dangerous People with Severe Personality Disorder* (1999). Shortcomings in the law were identified in this report following some highly publicised cases where serious offences were committed by people deemed not to be treatable under the

Mental Health Act 1983. The Inquiry into Ashworth Hospital (Fallon, 1999) highlighted problems in the management of the personality disorder unit and the proposals include a recommendation for the introduction of an indeterminate, reviewable sentence for offenders. The objective is to 'provide better protection for the public from dangerous severely personality disordered people' (Department of Health and Home Office, 1999). The two components of this requirement for better protection are to ensure that people 'are kept in detention for as long as they pose a high risk' and 'managing them in a way which provides better opportunities to deal with the consequences of their disorder' (Department of Health and Home Office, 1999). Much debate has centred on the human rights issues of whether indeterminate detention could or should be an option where an offence had not been committed but where someone presented extreme risk to others in the community. Assessing who does or does not suffer from a 'severe personality disorder', whether the level of risk they present is high, and when the level of risk is reduced enough for people to be managed in less secure provision are all fraught with difficulties as:

> …there is no consensus amongst clinicians on the nature of personality disorder, how it should be managed, or the extent of the role health professionals should be expected to play in dealing with those personality disordered people judged to be unlikely to respond to hospital treatment. This in turn reflects the lack of an adequate research base of evidence.
>
> (Department of Health and Home Office, 1999: p7.)

The government's response has been to develop pilot treatment services, which will be independently evaluated, and to fund 320 additional specialist places across the prison service and NHS plus 75 hostel places. Under the new mental health legislation, powers will be linked to a treatment plan, either to treat the underlying mental disorder or to manage behaviours arising from the disorder. Orders can be made by Tribunals for those not involved in the criminal justice system, or by the courts. The new act will simplify court disposals. There will be a single power of remand for assessment and treatment for 28 days that can be renewed for up to twelve weeks. The power to make a care and treatment order, following assessment, is limited to a six month period after which the

Mental Health Tribunal will make further decisions. A restriction order with similar powers to the present one will only apply where the care and treatment is to be provided in hospital. A hospital and limitation order is also an option with the effect of treating someone in hospital then transferring them to prison, once the clinical supervisor (consultant psychiatrist) deems treatment in hospital is no longer necessary.

Through the NSF, the government's agenda of tackling social exclusion is evident through outreach teams, and early response via crisis services. Historically, crisis services have been developed to meet initial 'assessment and intervention' and whist they have aimed to address admission figures, often failed to do so. The prioritisation, increased funding and the re-presentation of crisis teams under the modernisation agenda, may however effect change in the long term.

The Post-specialist Universe – Maintaining a Professional Identity Working Across Boundaries – The Future?

Although one in six adults, at any one time, may be suffering from some form of mental health problem, a series of filters exist which ensures that only a small proportion end up in receipt of specialist mental health services (Goldberg and Huxley, 1992). GPs are often the first port of call and may treat people themselves, offering counselling services or refer people to a range of supportive services. Changes in the funding arrangements for the voluntary sector, the development of Primary Care Groups or Trusts and the effects of contracting with the independent sector all affect the range, quality and diversity of service provision. As local authorities have moved to become 'enablers' rather than providers of services their relationship with the independent sector has changed. Traditionally the voluntary sector has become involved in areas, which have been poorly resourced by the statutory agencies: for example, homelessness, housing and employment (Patmore, 1987; Pilling, 1992). An increasing reliance on state funding through contracting arrangements may lessen the lobbying power

of some groups that have historically promoted service user's views. The user movement in mental health has been an important catalyst for getting change on the agenda, with activity from groups such as MIND and 'We're not mad; We're angry' gaining media attention to highlight poor practice and abuse of power within psychiatry. User involvement in planning services has been a feature in some areas and has led to imaginative community resources such as community cafes, a range of service user led groups and activities which are open at evenings and weekends. These can be supported by staff, but provide non-stigmatising support when service users want it.

In working across intra-organisational and professional boundaries, there are clearly identifiable indicators that highlight problematic areas:

1. Definition of health, ill-health and care.

2. Identification of health, ill-health and mental health.

3. Uneven patterns of service provision and therefore access.

4. Resources:
   - funding mechanisms
   - commissioning processes
   - contracting processes

5. Stimulation of the market to build and increase capacity.

6. User and patient involvement at an individual and strategic level.

7. Perception and involvement of carers and users and; significantly

8. A lack of shared understanding leading to a notion of partnership.

The introduction of the Health Act 1999 was an integrated piece of legislation, which enabled progressive partnerships to develop between Primary Care Groups or Trusts and Social Care Trusts. All three of these partnerships bring together health, social care, users, and carers and voluntary and independent sectors. Change therefore is at an organisational/structural level with facilitated power under the Health Act flexibilities to integrate service provision, pool budgets and jointly commission new and existing services. Theoretically, such partnerships pave the way to become Care Trusts with the systems and structures of partnership already developed. In reality, the difficulties remain and often pragmatic decisions and resolutions are made in order to achieve partnership, rather than a clear development of values, ideals, aims, objectives and professional practice. Whilst the majority of 'partnerships' are hosted by local authorities, it is likely that depending upon the service user group (Learning Disabilities, Mental Health) that the movement towards Trust status will lead to an additional reconfiguration between health and social care. The government have clearly stated that mental health should be the domain of health services and learning disability and older people the responsibility of care agencies. In the new era of partnership, new care trusts, whilst 'integrated' will have a specific health or social care focus.

Given this large scale reconfiguration of services, attention and resources are focussed upon intra-organisational design. Consequently, staff in managerial positions are required to manage this process of change, with a focus on outcomes rather than process. What is interesting to note is the lack of resources and attention to the 'partnership', 'integration' or even 'reconfiguration' of practice. The professional domains remains focussed upon 'how we can work together' rather than addressing common skills and values, which may lead to a 'generic', 'hybrid' or 'dually qualified' worker. The notion of performance management infers a 'top down' approach, which combined with service reconfiguration, questions the role, value and input of professional staff, service users and cares. The new welfare picture leaves users in a position of initiating, developing and maintaining links across many specialist areas (see Figure 10.1).

Whilst each agency is attempting to promote better partnership and communication at an organisational level, interestingly by changing service users for 'professionals' as in Figure 10.1. Clearly, at a time of infrastructure change, health and social care workers will require substantive skills across many areas. Initially these appear as:

1. Management of change.
2. Working within new organisations.
3. Working in partnership at macro and micro levels.
4. Integrating health, social care and the primary/secondary care interface.

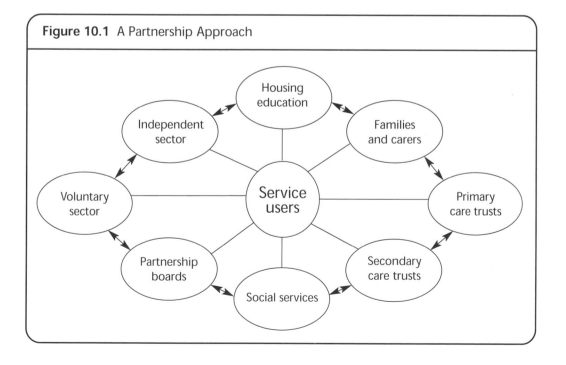

Figure 10.1 A Partnership Approach

5. Promoting the well being of families and communities.

6. Capacity building and regeneration of communities.

The challenge lies in achieving a synergy in practice in these five key areas!

Most local authority mental health social workers are now employed in Community Mental Health Teams. There has been a trend to develop multidisciplinary teams usually comprising social workers, psychiatrists, psychologists, community psychiatric nurses (CPNs), occupational therapists and support workers. Some have specialist remits to work with particular client groups within mental health services: for example, children and adolescents or older people, while others play particular roles: for example, assertive outreach or long term support workers. As Fagin and Chapman state:

> *Multi-disciplinary teams, practically by definition, attract professionals who are comfortable with the idea that the aetiology of mental disturbance is complex and multi-factorial, and not subsumed to single causal explanations.*
>
> (Fagin and Chapman, 1996: p15.)

The various disciplines in the team have their own specific areas of expertise and responsibility, although there is some blurring of boundaries and overlapping of roles. Psychiatrists, social workers and CPNs have professional responsibilities that are not shared. However, all carry out assessments and plan interventions. Trust, shared and agreed priorities, clear management structures and transparent decision making processes are all needed for teams to work effectively. Increasingly, the development of Community Mental Health Teams has, throughout the country, been an ad hoc and fragmented development. Whilst some areas have fully integrated services, others are only at the beginning of integration. Motivated by the 'Berlin Wall' of complex care cases and nursing vis-à-vis social care debates, the government issued Partnerships in Action (Department of Health, 1998) and the Health Act (Department of Health, 1999). These policy documents advocate closer links and pave the way for structural integration. None the less, Partnership in Action had an uneven effect,

later strengthened through the 1999 Act. Yet, despite government momentum, why does joint working and integration at a practice, organisational and structural level remain problematic?

Traditionally, social work and social care have resisted specialist forms of organisation and delivery, yet throughout the 1980s and 1990s, there was evidence of increase in the rise of 'specialisms' (e.g. Learning Disabilities, Mental Health). Despite the position advocated by CCETSW that the DipSW was a generic qualification, increasing specialism arose via 'pathways' as employers required workers with 'specialist' knowledge to meet the 'specialist' needs of high risk, vulnerable people. Given the wide-ranging social problems experienced by people with mental ill-health, it is essential that the skills and value base of social work are maintained in an overwhelmingly health led service. The qualifying and post-qualifying training for mental health social work needs to encompass both the skills for inter-disciplinary work and the specialist social work role.

With the move towards fully integrated statutory health and social care provided through joint mental health services comprising unified managerial structures, local authority social workers find themselves working in teams in which health professionals can numerically predominate. This has led to increasing numbers of social workers being managed by professionals who are not social work trained. This may in turn affect the nature of supervision offered, which needs to encompass the wide responsibilities of social workers especially in the areas of ASW work and linkages with child protection issues.

It will be the responsibility of these professionals to ensure that the integrated organisations become dynamic, different and forward thinking, ensuring that new inter-organisational barriers are not established, recreating old ones. Whilst resources and power often lie at the heart of failure to change, hopefully the integration of services, philosophy aims and objectives, allow the creation of encompassing policies and procedures reflecting the needs of services users and carers, thus avoiding practice being dominated by organisational difference.

Will the next five years see a movement from a post specialist universe to a specialist in organisational change or a universe led by integration on a specialist basis? *New World, New Order, New Partnership* – or business as usual?

Further Reading

Clarke, J., Gerwirtz, S. and McLaughlin, E. (Ed.) (2000). *New Managerialism New Welfare?* London: Sage.

Driver and Martell (1998). *New Labour: Politics After Thatcher.* Oxford: Polity Press.

Meway, B., Baciqalupo, V., Bornat, J., Johnson, J. and Spurr, S. (Eds.) (2002). *Understanding Care, Welfare and Community A Reader.* London: Routledge and The Open University.

Rogers, A. and Pilgrim, D. (2001). *Mental Health Policy in Britain (Part III).* Houndmills, Basingstoke: Palgrave.

Taylor, M. (2003). *Public Policy in the Community.* Houndsmill, Basingstoke: Palgrave.

Chapter 11

Learning Disabilities: Overcoming a Social Handicap

Roy McConkey and Theresa Nixon

Overview

Learning disability, or mental handicap as it used to be called in the United Kingdom, is the most prevalent handicapping condition throughout the world. The name can be misleading. An impairment to learning can result in social, emotional as well as intellectual handicaps. Indeed the most handicapping aspects of a learning disability are impaired communication; a paucity of social relationships and an inability for autonomous decision making.

For many generations such people were excluded from the mainstream of society. They brought shame to their families and were an economic burden to them. As the industrial revolution took hold, the solution was the provision of 'asylums' but these intended places of safety soon became institutions in which the 'patients' experienced a 'social death', to use Townsend's (1973) words.

The legacy of this shameful era still reverberates in our social policy, even though the aim is to have nearly all people currently living in mental handicap hospitals resettled into community housing within the next three years. But it will take much longer to break the mind-sets that such people require 'special treatment'; that 'they are better off with their own kind' and that 'they cannot be productive members of society'.

In sum, learning disability is primarily a social handicap. Hence trained social workers have a major contribution to make in ameliorating the handicapping effects of this disability. In this chapter, we focus especially on the contribution that is being made by social workers in fieldwork settings, who are mostly employed by statutory social services, and whose focus is on supporting families and individuals with a learning disability. Our aim is threefold:

1. To review the range of services that is evolving to meet the lifelong needs of this client group and the roles which social workers have in these situations.

2. To examine the unique and particular contributions that social workers can make in services and the key principles of good practice.

3. To reflect on the impediments to effective social work practice and possible ways of tackling them; in particular the value of working across specialisms.

Learning Disability Services

In this section we review the changes which have taken place to the meaning 'learning disability'; the new emphasis in services on inclusion and ordinary living principles and the range of services which are usually provided throughout the life span.

What does it mean to have a learning disability?

Whatever name is used to describe this disability – and around the world *mental retardation and intellectual disability* are more common – the impression is given of a unitary disability that is akin to visual impairment or a hearing loss. This is patently not so. We now realise that the term is best thought of as an umbrella label for a range of disabling conditions of diverse origins. Genetic factors are thought to account for around 60 per cent of people called 'learning disabled', of which Down Syndrome is the largest single group. Environmental causes have been implicated in the remaining 40 per cent; including maternal infection during pregnancy, diet and substance abuse, extreme prematurity and childhood infections (Mental Health Foundation, 1993). Obviously, such diverse causes produce different consequences on the development of children but even the same cause may produce marked effects in some individuals while others show minimal impairments. In sum then, there never can be a 'typical' person with a learning disability. But that said, there are a number of common features among people with a learning disability summarised below:

- Learning disability is generally a condition that is present from birth (or shortly afterwards) and the effects of it are lifelong.

- As the name implies, the person is slow to learn and to solve problems. This can apply to physical and social development as well as to intellectual development. They score markedly below average on tests of intelligence.

- Many people will experience difficulties in communication through impaired speech and language development.

- A child or adult with a learning disability has difficulty acquiring the skills required to function socially, such as safeguarding oneself from common dangers, caring for personal needs or travelling independently.

- The person needs extra help and support in comparison to their age peers. This applies in the family, at school, in leisure pursuits or to gain employment. But if they are given extra help, their competencies increase and their quality of life can improve.

- People can vary in the severity of their disability. The terms mild, moderate, severe and profound are often used to describe this. Although these categories were based originally on scores from intelligence tests, they now reflect the amount of help and assistance the person requires.

Re-conceptualising disability

Traditionally our thinking about disability is dominated by the 'mechanistic' model; namely, identify what is wrong with the person and then fix it! This approach has been pursued by doctors, therapists and educators. Disabled activists among others have been to the fore in promoting a different view, for example:

Disability is not a condition of the individual. The experiences of disabled people are of social restriction in the world around them, not of being a person with a 'disabling condition'. This is not to say that individuals do not experience 'disability', rather it is to assert that the individual's experience of disability is created in interaction with a physical and social world designed for non-disabled people.

(Swain et al., 1993: p56.)

In the *social model* of disability the role of services is to reduce the restrictions these citizens face and support them in leading their own life. This is increasingly recognised in policy statements. For example: the DHSS (NI) Review of Policy for People with a Learning Disability (1995) states that:

The vision of the future for people with a learning disability is one of inclusion which stresses citizenship, inclusion in society, inclusion in decision-making, participation so far as is practicable in mainstream education, employment and leisure, integration in living accommodation and the use of services and facilities, not least in the field of health and personal social services.

(Ministerial Foreword.)

Changes in services

By the closing decades of the twentieth century, remarkable changes had taken place in services for people with learning disabilities as the social model of disability took hold. Today, new opportunities in education, training, employment and housing are being devised as old institutions close, day centres are transformed into community resource centres and doors open in further education and employment (Gates, 1997). Present policy has been influenced by three international trends that have grown in strength over the past two decades:

Normalisation: Services need to be provided in as normal and as valued a setting as possible, if we are to reduce the perception of the clients as being different from their peers. As Wolfensberger states:

Normalisation starts from the premise that a major handicap of disabled people is their devaluation in society and it seeks to remedy this by enabling disabled people, as far as possible, to have experiences that are generally valued in society.

(1972: p1.)

Ordinary life: People with learning disabilities should have the opportunity to live an ordinary life and to participate to the full in their communities. An influential document published by the King's Fund spelt out this vision:

> Our goal is to see mentally handicapped people (people with learning disabilities) in the mainstream of life living in ordinary houses, in ordinary streets, with the same range of choices as any other citizens and mixing as equals with others and mostly non-handicapped members of their own community.
>
> (Towell, 1988: p9.)

Rights: The third big influence is the recognition that children and adults with disabilities have the same rights as any other citizen, particularly in the fields of education, housing and employment. The United Nations Declaration of Rights states:

> Disabled people, whatever the origin, nature and seriousness of their handicaps and disabilities, have the same fundamental rights as their fellow citizens of the same age, which implies first and foremost, the right to enjoy a decent life, as normal and full as possible.

Governmental reviews of services

In recent years, major reviews have been undertaken of services for this client group by the Scottish Executive (2000) and the Department of Health (2001) in England and Wales (2001). These reviews have enunciated the main principles that should underpin service provision. Four principles were noted for England and Wales; namely, rights, independence, choice and inclusion. These were amplified in the Scottish Review, summarised below:

- People with learning disabilities should be valued. They should be asked and encouraged to contribute to the community they live in. They should not be picked on or treated differently from others.

- People with learning disabilities are individual people.

- People with learning disabilities should be asked about the services they need and be involved in making choices about what they want.

- People with learning disabilities should be helped and supported to do everything they are able to.

- People with learning disabilities should be able to use the same local services as everyone else, wherever possible.

- People with learning disabilities should benefit from specialist social, health and educational services.

- People with learning disabilities should have services which take account of their age, abilities and other needs.

(Scottish Executive, 2000.)

Range of Services for People with Learning Disabilities

There is currently widespread agreement as to what constitutes a *minimum* set of services for people with a learning disability and their families in order to meet their needs and aspirations. These are dealt with more fully later but in summary, they are:

- Multidisciplinary teams to assess developmental progress and devise interventions to promote rehabilitation, self-reliance and social integration.

- The provision of specialised education and training opportunities both in childhood and in the adult years.

- Financial allowances and benefits to cover extra costs associated with the disability.

- Appropriate response to meeting their particular and additional health care needs, such as epilepsy, incontinence management and mental health problems.

- The provision of 'out of home' living accommodation (temporary or permanent).

- The creation of opportunities for employment, either in sheltered settings or on the open market.

- Opportunities for involvement in the life of the community and to develop friendships and relationships.

Some, but not all of these services, are underpinned by legislation, in particular:

- Chronically Sick and Disabled Persons Act (1970).

- The Mental Health Act (1983).
- The Education Act (1995).
- The Children Act (1989).
- Carers Recognition and Service Act (1995).
- Community Care Act (1996).
- Disability Discrimination Act (1995).
- The Human Rights Act (1998).

Services Throughout the Life Span

People with learning disabilities and their families have lifelong needs. However the nature and range of needs for services change over the life span of the person. In this section, we illustrate the range of service inputs which have developed in recent years and the contribution which social workers are making to them.

Services for babies and pre-schoolers

Three key roles are identified for social workers:

- Parental counselling.
- Provision of information about services and sources of support.
- Referral to services as appropriate (for example: health, social services and community services).

Parental counselling: With babies whose disability is evident at birth; parental counselling and support will help them adjust to the unexpected and for some distressing news. Social workers attached to paediatric units have a crucial role to play by giving information and time to the parents, enabling them to ventilate their feelings and mitigate, if possible, the sense of isolation and helplessness they may feel.

Many families appreciate being put in touch with parent associations, such as the Down Syndrome Association. Here they can meet with other parents who have had similar experiences to their own and who can provide a sympathetic listening ear, while answering the family's questions, based on their experiences. The arrival of a child with a learning disability can throw the parents'

relationship off-balance due to factors such as lack of sleep and the drain of coping with the child's demands. Referrals to marital counselling organisations such as Relate, or family therapy advisors may prove helpful.

Genetic counselling: If the baby's condition is thought to have a genetic component, families should also be offered genetic counselling to alert them to the implications for future pregnancies and provide advice for other family members.

Health services: The health visitor is probably the main contact between services and families in the early years. Although, it is likely that the child's developmental progress will be reviewed by hospital based paediatricians and/or the family's GP. With advances in medical science, there are a growing number of babies who survive but have complex disabilities. These infants and their carers require more intensive, specialised support and therapeutic inputs. Paediatric or learning disability nurses may also call to the family home if the child has specific nursing requirements or behavioural problems.

Pre-school facilities: In several localities, home teaching services are also offered to families, so that they can be guided in the play and learning activities they might use to promote the child's development. Increasingly, children with developmental disabilities are encouraged to attend local playgroups or pre-schools. Organisations such as the Pre-school Playgroups Association actively promote this and these children may also be given priority for placement in local nursery schools. In the pre-school years, families are mainly in contact with health and educational personnel. Only a minority will have regular social worker involvement and this is largely for reasons other than the child's disability.

Services during school age

Key roles for social workers:

- Providing social service advice on statements of special educational needs.
- Assessments for, and the provision of, family support services.

- Referral to services as appropriate

Education: In the United Kingdom, education authorities have a statutory responsibility for the education of all children in their area, which begins from two years of age. The local education authority are responsible for drawing up a 'Statement' of a child's special educational needs. They are 'required to seek parental, educational, medical, psychological and social services advice, together with any other advice which may be considered desirable' (p23). This can be quite a protracted process but the 'quality standard' is for it to be completed between six weeks and three months. If families do not agree with the Statement they can appeal to an independent tribunal. Social workers involved with families during the statementing process and appeals may find themselves in a conflict between their personal views, those of the parents and of their employing agency.

Family support services are also slowly developing to help families in their caring tasks. Social workers are required to assess both the child's and the carer's needs. The needs of siblings also need to be considered. Examples of family support services are:

- *Domiciliary help:* paid social care staff from either a statutory or a voluntary organisation such as Crossroads, come to the family home regularly to assist with designated tasks, such as caring for the child with the disability, assisting with household chores; taking the child out for leisure activities.

- *Respite breaks:* the child may be admitted for a number of days or weeks to a residential home or special unit to give the families a break. Respite care also can be provided by ordinary families who are paid to look after a child with disability in their own home.

- *After-school and holiday activities:* children may attend clubs and activities run by schools, voluntary or community organisations. Some of these take the form of residential holidays.

- *Fostering:* on a short term or long term basis with a substitute family is another option to help alleviate the chronic stress experienced

by some carers of children with learning disabilities. Foster parents need the same range of family support services as do natural parents. Social workers can draw upon the experiences of colleagues in mainstream fostering services when developing family placement schemes particularly in relation to the placement of younger children and teenagers.

The need for better family support services far exceeds the supply. It was hoped that the Children Act, in England and Wales, and the Children Order, in Northern Ireland, would enable, if not force, child health and childcare services to make substantial provision for all children with disability under the definition of 'children in need' within the Order. This has been slow to happen. Children's services are a vital area for prevention work and hopefully the Quality Protects agenda will offer some good opportunities for this.

Services for teenagers and young adults

Key roles for social workers:

- Contribute to transition planning and reviews organised by education.

- Undertake risk assessments with family carers and young people.

- Make referrals to further education, vocational training and employment programmes.

Transition planning: Under the Disabled Persons Act 1989, once a child turns fourteen years of age, the education authority has to seek an opinion from social services as to whether a child with a Statement is a disabled person who may require on-going social services when leaving school. A joint 'Transition Plan' should then be developed with the young person, their family, the school, the careers services, and health and social services. The plan should:

> *...identify specific targets which should be set as part of the annual review to ensure that independence training, personal and social skills, and other aspects of the wider curriculum are fully addressed during the young person's last years at school.*
>
> (p40.)

However this is also an opportunity to carry out a full review of the young person's wider needs and those of their family, to share information with families and for professionals and parents to work collaboratively. The plans should be reviewed and updated yearly.

Leisure pursuits: research has shown repeatedly the dearth of leisure activities and friendships for older teenagers and young adults with a learning disability. Youth organisations such as the Scouts encourage their local groups to facilitate the enrolment of children with disabilities. Some voluntary organisations have started special clubs for children and teenagers and befriending schemes have been introduced in some areas. Respite care and holiday schemes are also a source of growth and support for the young people if the focus shifts to their needs rather than merely a substitute caring role for families.

Transition to employment: One of the most exciting developments in the last ten years has been the growth of schemes to help older teenagers with disabilities prepare for employment and to give them work experience opportunities. Experience suggests that many are able to hold down part-time jobs and most aspire to doing so:

- *Further Education Colleges:* young people may undertake special courses at F.E. Colleges either alongside their attendance at special schools or after they have left school. Some courses are geared towards giving them work skills in areas such as baking and gardening. Trainees may be assessed for NVQs, usually at Level 1.

- *Supported employment:* in these schemes, young people are accompanied to the workplace by a 'job coach' who trains them on-the-job in both the specific task skills and the broader social skills needed to hold down a job. As the person becomes more competent in the work, the job coach gradually withdraws but remains in contact with the employer should problems arise. Initially, these placements are seen as training but the hope is that once the person proves their competence, they will receive payment for their work; albeit on a part-time basis.

- *Social businesses:* some voluntary organisations, with assistance from the European Social Fund, have started businesses to provide employment and training to people with disabilities. Examples include cafes, computer services and bottle-washing.

Service provision geared to the special needs of teenagers with disabilities has been slow to develop in the United Kingdom; mainly because of the divisive gap between educational and social services. Arguably, significant habilitation to community living could take place if a comprehensive range of services were targeted to this age group, and also if patterns of living could be established which would prevent some of the problems that become consolidated and even critical in adulthood.

Services for adults

Key roles for social workers:

- Planned moves from family care.

- Provision of productive daytime activities.

- Developing care packages for individuals.

- Providing counselling on relationships and sexuality.

- Working with sex offenders who have a learning disability. As this is a neglected area, we will pay particular attention to it in the next section on the contribution of social workers.

A home of one's own: a range of housing options need to be provided to suit the differing needs of individuals. Some may live independently while others need various levels of supported housing. Specialist support will be required for those with multiple and complex disabilities and also for those with severely challenging behaviours. Recent experience suggests that they too can be cared for in community houses. A growing number of people with learning disabilities now have their own tenancies with housing associations or local authorities.

Family carers may be reluctant to consider their son or daughter moving out of the family home. Given the dispersal of the nuclear family and the breakdown of the extended family in modern society, 'futures planning' is critical and helps to remove the most commonly expressed concern of parents, 'what will happen when we are gone'? A significant role of social workers is to listen to the wishes of the person with learning disability and of their carers; provide both parties with information about options and support them in coming to an informed decision.

Planning a move from the family home is best done on a developmental basis over a period of years. From childhood, people with learning disabilities should be helped to become self-reliant in domestic and community living skills and they should have opportunities for staying away from home for short periods, for example holiday breaks. Social workers have a major role to play in getting to know the families and supporting them through this process. Yet all too often their involvement is still triggered by a family crisis, which can result in an inappropriate placement with all the misery and upset that can bring.

Day-time activities: as noted earlier people with learning disabilities need to be offered a range of work, education, therapeutic and leisure options according to their needs and aspirations. Person-centred packages, which combine these options, are becoming more common. The advent of Direct Payments for people with learning disabilities may further assist this development although these have been slow to become established (Holman, 1998). One impediment to finding paid jobs for people on social security payments, has become widely known as the 'benefits trap', i.e. where people have to forfeit some or all of their social security payments for often low pay and insecure work opportunities. An added disincentive can be the reliance of families on this money to subvent the overall family income. Recent changes in social security regulations for disabled persons may alleviate this.

Counselling on relationships and sexuality: In the past, little attention was paid to relationships and issues around sexuality and conception were ignored. However, services that strive to provide 'ordinary lives' for their clients can no longer ignore these issues. Education about sexuality, advice on family planning and marriage preparation are issues which front line service staff and professional workers need to address as many family carers are reluctant or

feel unable to do so. Social workers could usefully provide a lead in doing this.

Services to older people

In the past, most people with learning disabilities died young. However the ageing population is now growing and social workers need to be involved in:

- Reassessing needs.
- Supporting family elderly carers.

Changing needs: as with the rest of the population, people with learning disabilities are living longer but little thought has been given to the needs of elderly persons. Service provision has been slow to come to terms with this new phenomenon. An obvious requirement is making available age appropriate services that will cater for the residential, occupational, leisure and health needs of older people who have additional or special needs associated with their disability. For example, there is increased risk of people with Downs Syndrome succumbing to dementia or Alzheimer's disease. It is crucial that social workers in learning disability have access to the expertise of colleagues working within the ageing specialism to assist them in accessing and developing an appropriate range of services to meet their clients' needs. Part of the debate is whether the needs of elderly people with learning disabilities should be met within specialist learning disability provision or whether mainstream services for older people can meet their needs. One of the difficulties can often be that staff in elderly services perceive themselves as not being equipped to meet the needs of people with a learning disability.

Elderly carers: throughout the United Kingdom, a growing number of parents in their seventies and eighties continue to look after a son or daughter with a learning disability – frequently as widows or widowers. Indeed they often become mutually dependent on one another and are often reluctant to separate. Family support services in this instance may need to serve a dual role and requires close co-ordination between services for the elderly and those for learning disability. If residential care becomes necessary for the parent, some services have found placements for both in the one sheltered housing facility, or else the person with the learning disability continues to be supported in the family home. The least preferred option, although sadly still the more common, is for the two to be separated in different residential establishments with few chances to visit one another.

Planning and Providing Services; The Contribution of Social Work

As the previous section illustrates, social work has joined medicine, nursing, psychology and professionals allied to medicine as an essential part of the multidisciplinary approach that is needed in supporting people with a learning disability to lead ordinary lives. In addition, social workers have both a unique function as defined by legislation, as well as particular contributions to make in learning disability services. The two unique contributions are in child protection and assessing, with doctors, the need for detention under mental health legislation. We then describe a number of other contributions which social workers are particularly well placed to make with a particular focus on working with sex offenders.

Developing stronger systems to protect children

With the introduction of the Children Act 1989 (and subsequently the corresponding statutes in Scotland and Northern Ireland) specialist social work teams were formed in many authorities for children with disabilities. When a child protection referral is received concerning a boy or girl with disabilities, particular care must be taken to consult with other specialist workers such as speech and language therapists and psychologists. They can assist the investigation in a number of ways; for example gathering appropriate information; facilitating the participation of those caring for the child and identifying particular ethnic or cultural considerations to be borne in mind.

Partnership working with child protection teams is essential. Substantial preparation time needs to be set aside by the investigating team, so that the child's developmental and communication abilities can be carefully

assessed. It is vital for the social worker to establish that a child has a reliable method of intentional communication and that the interviewer can understand their communication, through an 'interpreter' if necessary. The competency of the interviewer in communicating is the most crucial factor in determining whether a disabled child achieves their potential in the interview.

Social workers are expected to deal with children with disabilities and their families, as they would with other children. These same principles also apply when handling cases of suspected abuse of adults. This means knowing:

- The children's level of understanding of themselves, other people, places and time.
- The child's developmental level in understanding language as well as in expressive language.
- The extent of the child's vocabulary.
- Whether the child has words for body parts and sexual activity.
- The use of non-verbal signals to supplement or to carry meaning.
- The use of augmentative methods of communication such as sign systems.

Mental health admissions

A much higher incidence of mental health problems has been reported among people with learning disabilities, with estimates ranging from 20 per cent to 50 per cent of the adult population (Gravestock, 1999). Whilst there are differences in terms of the legislation and local mental health services across the countries of the United Kingdom, the same range of issues need to be addressed (see Chapter 10).

People with a learning disability can be detained in hospital for assessment, if they are suffering from a mental disorder, the nature and degree of which presents a substantial risk to themselves, and failure to detain them creates a substantial likelihood of serious physical harm to themselves or others.

Approved Social Workers under the Mental Health Act have powers to make an application for their assessment in hospital. They are required to advise patients detained or persons subject to guardianship of the relevant provisions of the Order, its effects and their rights. They also have a duty to consult and advise the patient's nearest relative. The role of the Approved Social Worker is to be both an advocate and a protector of civil rights, although paradoxically they also provide services and can be an employee of the controlling agency.

The social worker making a recommendation will need to consult with those professionally involved in the case, such as the GP or community nurse for learning disability. They must consider other options for giving the patient the care and treatment needed, such as guardianship, admission as a voluntary patient, provision of day care, or outpatient support/treatment, community psychiatric nursing support, primary care support, support from family/friends, relatives and voluntary organisations.

Guardianship

Guardianship is another way of requiring people to attend services in the community. Although it is usually presented as an alternative to hospital admission, there is no reason why it should not be used in aftercare as part of maintenance or rehabilitation programmes. Guardianship can provide an authoritative framework for the services necessary to support the person at home; facilitate an adequate monitoring level of persons in the community; and can assist in affording the person the protection they require. In almost all cases, guardianship is the least restrictive form of intervention that facilitates a planned programme of treatment and care. There is a legal framework provided in the Mental Health Act for reviews of the Order on a six or twelve month basis. One of the difficulties confronting social workers, in the use of guardianship, is that while they can require patients to attend certain services, with a Guardianship Order they cannot compel them to do so.

Working with sex offenders who have a learning disability

People who have a learning disability and who sexually offend are often a forgotten group. Usually they are deemed unfit to plead. Many would have had severely disturbed lives prior to the offence. The help they receive from social services and other professions is variable. Some find their way to prison, some to high or medium secure provision, others are put on probation with condition of treatment and some continue in community placements. Past experience indicates pockets of good practice in the assessment of risk but no coherent approach across the country. These matters require to be addressed by staff of learning disability and forensic services, social services, psychiatrists, probation officers and staff in voluntary organisations. Good social work practice can make a difference to the outcomes. The following two short case vignettes help to identify the type of common offender profile and address the essential elements for their effective care in the community.

Case vignette: John

John is 27 years of age, the eldest child of a family of seven, brought up by maternal grandparents. His mother left home when he was a baby due to excessive drinking. John never had any contact with his father. John, from an early age, had a borderline IQ and was very much seen as anti-social in his behaviour, was very solitary and often played on his own. He was viewed by his local community as the 'village idiot' and was taunted and teased frequently by his peers. He attended mainstream school but was unable to cope very well and was transferred to a special school because of his special needs at sixteen years of age. Prior to his transfer, he began to keep company with local youths involved in petty crime in his neighbourhood and began to abuse alcohol and solvents. During one such occasion, he attacked and sexually assaulted an elderly lady and was admitted to a specialist learning disability hospital on a Hospital Order for a period of assessment and treatment.

Case vignette: Martin

Martin is the second youngest of a family of four children. His father abused alcohol from his early childhood and his siblings experienced scenes of marital disharmony and domestic violence frequently within the home. Martin was sexually abused by an uncle who frequently stayed with the family from the age of six through to eleven years of age, although this did not become apparent until he was seventeen. He attended mainstream primary school, had a low IQ, poor concentration and impaired speech and had a Statement of Special Educational Needs issued at the age of sixteen. Then he was referred to a specialist school that could better meet his special educational needs. Prior to transferring schools, Martin was subjected to bullying within the school and began to play truant on a frequent basis. Social services became involved because he was beyond the control of his parents. He became involved in organised prostitution within his local area. He was charged with gross indecency at 17 years for sexually assaulting a nine year old girl. He was admitted on the fourth condition of a Probation Order to a semi-secure unit where he received specialist assessment and treatment over a four-year period.

During the period of treatment John was offered psychotherapy sessions by his psychiatrist and individual work was undertaken to enable him to cope with his anger and to understand the effect of the offence on his victim. Personal relationships training and social skills training were offered to both men by their social worker. They were also encouraged to join a 'speak-out' group which was run by the nursing and social work staff within the hospital that enabled them to address fears, anxieties and to identify support networks both within and outside the hospital in anticipation of their discharge to the community.

Social workers, and others in the multidisciplinary team, have a key role in ensuring that they follow guidance and protocols in relation to the discharge of detained patients who have sexually abused and in making appropriate aftercare arrangements for patients in the community. In the case of John and Martin this involved:

1. Taking part in a pre-discharge risk management meeting and making a systematic and comprehensive assessment of the patient's health and social care needs and their carers' needs.

2. Social services ensuring good co-ordination and communication between all those involved through shared protocols. Contact points, knowledge of each other's roles, contingency arrangements, needs assessments were made clear and easily understood by all parties.

3. A written action plan was agreed that

included the co-operation by participants in the delivery of various elements of the package of care.

4. Agreeing on the appointment of a key worker, which in both cases was a social worker. Their role was to keep in close contact with the patient, to monitor by contact those delivering the care, ensuring that the agreed programme was given and immediate action was taken with those responsible if the agreed programme of care was not delivered. Close monitoring was required in case of any non co-operation, change of address or disappearance. This included warning those involved in the delivery of the care that in the light of any non co-operation, detention or guardianship would be considered under the Mental Health Act.

These options and the patients' progress were considered and reviewed at agreed regular intervals by the social worker and the multi-disciplinary team involved.

This work is very resource intensive but necessary in order to balance the rights of the person against those of society and to provide opportunities for therapeutic interventions and rehabilitation.

Particular Contribution Made by Social Workers

In this section we describe some areas of work with people with learning disabilities in which social workers have, we feel, a particular contribution to make. This is not to imply that other professionals should be uninvolved but rather that the training and role of social work makes them well placed to undertake these tasks.

Person-centred planning

Person-centred planning is an essential tool that places each person at the centre of the decision making process about service planning and which requires families, carers, friends and professional staff to focus on the aspirations and needs of each person with whom they are in contact. Typically, the group will meet together on a number of occasions with the person to identify their needs and explore ways by which they can by met (Sanderson et al., 1997).

The contribution of social workers lies in their ability to assess needs, make risk assessments, formulate plans, assist in their implementation and evaluate outcomes for service users. This process demands time, resources and requires flexibility from social services management, resulting in a change in the role and function of social workers and social care staff. For example, social workers are more likely to spend time connecting their clients with other people in the community and their working hours often need to be arranged around the help the person needs. Social workers in learning disability latterly have had to learn to support people without controlling them, to be loyal to people without owning them and to open up connections and opportunities 'out there' in the community rather than creating a parallel world within specialist services.

Care management

Many social workers carry a care management role which has much in common with person-centred planning in that it aims to fulfil the themes of co-ordination, cost effectiveness and continuity from the person's perspective rather than from the systems' perspective. Cost effectiveness matters to the person. People want the money that is available to be spent on the things that are most important to them. Co-ordination is about developing a shared understanding of the person's situation and strengthening a shared commitment to support the person as well as

making sure that support and services are scheduled in response to the person's needs rather than those of the system. However care management has not driven change as quickly as some people had hoped (see Chapter 10). The failure of care management to create a change of pattern in service provision has been one of the reasons for the government agreeing to introduce Direct Payments legislation. However, the take up of Direct Payments has been very low for people with a learning disability (Community Care Development Centre, 1999).

Multidisciplinary team working

Social workers are often well placed to take on the co-ordinating role in the multidisciplinary team especially in liaising with family carers and building an on-going relationship with the person with a learning disability. They can ascertain the extent of the family's and person's existing support networks and identify particular gaps. Social workers are often most effective in helping families and clients if they are locally based and have a good working knowledge of local services; for instance knowing the local hairdresser who cuts hair at home, the grocer who delivers orders or a sympathetic home help. This can strengthen the fabric of social life for many families of people with a learning disability.

The emphasis on inter-disciplinary practice has led to shared training opportunities on key issues such as protection of vulnerable adults, child protection and Code of Practice for Special Educational Needs. There is increasingly a move for professionals to share one file, to have a common assessment of need and one review system between residential, day care and fieldwork services. Changing models of primary care services in the community have implications for the work of social workers and also calls for greater involvement with GPs and local commissioning teams in the future.

Protection of vulnerable adults

As detailed in Chapter 7, people with learning disabilities have been subjected to abuse by family members, other service users, staff in services, volunteer helpers and members of the public. Most agencies have now developed a policy regarding the 'Protection of Vulnerable Adults' aimed at preventing abuse by:

- Promoting a multidisciplinary approach to vulnerable adult protection.

- Providing a basis for identifying those in need of protection.

- Outlining the process of intervention.

- Raising awareness among professionals and the public of vulnerable adult abuse.

When an instance of abuse is reported, an inquiry will be undertaken by a designated officer (who may or may not be a social worker). Once this has been completed, a case conference is usually held both to establish any on-going risk to the individual and also to determine the actions required to monitor the safety of individuals or others who may pose a risk to the person with a learning disability. Support to the person with a learning disability is crucial and may need to be on-going over a period of time.

Carer support

A fundamental question for social workers is 'who is the client?' Is it the person with the disability, or their carers – each of whom have individual needs that may at times conflict? As a generalisation, parents may wish their son or daughter to be placed in a protective environment, whereas the person wants to have the same opportunities as their siblings. Balancing these demands is not easy. Helping to reconcile these disputes requires diplomacy and negotiation alongside a careful assessment of risks and the adoption of ways of risk minimisation; for example, in using public transport; undertaking a work placement and in protection from abuse. Engaging families in identifying and implementing training programmes is also an essential factor to successful resolution of disputes.

Belatedly, it has been recognised that carers have needs in their own right. A Northern Ireland survey of carers by Evason and Whittington (1995), found that caring often had a detrimental effect on the physical and mental health of carers. The rights and needs of carers in the UK have been recognised with the introduction of the Carers Recognition and Services Act (1996). However, the legislation falls short in a number of respects. Whilst there is an obligation to assess the carer's needs, this obligation does not extend to the provision of services to meet these needs. Secondly the Act does not fully define what constitutes a substantial amount of care on a regular basis and this has led to differing interpretations of this in different areas.

Liaison with police and role of 'appropriate adult'

Offending behaviour by people with a learning disability is uncommon (1% of the population) and is virtually confined to those with mild/moderate intellectual handicap (Hodgins, 1992). A person with learning disabilities who offends should not automatically enter the penal system and should be assessed and most often dealt with under the current Mental Health legislation. A range of services is required for offenders sentenced by the court and for those who do not reach the courts. Members of the community learning disability teams, probation officers and specialist social workers should work together to make explicit recommendations to the courts regarding such patients (for example in terms of Supervision Orders, Guardianship Orders and Hospital Orders). Specialist social workers in learning disability are often asked to take on the role of *appropriate adult* when a person with a learning disability has been detained and is to be interviewed by the police. Their presence is to ensure fair treatment and to facilitate communication between the investigating officer and the interviewee (Hayes, 1998).

Creating More Effective Social Work Services

In this final section, we explore some of the ways in which social work services could become more effective. At the outset, we admit there is a dearth of studies that provide objective evidence on this issue and urge that practitioners and researchers attend to this with some urgency in the future.

Sharing resources to meet needs

One of the most common difficulties encountered by social workers is the perceived inadequacy of resources available to deliver preventative services that enhance the quality of people's lives. Funding continues to be directed at solving crises (Clegg, 1998). Three actions would produce more cost efficient services:

1. Substantial inputs to children with learning disabilities and their families can provide dividends at a later age and reduce the need for some services into adulthood.

2. Service supports should be built around individual needs and wants rather than individuals being slotted into services.

3. If people with learning disabilities are seen as more similar to than different from people without disabilities then ordinary community services can undertake much of the routine work presently being done in specialists services and avoid duplication of effort.

Integrating health and social care

Recent *Partnership In Action* proposals (Community Care Development Centre, 1999) include the ability to pool budgets to purchase health and social care, transferring commissioning responsibility from one agency to another, and integrating provision. The flexible 'Partnership Approach' is also embodied in centrally driven requirements to be locally developed across agencies (for which 'jointness' is a criterion for funding) and national and local standards by which the performance of authorities will be measured. These are embodied in government initiatives such as Joint Investment Plans, Health Improvement Programmes, the Partnership Grant, National Service Framework and National Priorities Guidance.

However, social workers are employed as part of a complex bureaucratic system designed to disperse public money. Each specialist area is unlikely to produce a difference unless co-ordinated efforts are made to refocus social services. This will involve:

- Joint provision of health and social services which is a reality in Northern Ireland.

- The pooling of budgets under one manager.

- Establishing monitoring systems linked to demonstrating good joint working.

Management of caseloads

The uniqueness of each person requires that social workers employ an individual approach to the person's needs at different stages in the life cycle. This may mean that people do not move on easily and results in more people with a learning disability getting a lesser service. One of the difficulties of working within a specialism is that instead of considering referrals to other agencies such as family therapy, marital counselling and psychotherapy, social workers may try to deal with all difficulties presented to them. This should be tackled in a multifaceted way:

- Specialist social workers need formal supervision aimed at facilitating competent, efficient and accountable practice within achievable time frames.

- Social work managers need to prioritise cases with statutory components over six months duration or if there is any change in the circumstances.

- Explicit referral routes need to be developed between families, primary care teams, education and adult services if users are to access services effectively and efficiently.

Co-ordinated working

Social workers also face a difficulty in maintaining effective interfaces with a range of provider agencies and professionals both in mainstream services and in community agencies. Collaboration between such agencies is however integral to the development of effective support services and partnerships, and to avoid waste and duplication of effort. This is more likely to be achieved if:

- Each professional or service clearly defines its role and responsibilities.

- Adequate structures, processes and protocols are in place to involve each other in inter-agency needs assessment and service delivery.

- The parties demonstrate mutual respect

for each other's contribution and foster good working relationships amongst the professionals involved.

Role of specialist social worker

Since the 1990s, there has been a move to a more specialist focus in social work practice, but this is not well reflected with regard to learning disabilities in social work training or even in Approved Social Work training courses under the Mental Health Act. Only a few days are devoted to covering the many aspects of this specialism. This ambiguity needs to be addressed. We believe there is a role for specialist social work practice in the field of learning disabilities; to fulfil statutory functions, to support family carers and to lead on significant issues such as child protection, person-centred planning and protection of vulnerable adults from abuse. This will require:

- A cadre of suitable mentors and managers being available to nurture this development.

- An explicit commitment by health and social services to recognise this grade of staffing.

- A clear role and focus for community learning disability teams with the experience, leadership skills, expertise and commitment in health commissioning with identified lead roles to encourage partnership working.

Social worker training

The changing nature of learning disability services means that social work training also needs to change. The current changes to social work training with a specific requirement to focus on disability should impact on practice standards and the promotion of good practice. The training should be based around the skills required to meet the needs of clients. However, there is no agreement among social workers on common goals and techniques:

- The profession needs to place greater emphasis on evidence-based practice; determining what generally works and what does not.

- Tutors must have recent and on-going practice experience to share with students.

Joint appointments between services and universities can help achieve this.

- Greater integration of training and opportunities for specialist postgraduate training with other professionals, notably community nursing, is also an essential component for any future direction.

Empowering individuals

Although we come to this last, empowerment is arguably the most crucial development in the new century. This can unlock new resources; make social inclusion more of a reality and ensure that services meet people's needs (Ward, 1998). Social workers have an important role in promoting client empowerment by:

- Listening to the views of people with a learning disability and letting these views directly influence service development.

- Fostering the development of self-advocacy by supporting groups and individuals access to training and support services.

- Encouraging the formation of citizen advocacy schemes in their locality so that volunteer advocates can speak up on their behalf.

- Strengthening and generating informal social networks or circles of support so that people with a learning disability are assisted to integrate and feel part of a local community.

- Finding ways of discharging their statutory duty to care while at the same time taking risks in letting go of the power social workers hold in the planning and implementation of support services for people with a learning disability.

Conclusion

As we move forward in the new century, there is good reason for many organisations and individuals to reflect and feel proud of their achievements in striving for the inclusion of people with a learning disability as the accepted norm.

However, specialist social workers in learning disabilities must not lose sight of the need to think and respond holistically to the needs of people with disabilities. In implementing policies, social workers must ask three questions of themselves and of others involved in planning and delivery of services:

1. What steps are they taking to ensure that people with learning disabilities are truly empowered to participate?

2. What steps are they taking to help users understand issues being discussed and to feel confident that their views will be considered and valued?

3. What opportunities are they making available to help people settle and integrate as full participants of community life?

A number of obstacles still exist in the continued development and implementation of care policies by specialist social workers in the community. Chief amongst these is the tightening of funding which can make new service developments prohibitive. Yet, specialist social workers need to be unequivocal in their commitment to care in the community and continue to push for good quality services. They now have a better view of the type of local service they wish to see. It does not require as much money as we sometimes think. However, it does demand a much better use of the resources we already have and to ensure that there are clear targets and criteria set out to attract new funding. The best resource in learning disability services is the people who are involved in the service, namely the staff, the families and people with a learning disability themselves.

In the past, specialist social workers in learning disabilities tended to focus on accessing services. However, in future they must recognise that they will need to focus more on setting standards and ensuring that the national agenda and priorities include services for people with a learning disability and their carers, and working alongside them to provide additional education, training and support. A key objective should be to define, set and audit service standards that will in turn provide a framework for measuring outcomes and ensure that performance measures reflect specific progress on objectives for services. Learning disability services could swing from a more medically-based responsibility to a social work responsibility but in reality, both inputs are necessary and extant systems do not make this easy to change.

In sum, the specialist social worker will need to be responsive to changing service demands and legislative needs, be accountable in a transparent way for their own practice, while promoting their specialist role within a multidisciplinary context and nurturing best practice through research and staff development.

Further Reading

Department of Health (2001). *Valuing People: A New Strategy for Learning Disability for the 21st Century*. London: HMSO.

Gates, B. (1997). *Learning Disabilities*. Edinburgh: Churchill Livingstone.

Mental Health Foundation (1996). *Building Expectations: Opportunities and Services for People with a Learning Disability*. London: Mental Health Foundation.

Mittler, P. and Sinason, V. (1996). *Changing Policy and Practice for People with Learning Disabilities*. London: Cassell.

Robinson, C. and Stalker, K. (1998). *Growing Up with a Disability*. London: Jessica Kingsley Publications.

Schwartz, D. (1997). *Who Cares? Rediscovering Community*. Oxford: Westview Press.

Chapter 12
Working with Older People to Challenge Ageism
Stephen Pugh

Introduction: Continuity of Provision

Service provision for older people has a long tradition, which in some aspect stretches back into the middle ages. Sheltered accommodation, for example, has its origins with almshouses developed as the church's response to social problems. Equally, workhouses, which were established by the Poor Law (Amendment) Act 1834, can be seen as the origins of residential care for older people. This sense of continuity is important for some users of the services, particularly given that in many instances the physical fabric remained the same pre and post repeal of this Act, as reported by Townsend (1962). Indeed, in 1948 some buildings previously used as workhouses became homes for older people. It must, however, be quickly established that the atmosphere and the environment in which care is currently offered has changed considerably from the workhouses to the current residential care provision.

Continuity of provision has had its implications for both the users of the services and the workers employed to deliver the service. For some of the current and potential users of residential care, the historical backdrop is very real as memories are still held of the workhouses; the type of care which was offered and the stigma that resulted from admission into the workhouse. The current influences of these memories come into play strongly at the point that residential care may be seen as an appropriate resource to access. In many instances, whilst a needs-led assessment may well conclude that residential care is an appropriate outcome for a given situation, memories held from early adult life, of the workhouse, can have a considerable influence on the decision whether or not to accept such a service.

The continuity argument may suggest that those who work with older people have not been particularly innovative in their approach to service development. However, this is not the case, as we will see in this chapter, enormous strides have been made to improve existing service provision and to develop new approaches to practice.

Working with Older People: Perceptions and Values

An essential prerequisite for social work practice with older people is that the practice must be built upon fundamental elements, in particular, of respect, honesty, validation, choice and openness. Working with adults requires the use of skills associated with negotiation, conflict resolution and on occasions, managing difficult and seemingly intractable situations. A prerequisite for good practice is an understanding of ageism as a system of oppression; the importance of rights as incorporated into practice; the significance of past events in understanding the present and finally how the person has lived their life – a biographical approach to practice. These are explored in detail below.

Ageism

Ageism as a system of oppression has only recently been acknowledged and was defined by Butler (1987) as:

> ...a process of systematic stereotyping of, and discrimination against, people because they are old, just as racism and sexism accomplish this for skin colour and gender.
>
> (Butler, 1987: p22.)

The stereotyping which is a product of oppression assumes that every older person has the same characteristics and they are thereby treated as a member of a homogenous group who all have the same needs, wishes and aspirations. Older people are seen to have characteristics, which are exhibited by all in the group and more importantly recognised by everybody else (i.e. they are forgetful, are slow, they live in the past!). Being old is presented as a condition that should be avoided.

As a result of these generalisations and the assumption that often operates that all older people are the same, we, as a society, are guilty of grouping together people whose ages may be forty years or more apart, all of which is based upon a socially constructed age transition – retirement. At no other point in the life span do we undertake such a grouping. We would not for example assume that the needs of a 15 year old are the same as a 55 year old. This is however, viewed as legitimate practice in all service areas responding to the needs of older people.

As an illustration of this point, if we look at the differences in life events between two fictional people, one of whom is currently aged 100 years and the other aged sixty years, there is a phenomenal difference between these two individuals. Consider the following life histories: the 100 year old was born in 1902 – one year after the death of Queen Victoria. They were aged twelve at the outbreak of the First World War and sixteen at its close. It is likely that in some way, the war touched their life. Through the 1920s they themselves were in their twenties and probably started their family. They were bringing their family up through the 1930s and the great depression and were aged thirty-six years at the outbreak of the Second World War. It is likely that they saw some form of compulsory service during the war and would have been aged forty-three years at the end of hostilities. They retired (given that due to differential mortality rates, this is likely to be a woman) in 1962 at the age of sixty years.

This fictional person has lived in retirement for forty-two years, through the swinging sixties, through the seventies and the Thatcher period. They have seen changes which are incredible; flight, disease control, changes in quality of life and the advent of the mobile phone amongst others.

In contrast, the person currently aged sixty years was born in 1942, was aged three years at the close of the Second World War and probably had their family in the 1960s just as the other person was retiring. They are likely to have been at work during the Thatcher years and probably only retired a couple of years ago; alternatively, they may still be at work. These two fictional people's life stories are so very different, but because they have both crossed an age related transition – retirement, we regard them as the same or at best very similar and expect the same services to meet their needs.

Ageism is a pervasive system of oppression, but this on its own cannot provide a complete explanation of the situation in which older people are placed. The concepts of 'jeopardy' and 'multiple jeopardy' may assist in providing

a broader understanding of the day-to-day reality of the lives of older people. In describing the situation of older black people who are living in a second homeland, Norman (1985) has used the term 'triple jeopardy'. She comments:

> They are not merely in double jeopardy by reason of age and discrimination…but in triple jeopardy. At risk because they are old, because of the physical conditions and hostility under which they have to live, and because services are not accessible to them.
>
> (Norman, 1985: p1.)

This approach identifies the existence of multiple systems of oppression, which intersect and have differing emphases as individual lives are being lived. For example, an older lesbian may experience oppression related to her age whilst out shopping and in doing so, she may overhear a pejorative conversation about same sex relationships and feel uncomfortable about the tone of the conversation given her own sexuality. If this woman was black or experienced a disability, she may equally encounter direct hostility related to her skin colour or her disability. In this respect, this particular older woman's life has been affected negatively by ageism, homophobia, racism and disability oppression at different times as she conducted her day (Pugh, 2002).

In terms of social work with older people, it is vitally important that practitioners do not incorporate expressions of ageism into their practice. This entails viewing older people positively, as individuals with a past and a future, with strengths as well as difficulties. Of equal importance in practice is the challenge to ageism thus ensuring that appropriate resources are accessed and not denied by such statements as 'what do you expect at your age?'.

Hughes (1995) identifies the elements or constituents of anti-ageist practice as being:

- *Empowerment:* the process and outcome of practice should be aimed at changing the relative power between the older person, professionals, family if necessary and other significant people to ensure that the older person continues to have, or acquires, control over their own life and all that goes with power and control – freedom, autonomy, dignity and feelings of personal self-worth.

- *Participation:* the meaningful sharing with, and involvement of, the older person in practice is both a key principle in its own right as well as a means of demonstrating commitment to empowerment.

- *Choice:* the ability to make choices and to determine as far as one can the outcome of events is an important means of personal validation, as well as a right in terms of personhood and citizenship.

- *Integration:* as far as possible, people seem to want to live in mixed communities and not segregated with people with whom they might share one particular characteristic. Celebrating old age as a valid point on the continuum of life, and not a separate, different end phase, means integrating older people into the mainstream of life at every level.

- *Normalization:* involves making available whatever is necessary to enable old people to carry on living in the same way, with the same or better quality of life as other people in society.

(Hughes, 1995: p47.)

Whilst Hughes (1995) asserts that this represents an expression of anti-ageist practice, the reality is of course that the elements outlined above form part of anti-oppressive practice and should be integral to all social workers. What is missing in this listing is the need to challenge ageist language – such as the use of the term 'the elderly' and ageist attitudes. Challenging ageism features in Standard One of the National Service Framework for Older People (2001). Given the need for an anti-ageist service response, it becomes somewhat anachronistic that we have in fact service provision for older people at all! Surely, anti-ageist social work would require the dissolution of service provision, which is based on age. A more recent trend has in fact resulted in the establishment of 'adult' teams which do away with these age related service definitions.

Moreover, social work with older people is, on the whole, social work with older women. As such, additional concerns of gender become an integral part of social work practice. This therefore has to reflect both the current experience of being an older woman as well as the influence of cohort effects based on gender. The issue of power becomes an important feature of social work with all older people but in particular older women especially when this is focussed upon gender issues.

Significant and past events

The influence of a 'life lived', of seventy or eighty years of living is and should be, a very important aspect of working with older people. This reflects how the person has coped with life events; marriage, children and death and how the individual older person may be responding to their current situation. The memories of the past can be particularly important when we consider that it was not until the enactment of the National Assistance Act 1948 that the Poor Law was repealed. People who are currently in their eighties were in their thirties when this legislation was enacted.

The shared experience of cohorts is particularly important when exploring issues pertinent to older people. On a broader scale, historic national and international events, which have impacted on groups of people, can be referred to as *cohort affects*. As an example, the post war settlement of the late 1940s – the Welfare State – promised 'cradle to grave' state support for the individual: thus the state was involved in providing health care, employment, education, housing, income support and social services. This settlement becomes a cohort effect because, quite simply it affected all the cohorts who were part of it. Images of paying into a system when at work through taxation and national insurance and drawing upon that accumulated reserve are powerful. Strictly speaking, this imagery is inaccurate, but the ideas have left a clear sense of obligations, which are a reflection of this cohort effect. Later cohorts, post the late 1980s have seen a very different culture and therefore expectations of the state's involvement in their lives. This of course reflects the political ideology of the Conservative government, which had made substantial inroads in to dismantling aspects of the Welfare State under the auspices of freeing the individual from the 'Nanny State'.

In attempting to understand this effect in more detail, Ryder notes that 'each cohort has a distinctive composition and character reflecting the circumstances of its unique origination and history' (Ryder, 1965: p845). Jacobs provides a definition of the cohort effect, which is 'distinct political and economic experiences (which) separate generations and have lasting impact' (Jacobs, 1990: p350).

A further complication to this notion arises from the concept of 'period effects', which 'emerge from the major events that shape the lives of persons who experience them' (Morgan and Kunkel, 1998: p39). For example, the virulence of tuberculosis before mass immunisation gave rise to particular services, such as open access x-ray units and sanatoria. At the time, this anti-TB measure affected all cohorts and represents a period effect. However, mass immunisation has confined this affect to medical and social history, but represents real memories for those who were affected.

As a further example, it is only recently that older lesbians and gay men have begun to be recognised. Reflecting on the impact of cohort effects on this group of people we need to understand the dominant attitudes towards same sex relationships fifty years ago and perhaps even further into the past. Sex between men was criminalized with severe sanctions until the enactment of the Sexual Offences Act 1967. This had the result that many gay men lived with aspects of their lives hidden or entered heterosexual relationships in the belief that this was *normal* and in which they could avoid public scrutiny. Whilst criminal sanctions were imposed on gay men, lesbians, who were not subjected to the same legislation, were faced with very severe social sanctions and may have lost custody and contact with their children because of their sexuality.

This atmosphere of sanction, fear and extortion patently would have affected both lesbians and gay men as they grew up. Such pressures necessarily influenced how the individual lesbian and gay man viewed themselves and how they interacted with other lesbians, gay men and heterosexuals. This deep secret was after all so important with such severe consequences that it must never become known. The atmosphere prior to the late 1960s on the whole viewed lesbians and gay men as perverted and unnatural, thus many gay men and lesbians were both individually and by association, labelled as 'sick by doctors, immoral by clergy, unfit by the military, and a menace by the police' (Kochman, 1997: p2).

Given this, lesbians and gay men had, because they had to, constructed lives that reflected their own circumstances. Lee (1989) identifies two solutions for gay men before the changes in legislation. The first was to marry and possibly

to conduct same sex relationships in secret with an expectation of never living with a lover. The other solution was to remain single with the air of asexuality or disinterest in sex, which by its nature was less of a threat and thereby facilitated the acceptance of the individual gay man. In family histories, how many uncles and great uncles remained bachelors thereby hiding their gay sexuality (Pugh, 2002).

These examples of cohort and period affects are very real and continue to influence older people's lives today in the manner in which life events are viewed and sometimes how particular issues are understood. Social work with older people must therefore, as part of its specialist knowledge, acknowledge the impact of these affects on the current situations in which older people are placed. One aspect of this is how the social worker presents themselves to the older person. As an example, a social worker who exudes heterosexuality through images and discussion may not be trusted with personal information by an older lesbian or gay man who has had to live their early adult life in fear of being 'discovered' and being careful about how others react to them. As a result, social work with older people needs to explore and assess the present as influenced by the past.

Understanding the past and how it informs the present and the future – cohort and period effects – is in essence the cornerstone of the *biographical approach* to practice. This identifies that older people have experienced different careers in their lives which allows for the process of ageing to be viewed '...as a complex of strands running for various lengths of time throughout the biography and moulding its biography' (Johnson, 1976: p109).

The implications for social work practice, as Johnson (1976) argues, are that care would be planned with older people and not done to them. It would also prevent the assessment of the older person being made from the standpoint of the professional and therefore encourage the recognition of remaining capabilities and strengths as opposed to just the identification of problems. Johnson (1976) goes on to comment:

> *Only within (the) context of personal priorities is it reasonable for professional helpers of any sort to impose major changes on the lives of older people. Hospitalization, for example, should only be offered along with realistic estimates of outcomes so that the individual may choose. So often, the condition is preferable than the 'cure'...*
>
> (Johnson, 1976: p111.)

In reference specifically to mental health problems in later life, Johnson (1988) goes on to comment that:

> *Like fingerprints, life histories are individual and unique. They are influenced by the common experiences of their cohort contemporaries…and the prevailing pressures of culture, fashion, politics and social order. Yet, within this framework of external structures, each life is significantly different from all others. When 'helpers' enter the lives of elderly (sic) people to deal with behavioural changes, which might be represented as disorders, it is this uniqueness that must provide the backcloth to assessment and assistance.*
>
> (Johnson, 1988: p141-2.)

It is in this last comment of Johnson's that the importance of cohort effects and the biographical approach for social workers working with older people rests. Knowledge of critical events and their impact on the individual older person becomes part of the skills base of specialist social work with older people. Moreover, reflecting on how the social worker views the older person and how they then assist them becomes essential in practice. Brian Gearing identifies this in the commentary on Hughes (1995) work. Older people are seen as:

> *…citizens, first and foremost, rather than consumers. Her (Hughes) 'fundamental values', which provide a foundation for principles and practice, are personhood (older people are people first and old second), celebration (of age), and citizenship. Arising from this value position is her (Hughes) advocacy of a professional model, rather than an administrative model.*
>
> (Hughes, 1995: pix.)

The approach adopted by social workers working with older people is vitally important and is part of the claim to specialist knowledge and practice. Viewing the older person as a person in their own right and as an equal begins to establish a relationship based on trust and honesty; a relationship that recognises both the influence of the past and how that person has coped as part of the present. To do otherwise is to reinforce ageism and in some respect change the older person in to a commodity, rather than someone with whom one works.

The re-emergence of a specialism

The re-emergence of specialist social work with older people began in the late 1980s and early 1990s and coincided with the development and recognition of practices, which reflected the particular circumstances of such work with older people. This culminated with the implementation of the National Health Service and Community Care Act 1990. The Act had both fiscal and practice elements, as access to social security benefits to pay for residential care were withdrawn but in practice terms, the Act enshrined into legislation what had become accepted as good social work practice.

The assertion of specialist knowledge and practice requirements whilst being seen as a reaction to the dominance of working with children in social services departments did not in itself provide parity of status in working with older people. In a parallel with the health service, social work with older people was viewed as a Cinderella area staffed by either failed childcare workers or by people who intrinsically could not work with the stresses of children and family services.

Demographic factors have also played their part in the re-emergence of specialist working with older people as the population aged and in particular, the numbers of people in very late life increased significantly. Differing mortality rates between men and women have the result that overall the experience of very late life is in fact the experience of women. Arber and Ginn (1995) identified this demographic effect as the 'feminisation of late life'. The practical result is that much of social work with older people is in fact social work with older women.

Social work with older people pre-1993

Before 1993, legislation concerning social work with older people was fragmented and issue related. Thus, some aspects of the National Assistance Act 1948 remained in use, such as:

- Part III of the Act established local consent to run residential care homes.

- Section 46 involved provisions for the compulsory removal and detention of older people in particular circumstances.

- Section 47 provided a requirement to protect the moveable property of anyone admitted to hospital (including pets).

The Chronic Sick and Disabled Persons Act 1970 also provided a base for aspects of social work with older people. However, overall the absence of a parallel to the comprehensive legislation that is the Children Act 1989 had a number of consequences. The first of which was the variable nature of social work practice with older people, which was made even more complex by changes in the social security legislation related to the payment of fees for residential care. The fragmentation of legislation has meant that social workers working with older people have required a detailed and broad understanding of the law. This necessarily includes an appreciation of how an adult is viewed by legislators, which has in turn informed the nature of legislation, and the presumptions, which lie behind this. This knowledge base represents a further reinforcement of the specialist knowledge that is required by social workers working with older people.

The Griffiths Report (1988) identified that the then arrangements for payment of residential care fees represented 'a perverse incentive for residential care'. In reality, it had become easier for social workers to direct older people into residential care than to assist them to make arrangements to be supported at home.

Care management, an import from North America, was seen as the process by which multiple inputs of care could be managed and co-ordinated. The emphasis on needs-led assessments as opposed to service driven assessments was becoming increasingly influential. No longer could social workers fit the service user to existing service provision, and hope for a good match, instead the person had to be assessed to reflect their individual needs and then services engaged to meet these needs. However, Cohen and Fisher (1988) maintained that care managers did not have to be social workers; moreover, that social workers were not the most suitable professionals to undertake this role. This comment echoes in some respect the issues raised at the end of this chapter about what it is that social work can bring to the care of older people. In practice, the number of unqualified assessors increased, although it could be argued that many of these assessors were present prior to the enactment of the Act as domiciliary care assessors.

Another practice development arose from the recognition that older people were set in families and had relationships with others upon whom they may depend on for their care. The influence of carers and their needs eventually led to the Carers (Recognition and Services) Act 1996.

Having recognised that older people were no longer excluded from having personal relationships and that they were a part of dynamic systems, it was inevitable that the potential for the abuse of older people within these systems was established. Whilst there is no comprehensive adult protection legislation, this process did culminate in the Department of Health document *No Secrets* (2000) (for more detail see Chapter 7). It is not the intention of this work to review the literature, which exists related to the abuse of older people, although it should be noted that there is a considerable literature on this topic (Biggs et al., 1995; Pritchard, 1999; Pugh, 1996).

Social work with older people post-1993

April 1993 saw the full implementation of the National Health Service and Community Care Act 1990. This move was long awaited as the government had vacillated about which agency was to take lead responsibility for the community care aspects of the Act. The Act contained both financial and practice elements and represented a readjustment of the balance in the care of older people between the state and the family with the emphasis being moved towards the later. For example, from April 1993, access to social security budgets, which were being used to pay for residential care fees for older people was removed. No longer could older people enter residential care with the expectation that the state would pay the fees without first having an assessment of their needs and that their identified needs suggested that such resources were appropriate. The accompanying government rhetoric emphasised that the support of older people in their own homes as the desired objective of older people themselves.

Most importantly, the new legislative framework required a split between service assessment and service provision (the purchaser/provider split). This was seen as essential by government, providing a structural prerequisite to enable social workers to develop the skills required to undertake needs-led assessments (as required by Section 47(1) of the Act). This arrangement also established the management of care that was required to enable older people to live in their own homes. Hence, the post-1993 reforms represented a significant change in practice as social workers became used to a different approach to assessment and different organisational arrangements as local authorities were given responsibility to develop a market in social care. As a direct consequence, local authority residential care provision has become increasingly rare, as such establishments were either sold off or moved into not-for-profit trusts and home care support was increasingly purchased from a variety of private and not-for-profit organisations.

Current Debates

There are a number of policy and practice debates about social work with older people. First, concern has been expressed about the current *cost of care* at a time when the absolute numbers of older people are still rising. The Sutherland Report (1999) explored a number of options to pay for both nursing and residential care of older people concluding that:

● *Long-term care is a risk that is best covered by some kind of risk pooling…*

● *Private insurance will not deliver what is required at an acceptable cost, nor does the industry want to provide that degree of coverage.*

● *The most efficient way of pooling risk, giving the best value to the nation as a whole, is through services underwritten by general taxation, based on need rather than wealth.*

● *A hypothecated unfunded social insurance fund would not be appropriate. a prefunded scheme would constitute a significant lifetime burden for young people…*

● *The answer lies in improvement in state provision…the elements of care which relate to living costs and housing should be met from people's income and savings, subject to means testing…while the special costs of what we call 'personal care' should be met by the state.*

(The Sutherland Report, 1999: pxviii.)

The overall cost of care is set to continue to rise. In Scotland the cost for the individual is very different to that for older people living in England and Wales.

Whilst the National Health Service and Community Care Act 1990 has changed the basis upon which some of these costs have been derived, in terms of current practice, the same constraints are placed upon the service response to the needs of older people.

Second, the debates around the relationship of health and social care provision for older people, which surround *joint working with the health service*. The establishment of differing organisational arrangements for the health service; trusts, community health trusts, have thrown in to the debate the relationship between social work and health provision. Various reports have suggested differing organisational arrangements with the lead being placed within a health service context. Almost fifty years ago, the Guillebaud Report (1956) recommended, primarily on efficiency grounds and the needs of older people, that welfare departments should be assimilated into the health department. Similarly, the Herbert Report (1960) commented:

> *…in view of the fact that so high a proportion of the work of the health department and all its branches in a county or county borough is concerned with the domiciliary care of older people, it is only logical and sensible that the health and welfare departments should be combined, with perhaps separate sub-committees looking after the residential homes and needs of the handicapped.*

(Herbert Report, 1960: p213-4.)

During the 1960s, the assumed primacy in the delivery of care, The Gillie Report (1963) suggested that: the family doctor was best placed to 'mobilise and co-ordinate the health and welfare services' (Gillie Report,1963: p9). with the help of the domiciliary team of workers, which the preventative service can supply (Gillie Report, 1963: p38). Recent debates have brought issues of joint working between the health service and social services to the fore again. The emergence of primary health care trusts and such standards documents as the *National Service Framework for Older People* (2001) have placed a dynamic on the process of joint working which could finally result in organisational change. NSF (2001) *Standard 2 – Person Centered Care*, may be the instrument of change.

Social work with older people – organisationally may as a consequence be located within health service structures. The question that needs to be asked therefore, is what do social workers bring to the care of older people that is unique to social work? If as seems likely, assessments are to be undertaken jointly, the skills associated with assessment are not unique to social workers and these skills can obviously be learnt by other professionals. Social work could make a claim for this uniqueness based on experience of community provision and in particular risk assessment and the management of risk. As long ago as 1950, a leader in the journal *The Medical Officer* stated:

> *If health visitors can be adequately trained and be recruited in sufficient numbers we can think of no more suitable persons for the visitation of the aged, not only because they are best fitted to assist in the prevention of disasters which at present unfortunately afflict too many in late life, but also because the employment of one nurse in the district for all preventative health service is a sensible and economic way of securing adequate visitation without multiplication of visitors.*
>
> (*The Medical Officer*, 1950, Leader on The Aged in Hospital and at Home 15 July: p26.)

Hence, social workers may be vulnerable to having part of their current functions performed by health professionals. Traditionally, the employment status (being employed by the local authority) and the educational background of social workers has enabled them, in the interface with health professionals, to advocate for service users within the context of the dominance of the medical model and the power of doctors.

The current government's objectives of modernising and improving the quality of public services has resulted in such initiatives as Best Value, Performance Assessment Framework and the establishment of the National Commission for Care Standards.

The result has been increased scrutiny and management of public provision through the establishment of a series of national minimum standards. An example of this is care homes for older people: national minimum standards (2001) issued through Section 23(1) of the Care Standards Act 2000.

The concept of 'Best Value' was introduced through a White Paper in 1998 (DETR, 1998) and the Local Government Act 1999. These required local authorities to consult and engage with local communities, set targets for continuing improvement and introduce competition in the delivery of public services whilst undertaking reviews of public services every five years. A number of principles were established within the Best Value framework to assist the review of service provision. These being:

- challenge
- compare
- consult
- compete

Local councils have been required, since April 2000, to develop Best Value performance plans and to review all their services over a five-year period applying Best Value principles (Department of Health, CI 2002: p2). This has been translated into a number of indicators of performance for the year 2002/3 which include:

- **BV52:** cost of intensive social care for adults and older people by reference to the average gross weekly cost of providing care for adults and elderly people.

- **BV53:** intensive home care per 1,000 population aged 65 and over.

- **BV54:** older people helped to live at home per 1,000 population aged 65 or over.

(DTLR, 2002.)

In a broader context, the Performance Assessment Framework, first published in consultation in 1999 (Department of Health, 1999) is part of the modernising agenda for social services, which was issued a year earlier (Department of Health, 1998). The Performance Assessment Framework (PAF) establishes and requires information to be collated from differing sources that then enables a review of the performance of each social service department. This process equally involves Social Service Inspectorate inspections (SSI) and joint reviews with the Audit Commission all exploring the performance of social service departments. This process has led in May 2002 to the publication of a star rating of individual social services.

Best Value, performance assessment, SSI inspections and joint reviews, have all changed the environment in which social work with older people is undertaken. The result is that in many ways core activities are in danger of becoming a commodity rather than a process. The obvious example here is that of the social work assessment which is described by Coulshed and Orme (1998) as an on-going process. The collection of performance data has the ability to turn the assessment into an event which is measurable and that has a clear and definable ending. Whilst this facilitates the ability to compare the performance of social service department and individual social workers, it does not provide a great insight in to the quality of the interaction with the service user.

The establishment of the National Commission for Care Standards was first highlighted in

Modernising Social Services (Department of Health, 1998) and was finally established in April 2002 with the enactment of the Care Standards Act 2000. The Commission brings, under one management structure, the individual health and local authority inspection units in England with similar structures in Wales, Scotland and Northern Ireland.

The Commission, with its new legislative framework, the Care Standards Act 2000, aims to apply a consistent approach to the inspection and regulation of many care services with the objective of improving services through the application of national minimum standards.

The outcomes for the users of the services, for individual older people, it is hoped will be an improvement in the quality of the services which is applied consistently across the country. Whilst these frameworks are busily trying to achieve their objectives, it is difficult to assess exactly what impact these will have and whether they will indeed result in a raising of standards.

There have been some notable absences from the national policy debates.

First, the nature and lack of adequate provision for black older people has been identified in the work of a number of researchers and commentators (see for example, Ahmed and Atkin, 1996; Blakemore and Boneham, 1994). The needs of black older people were highlighted and prompted a rethink of the nature of service provision and a critical review of the context of white European services.

Second, lesbian and gay older people in some respects have suffered a similar absence from the policy and practice agenda. In social gerontology, issues related to lesbian and gay older people have not featured in any of the major texts, although interestingly there is substantial literature available. Equally, the power of ageism is such that all older people are viewed as asexual and therefore sexuality is not an issue of concern for practitioners. When sexuality is recognised, on the whole, this is pathologised. The assumption is of heterosexuality.

Key Issues in Working with Older People

Contract culture

The emergence of a *contract culture*, post implementation of the 1990 Act, has brought social workers into contact with the commercial and financial reality of care provision for older people. Hence, social workers are now involved in monitoring contract compliance. This requires the social worker to review how the care package is working and whether the contracted organisation is providing the care that is required to support that older person as specified in the contract. Large sums of money can be involved in individual or block contracts. Social workers must avoid being influenced to provide a particular agency with contracts with the possibility of financial rewards. Many local authorities are currently employing reviewing and monitoring officers to review the care in residential settings or in the person's own home. Hence, a different person reviews the situation, the benefit of which is the independence of approach.

Home support or residential care

If the cost of support in the home exceeds that of residential care then the institutional option becomes the most cost effective way of supporting the older person. In contrast, home support packages for younger adults can cost many hundreds of pounds. This does establish a tension between the costs of supporting older people and that of younger adults even if the presenting problem is the same. This highlights issues of equal rights and the practice of agencies in the light of Standard 1 of the National Service Framework for Older People and the challenge to ageism.

The existence and widespread acceptance of residential care as an option to meet the needs of older people, can be seen as having a significant impact on the cost of other service outcomes. In contrast, residential care for younger adults is much less easily accessed and as a result has less of an impact on the overall cost of care for this group.

The nature of support in the home, which reflected the needs of the individual became more difficult as costs increased, the free market developed and much greater emphasis was placed on new styles of management and unit costing of care. Particular 'blockages' were identified which became crucial decision making points in continued care at home. Initially, the cost of support through the night became the issue, which determined whether care could be continued to be offered at home within safe parameters. As this was overcome the provision and cost of equipment became the issue that in particular focussed on hoists.

Rights based social work with older people

Social work with older people is in part a reflection of the absence of a comprehensive legislative framework and in part because this involves working with adults. As a result, social work with older people has had to acknowledge and respond to the issues of *rights* long before the Human Rights Act 1998. Although in common usage is the idea of 'putting' someone in a home, such a move, on the whole, cannot be undertaken without the consent of the person concerned.

Rights based social work would have at its core the issue of consent. This would necessarily involve the worker undertaking an assessment *with* the person concerned; sharing that assessment and outlining the options and risks concerned. Such an approach equally involves working at least with consensus and at best in partnership with all those involved.

Working with Other Specialists

As specialist knowledge developed so further areas of sub-practice have developed. One such area is dementia services and promoted through the establishment of dementia teams in some authorities. Mental health services have at times reflected ageist attitudes vis-à-vis compulsory admission and the reluctance to enforce legislation based on an assessment of need. Equally, such service provision has been dominated by the organic, dementia, to the detriment of people who experience functional mental illness. As a result, mental health service provision was based on the idea that being old and having mental health problems meant dementia. Very little acknowledgement has been given to the idea that people who have functional mental illnesses in earlier life do age and that equally a depressive illness can occur in late life. Sub-specialist teams within the general field of social work practice can in part address some of these difficulties.

The need for specialist social work with older people

Given the pessimistic discussion outlined above, the question that we need to ask, 'is whether

social work with older people has any future?' The answer to this question lies with existing practitioners and academics who need to establish a very clear remit for social work and a clear understanding of what it can bring to the care of older people. In this debate, we cannot rely on social work having a role based on inertia or the establishment of a role by picking up the tasks that are not wanted by other professionals. Equally, we can rely on potential overload of other professionals such as nurses who amongst other processes are taking on additional tasks that have traditionally been undertaken by doctors.

The claim to specialist knowledge which has been outlined in this work – of understanding how the past informs the present and the future, knowledge of the law, of being with older people, is a start in this process. The approach that social work can bring to the care of older people relates to the different influences in understanding the situation in which an older person is placed. This is partially informed by the education and training of social workers, the adoption of a social model, but equally seeing potential so that older people can have choices and thereby own the outcomes.

The existing roles of enabling, advocating, standards monitoring and presenting a challenge to ageism whilst forming part of the functions of other professionals should become the raison d'être of social work with older people. These need to be seized and trumpeted by the profession or be damned by its own inaction.

The other question that needs to be asked at this point is whether older people themselves want social workers. This is a large area to develop and not the remit of this work but the answer would make interesting reading and reflection.

Further Reading

Andrews, M. (1999). The Seductiveness of Agelessness. *Ageing and Society*, 19: p301-18.

Arber, S. and Ginn, J. (1995). *Connecting Gender and Ageing*. Buckingham: OU Press.

Hughes, B. (1995). *Older People and Community Care: Critical Theory and Practice*. Buckingham: OU Press.

Means, R., Morbey, H. and Smith, R. (2000). *From Community Care to Market Care?* Bristol: Policy Press.

Chapter 13

Making Links Across Specialisms: Education, the Panacea for Good Practice?

Jan Horwath and Steven M. Shardlow

Specialist – a man (sic) who knows more and more about less and less.

(Cited by Charles Mayo in Modern Hospital, 1938.)

Gender specific language in original.

Introduction

As social workers grapple with complex policy and practice developments in their particular field, there is a danger that they become the type of specialist described by Mayo, *knowing ever more about less and less*. Yet, as highlighted throughout this book, better outcomes for service users are dependent on practitioners working effectively across social work specialisms. Hence, the task for the educator is to reverse Mayo's dictum and to enable social work specialists to learn *more and more* about more and more. The benefits of education across specialisms are similar to the benefits of interprofessional education, as identified by Barr et al., (1999). These include: establishing a common knowledge and value base; increased motivation to collaborate; a change in attitudes through countering prejudice and challenging stereotypes; and developing collaborative relationships. However, if the benefits described above are to be achieved, educators and operational managers must first recognise and address the problems of education across specialisms. These problems can arise for a number of reasons. First, workers may differ in their perceptions of education and its relevance across specialisms. Second, social workers may be resistant to education beyond their own specialist area of practice. Third, the specialist educator may consider they are ill equipped to educate across specialisms. In the first part of this chapter, we explore these issues in detail. In the second half of the chapter, we provide exercises that can be used and adapted for joint education of different social worker specialists.

Organisational Perceptions of Education

Professional education in social work organisations is sometimes treated as an entity in its own right, separated from organisational structures, policies and procedures. Something rarefied, almost as if distilled from other organisational components. Hence, a common response to the introduction of new guidance (such as, that emanating from the Department of Health) or the resolution of practice problems within an organisation is to provide educational programmes (see for example, Buckley and Caple, 1995). Such education may be appropriate both in raising the awareness of practitioners and managers about practice developments and also in helping to develop their knowledge, values and skills. However, whatever the quality, education alone is often insufficient of itself to change practice. Therefore, facilitators[1] and operational managers need to consider whether better outcomes for service users can be achieved through staff development alone, or whether operational changes are also required. For example, in order to work effectively with service users who have been affected by domestic violence, social workers need to recognise the impact domestic violence can have on individuals – this can be learnt through education. However, social workers also require practice guidance as to their role, once they have identified domestic violence – an operational responsibility. If such operational components are not in place the facilitator can adopt a facilitation role, by working with senior managers to identify organisational changes needed to provide the framework for practice.

Unfortunately, not all facilitators are in a position where education and staff development are clearly linked to operational

---

1. We have used the term 'facilitator' throughout this chapter to describe those employed in staff development units, educators who work within organisations to facilitate the learning of employees.

services. Stickland (1992) uses a continuum to describe the different relationships that may exist between an education unit and senior operational managers. These different types of relationship may also exist within organisations, between specialist facilitators and the senior managers for specific services. The continuum proposed by Stickland has been adapted to show these different types of relationship in Figure 13.1

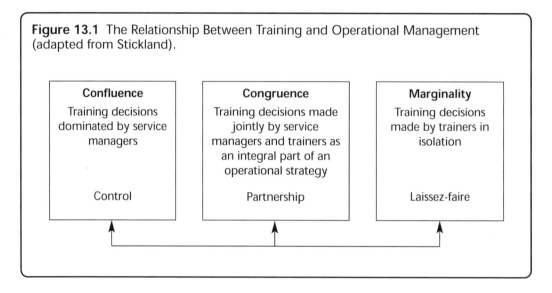

Figure 13.1 The Relationship Between Training and Operational Management (adapted from Stickland).

Stickland refers to *confluence* existing at one end of the continuum. In this situation, education is incorporated into service management, where the message given to the facilitator by operational managers is 'do what I say'. Hence, the operational managers are in control. For example, new guidance is introduced for use when assessing home care services for older people. Senior managers of the service decide exactly what education to provide, to whom, and give a specific brief to the facilitator who is knowledgeable about work with older people. Stickland refers to *marginality* at the other end of the continuum. In this position, the facilitator is remote from organisational systems and can 'get on with it' with no direction from operational managers who have a laissez-faire attitude towards education. Using the example above, managers may decide to either provide information sessions on the guidance themselves or leave the facilitator to ascertain what if any education is relevant for staff. Stickland, refers to the mid-point of the continuum as *congruence*. In this situation, education is an integral part of the operational strategy. Facilitators 'work together' in partnership with operational managers. In the case of education to use the new guidance for assessing home care services for older people, the facilitator and senior managers would incorporate the education strategy into an operational implementation plan.

The continuum shown in Table 13.1 above has been discussed in terms of the relationship between facilitators and the operational managers for one specialist service. Relationships become more complex when facilitators and operational managers make links across specialisms. For example, facilitators from two agencies or services may come together to deliver education. Each facilitator may have a different relationship with the operational managers for their particular service. For example, one facilitator may work with operational managers who are controlling while the other may work with managers who want to work in partnership. These differing relationships between facilitators and operational managers can have a significant impact on the role of facilitators working across specialisms as shown in case example 1.

Case example 1

Facilitator A specialises in mental health education. The mental health operational managers have a controlling approach to education. These managers have concerns arising from a 'Best Value Review', that staff within the service do not meet the needs of people who are learning disabled and have psychotic conditions. The operational managers believe the quality of service could be improved, if staff from both mental health services and also services for adults with disabilities received joint education. These managers become the driving force for an education initiative. They liaise with managers from disability services and they outline the course aims, objectives and education content. They give facilitator A a very specific brief, making clear that they expect facilitator A to provide the education. They have negotiated with operational managers, from services for adults with disabilities, that facilitator B who specialises in education about learning disability will deliver the education with facilitator A. Facilitator B works with operational managers who take a laissez-faire approach to education. The idea of joint education had not occurred to them before they were approached by the managers from mental health services. However, mindful of the 'Best Value Review' they go along with the education initiative. The managers from disability services leave facilitator B to decide who should attend the education, the education aims and objectives and the course content. In this situation, the facilitators are in a position where the clarity of the education specification of the mental health operational managers is likely to dominate the design and delivery of the education programme.

Table 13.1 describes the impact of the different permutations of organisational relationship between operational managers and facilitators in respect of education across specialisms. This relationship can influence the co-working dynamics between facilitators delivering education across specialisms. For example, in case example 1 facilitator B may feel a lack of ownership towards the education programme, as it reflects the requirements of the managers from mental health services. This can result in an unequal co-education relationship between the facilitators. For example, facilitator B may expect facilitator A to take lead responsibility for course delivery. The organisational relationships between facilitators and managers will also impact on the quality of the learning experience. Using the case example above, participants from disability services may experience the course as irrelevant and believe that it does not meet their learning needs because the content is designed to meet the needs of staff from mental health services. A course that does not meet the needs of staff from both specialisms can reinforce or mirror preconceived ideas amongst learners about the status of one specialism over another. This in turn can lead

to a resistance to both train and also work together across specialisms.

Issues, Tensions and Resistance in the Training Room

Issues, tensions and resistance during an educational event can as described above, be a product of the organisational relationship between operational managers and facilitators. Tensions may also result from bringing together specialist social workers who work in different settings. As identified in Chapter 1, there are a number of different types of specialist social work practice. This can lead to education programmes being offered to social workers on an intra-agency, inter-agency or multidisciplinary basis. For example, workers employed by the same agency who provide different services within the agency may come together for specialist education, across specialisms, as part of an intra-agency educational programme. Alternatively, staff who work for different organisations may attend education across specialisms as part of an inter-agency education programme. Social workers may also attend multidisciplinary

Table 13.1 The Organisational Relationship Between the Management of Operations and of Training and the Impact on the Delivery of Training Across Specialisms

Control/control In this situation there is an expectation by the operational managers from both specialisms that they will determine the content of training programmes. Facilitators may be placed in a situation where the operational managers have very different views on content and will not negotiate. The training programme could reflect organisational conflict and issues of working across specialisms rather than strengths	**Control/laissez-faire** Here one specialism is likely to dominate in terms of defining course content. The training could be biased reflecting the needs and views of only one of the specialisms
Control/partnership Once again one specialism is likely to dominate. However, this will be determined by the degree that the operational managers of the other specialism are prepared to accommodate the needs of the former	**Laissez-faire/laissez-faire** Both sets of operational managers are disinterested in the training and the facilitators are left to design and develop their own programmes. The effectiveness will depend on the personal links that the facilitators have with practice and their ability to deliver training that reflects the practice needs of both specialisms
Laissez-faire/partnership One specialism is likely to make great efforts to engage operational managers in developing a training programme. If they sense a lack of interest from the other specialism the effectiveness of the training will depend on the ability of the facilitator from the laissez-faire specialism to work with the partnership specialism and make the needs of this specialism clear	**Partnership/partnership** This combination is likely to produce the most effective training programme. Operational managers and facilitators from both specialisms will work together to identify both training and operational needs. In this situation training is likely to be relevant, targeted and set within a broad operational strategy

education across specialisms. Such multidisciplinary courses bring together a range of professionals. The issues and concerns of practitioners and managers attending training events will vary depending on whether the training is multidisciplinary, intra-agency or inter-agency. Consideration is given in Table 13.1 to the issues encountered by both course participants and facilitators in the different training settings.

As can be seen from Table 13.2 course participants bring with them a history of working across specialisms. As part of an education programme, facilitators need to

acknowledge the impact of this history on the learners' values and attitudes towards engaging and delivering social work practice across specialisms. In addition, learners need an opportunity to explore the way in which these experiences can influence practice. Brookfield (1986) notes that facilitators should provide learning opportunities that assist course participants to critically examine their values, assumptions and practice enabling them to work more positively. These learning opportunities should seek to:

● Counter prejudice and the negative stereotypes that exist between specialists.

Table 13.2 Types of Specialist Training and the Implications for Participants and Facilitators

Type of training	Issues for participants	Issues for trainer
Inter-agency training refers to training that is delivered to staff from more than one agency. For example, social workers and probation officers	Participants will have different professional backgrounds and training experiences. The task and priority may vary amongst participants depending on agency function. Myths may exist about the different agencies that can influence attitudes to working together	Training staff from an unfamiliar agency context. The facilitator will have to manage issues relating to differences in organisational cultures
Single agency training or *intra-agency training* refers to training that is provided by a single employer to meet the needs of their employees. For example, social workers employed in adult and children's services within the same social services department	Participants may bring operational conflicts and tensions into the training room. Different perceptions of task and process may exist amongst participants dependent on setting. Historical differences and stereotyping may become apparent between the specialist groups. Certain service areas may be perceived as having more status, funding etc. than others	The facilitator may either be known as an in-house trainer responsible for a certain area or be considered an expert in one area and is therefore perceived as unable to appreciate other specialist functions
Multidisciplinary training refers to training that is provided to a range of professionals employed by one or more employers. For example, a course for staff working in a community mental health team may be made up of staff employed by a local social services department and a care trust	Status issues, professional conflicts and rivalries may emerge. Different learning styles, variations in working together being central to role differences in levels of power and authority. Variations in approaches to learning will exist amongst the group dependent on professional education	Facilitators may train professionals from different professions with different roles, responsibilities, perceptions of the issues and understanding of each others roles and responsibilities

- Develop an understanding amongst course participants of different roles, responsibilities and values informing practice.
- Ensure participants recognise the impact of national guidance, local policies and agency remits on collaborative practice.
- Provide opportunities for learners to develop strategies for effective co-operation and collaboration.
- Address communication barriers.

Course participants will only make use of the learning opportunities if the climate is conducive to learning. Creating a positive environment for learning begins before the education event. The most effective education occurs when learners have a sense of identity and security. In education groups, this comes from individuals recognising that they share at least some similarities with others (Brummer and Simmonds, 1992). Facilitators can begin to create this sense of security and identity by careful consideration of the following key questions at the planning stage:

- Is the purpose of the training clear?

- Is there an understanding of the practice issues from different specialist perspectives?

- Are the needs of all participants likely to be met?

- How can the facilitator/facilitators ensure they model sound collaborative practice?

- Have the facilitators considered co-working issues such as: clarifying roles; power issues; and approaches to conflict resolution within the group?

Once course participants enter the education room, the task for the facilitator is to create a group environment that encourages learning. Facilitators are likely to create an effective medium for learning if they can positively answer the following questions in relation to their education programme:

- Do education methods recognise the different learning styles of course participants?

- Does course content reflect the needs of the different specialists?

- Do the initial training activities facilitate group cohesion by focussing on commonalities between specialisms rather than difference?

- Once the group is established, are there exercises that enable learners to explore tensions and differences between specialisms in a meaningful manner?

Locality based training can be an effective arena for specialist education as it has been found to have a positive impact on collaborative practice (Barr and Waterton, 1996). Locality based training refers to education that brings together practitioners or managers who work together. This approach encourages communication and networking and provides a forum for addressing the local issues and tensions that can exist between the specialist workers. A focus on case studies based on local issues is an effective method for exploring local practice dilemmas. However,

Shaw (1993) found that the benefits of collaborative education such as greater understanding of different roles were generally lost after six months, if organisational and managerial systems did not support the learning gained from education courses. Norman (1998) cited in Glennie and Norman (2000) notes that on-going locality based events designed to explore different roles and responsibilities, as well as current relevant local and national issues address this issue. She notes that this approach makes a difference to working together because participants have structured opportunities to review practice and address emerging issues. Further, she emphasises the importance of the role of group facilitator and concludes:

> *When well managed, education structures, which mirror the inter-professional working system and are sensitive to current practitioner need, make an important contribution to the maintenance of effective working relationships.*
>
> (Glennie and Norman, 2000: p57.)

Co-education: Managing the Challenges of Education Across Specialisms

In this chapter, reference has been made to issues encountered by facilitators when working across specialisms. For example, facilitators need to balance the requirements of operational managers with the needs of learners and they have to manage the tensions evident between different specialist workers during an education event. Facilitators delivering inter-professional education across different agencies have experience of addressing these issues. The lessons learnt would seem to be applicable to facilitate education across social work specialisms. For example, Barr and Waterton (1996) note that inter-agency education is more likely to be effective if two facilitators, representing the different agencies or professional groups, are involved in course planning and delivery. Barr and Waterton argue that this ensures that differences between agency practice can be explored without participants feeling that they are being placed in untenable situations. In addition, course participants may consider that their needs are more likely to be met if at least one of the facilitators can identify with their needs. This seems directly relevant for education across social work specialisms. Yet, co-education is a difficult process that requires commitment, honesty and the ability to value difference (Horwath and Morrison, 1999). One of the most difficult issues for facilitators to recognise, acknowledge and address, concerns differences in power and status between the facilitators. Cross (1994) vividly describes the tensions that can exist when a child protection facilitator, who may frequently be perceived by course participants as being of high status, co-trains with a facilitator from disability services, a service that is often marginalised within social services departments. Issues can be further exacerbated if the facilitator from disability services also has a disability. In this situation, Cross believes both facilitators need to acknowledge their ignorance of the other specialism, admit that a power imbalance exists, analyse the nature of the power differences and consider how these issues will be managed during the training course. If this issue is not addressed then the facilitators may mirror the stereotypical images that course participants already hold.

Training together across social work specialisms is not an easy task. Yet, the benefits of effective education are far reaching and can help to lay down the foundations for forms of practice that promote better outcomes for service users.

Who requires what type of education?

One of the most striking themes running through this book is the recognition by all the authors that practice across social work specialisms is a complex task that requires a diverse range of knowledge, values and skills. The authors have also made clear that effective, innovative practice demands that practitioners and managers challenge current approaches to practice and think creatively about ways in which social work specialists can use each other's expertise to benefit service users. Education programmes should support and encourage this creative thinking. Such creative thinking cannot be achieved through one training programme alone, rather a training strategy is required that addresses the different needs of workers. This training strategy should

provide a developmental pathway for learners, which enables the learner to understand the reasons for working across specialisms and then to build upon this understanding to develop their practice in this area. This can be achieved by offering education at a number of different levels, including: awareness raising; developing the knowledge and skills for effective specialist practice; and advanced education in terms of managing complex work across specialisms. Each level is considered in detail below:

1) *Awareness raising*

The purpose of training at this level is to ensure that social workers understand the rationale behind working across specialisms and recognise the changes in their role and responsibilities that this type of work requires. All social work staff should receive this education. Education at this level should provide course participants with opportunities to explore:

- Reasons for working across specialisms, in terms of legal frameworks and research into effective practice.

- The costs and benefits of working across specialisms.

- The roles and responsibilities of staff.

- National guidance, local procedures and arrangements and resources.

2) *Developing knowledge, values and skills amongst staff*

At this level learners should be aware of the rationale underpinning work across specialisms and understand the skills and knowledge needed to practise effectively in their roles. These learners need to develop the skills to work together effectively across specialisms and have the knowledge and values to support their practice. All social work staff who are likely to work across social work specialisms should receive this education. Education at this level should include learning opportunities to explore:

- Research and practice developments regarding current practice across specialisms.

- Skill development in line with roles and responsibilities.

- The principles and processes that promote effective practice across specialisms.
- Factors that promote collaborative practice applied to the local situation.

3) *Developing specialist practice*

This level of education is required by social workers who work together consistently across specialisms or who are involved in complex practice across social work specialisms. Education should provide learners with opportunities to explore:

- Collaborative practice in complex cases.
- Local issues and tensions.
- Establishing and maintaining effective working relationships across specialisms.

Meeting the needs of managers

Effective social work practice across specialisms is not only dependent on practitioners having appropriate knowledge, values and skills to work together effectively to meet the needs of service users, but it is also dependent on practitioners working in an environment that encourages and supports collaborative practice. Hence, managers at different organisational levels require education to enable them to create an operational framework such as the one described in Chapter 1, which facilitates work across specialisms. In addition, front line managers need to develop skills in supervising staff working across specialisms ensuring that collaborative practice promotes better outcomes for service users.

Education Materials

This section consists of education exercises that can be used as part of the training strategy described above to develop the knowledge, values and skills of practitioners and managers working across specialisms. These exercises have been developed using material from this book. The first four exercises are designed to provide learning opportunities for course participants to consider the benefits and dilemmas related to working across social work specialisms. These exercises can be adapted for use on management training programmes. The remaining exercises focus on specific practice issues.

Exercise 1   Why Work Across Specialisms?

Aim: The purpose of this exercise is to enable participants to consider the benefits of working together across specialisms.

Target group: This exercise is relevant to practitioners and managers.

Time required: 60-90 minutes.

Preparation: Prepare a case study that involves contributions from all the specialisms represented by the course participants. The case study should focus on either an assessment of need; or the assessment of risk; or the provision of services.

Method:

Method A to be used when participants from only two specialisms are involved in training.

As the facilitator:

1. Give a brief introduction to the exercise using the key aim outlined above.
2. Divide the group into three small groups: one consisting of course participants from one specialism; another consisting of participants from the other specialism; and one group of participants from both specialisms. Give each group the same

prepared case study. Ask the specialist groups to begin to consider either how they would assess the situation described in the case study or complete a care plan using their specialist knowledge. However, for the third group ask them to work together to complete the assessment or care plan. Ask each group to capture their responses to the case study on flipchart paper.

3. When the groups have completed the task display the responses on the wall and ask individuals to read them. Once they have done this, ask the course participants to return to their subgroups and consider what seems to be different across the groups about the assessments/planning strategies from the following perspectives:

   ● the service user

   ● the workers

   ● the organisations

4. Ask, 'What are the gains and losses of working separately and across specialisms?'

   Invite participants to reform as the large group and the facilitator should then record their responses and initiate a discussion on the advantages and potential problems of working across specialisms.

Method B *for use with a group consisting of participants from a range of specialisms.*

1. Divide the education group into specialist groups and ask each group to work on the case study from their particular service perspective. Inform the group members that they will need to keep individual notes to use for the second part of the exercise.

2. Re-divide the groups to form multi-specialist groups and ask these groups to complete an assessment/care plan using their specialist contributions from stage one.

3. Once the assessment is completed, ask course participants, within the sub-groups, to consider the differences between completing the assessment/plan in specialist groups and taking a joint approach. Suggest that they have this discussion focussing on the following perspectives:

   ● the service user

   ● the workers

   ● the organisations

4. Initiate a large group discussion by inviting feedback from the sub-groups (invite comments on key themes not full extended reports from each group). Tease out the common themes and the key benefits and issues related to working together. You may wish to display this list of benefits and issues and refer to these as appropriate during the rest of the course.

Exercise 2   Working Together: Blocks and Barriers

Aim: The aim of the exercise is to identify some elements that promote and inhibit working across specialisms.

Target group: This exercise can be adapted to meet the needs of either managers or practitioners. It works best with groups of less than fifteen.

Time required: 60-90 minutes.

Preparation: Prepare a 'wall' consisting of three sheets of flipchart paper pinned next to each other. Head one sheet *service user*, another *professional* and the final one *organisation*.

Familiarise yourself with the general issues regarding working together across specialisms as identified in this book. Chapter 1 may be particularly useful. In addition, ensure that you are aware of any particular local issues.

Method:

As the facilitator:

1. Introduce the exercise by explaining that the flip chart 'wall' is separating the specialist areas of practice. Give each member of the group some 'stickies' and ask them to list their reasons for keeping the 'wall' in place in terms of implications for service users, themselves as practitioners and the organisation. Remind them to put each reason on a different 'stickies' and place their 'stickies' on the appropriate section of 'wall'.

2. Once this is done, take down the wall. Divide participants into three groups, each one to collate the 'stickies' for each section of the 'wall'. You may wish to allow participants to self-select into the three groups. Remind the participants they will all have an opportunity to find out what was written on each section of 'wall'.

3. Ask each sub-group to collate the responses under themes and to consider *strategies* for addressing the blocks to working together.

4. Reform participants into a large group to share their *blocks* and *strategies*. In discussion, draw out common themes and identify differences, exploring the implications for effective practice across specialisms.

Exercise 3   **Audit of Current Practice**

Aim: The purpose of this exercise is to provide opportunities for course participants to reflect on current practice across specialisms.

Target groups: This exercise can be adapted to meet the needs of either managers or practitioners.

Time required: 90-120 minutes.

Preparation: Devise at least fifteen short scenarios that would require practitioners to work together (using the specialisms represented by the course participants). Write each scenario on a separate small card. For example:

> *Jamie is a fourteen year old young carer with a hearing impairment. He lives with his mother who has multiple sclerosis and is wheelchair bound.*

Have as many sets of the scenarios as there are anticipated sub-groups.

Method:

As the facilitator:

1. Divide the group into sub-groups each consisting of five to six course participants (ensure a mix of specialists in each group). Give each group a set of scenario cards.

First ask the groups to consider how they would work currently to address each situation described on the cards. Second, the groups should consider ways they would wish to practice 'working across specialisms' in order to promote better outcomes for the service users.

2. Based on their discussions, ask the group to remain as sub-groups and to list what would need to change to promote effective practice across specialisms in terms of:

- policy
- practice
- resources
- management

3. Ask each group in turn to feedback their views and as facilitators draw out common themes.

The following questions to the whole group can be used to 'trigger' ideas about current practice:

For managers:

- What systems are in place within the organisation and between organisations to ensure that information can be shared, assessments made and interventions co-ordinated?
- Are systems in place that enable joint commissioning and planning of services?
- Are polices and procedures in place which enable issues relating to conflicts of interest between service users to be addressed?
- Do local service level agreements encourage and facilitate joint work across specialisms?
- Are joint education strategies in place for both practitioners and managers?

For practitioners:

- Do I recognise the potential needs of all family members, when working with a particular service user?
- Do I know how to refer to appropriate services?
- What assumptions do I make about other family members?
- Do I know who to contact within my own or other agencies if I have concerns regarding particular issues beyond my specialism?
- How do I attempt to work with professionals from other services when identifying and meeting the needs of the service user and their family?
- How would I manage conflicting views and opinions between myself and social workers from other services?

These questions could also be used for an exercise in its own right aimed at enabling course participants to audit their current practice.

Exercise 4　Defining Vulnerability Amongst Adults

Aim: The purpose of this exercise is to enable course participants to begin to consider what is meant by the term 'vulnerable' adult and the implications of the term for work across specialisms.

Target group: Practitioners.

Time required: 60 minutes.

Preparation: Read Chapter 7 by Penhale and Parker on *The Protection of Vulnerable Adults: The Role of Social Work*. Prepare enough copies of the scenarios, detailed below, such that there are enough for each course participant to have a copy. Alternatively, prepare scenarios that reflect the areas of vulnerability you wish participants to consider.

Scenario One
Enid, is in her 80s, and has rheumatoid arthritis, which particularly affects her hands and feet. She is finding it increasingly difficult to use cooking equipment, such as the cooker, tin opener, and to lift pots, pans and the kettle. Recently, she dropped a pan of hot soup, which narrowly missed spilling over her. Enid was so shocked by this incident that she asked her GP for advice about this matter. The GP referred Enid to the local social services team for adults who assess her needs for support and assistance with daily living tasks.

Scenario Two
Janet (aged 53) lives in a hostel for people with learning disabilities. She had lived in a long-stay hospital for forty years, from childhood, and has spent twelve years living in a hostel. She has developed recently a life-threatening physical illness that needs surgery. Janet refuses to go into hospital because of her past experiences. Without surgery she will die. However, she did not appear to understand this fully.

Scenario Three
Edward is in his mid 70s and is experiencing the early stages of dementia. He is also quite depressed and uncertain about what the future might hold. He is very clear that he wishes to remain living at home. His wife, Doris, indicates that she wishes to continue caring for Edward. Recently, Edward's mood swings, which include an aggressive component, develop into physical violence directed towards his wife, and on occasion other members of the family who attempt to intervene. Doris contacts social services for assistance and support, recognising that this change is too great for her to deal with on her own. Edward, however, refuses all help, failing to recognise the effect that his behaviour is having on his wife. His refusal is at times aggressive, which serves to worsen the situation, and at one point he is compulsorily admitted to hospital in order to ensure the safety of his wife.

Method:

As the facilitator:

1.　Introduce the exercise, using Chapter 7 to illustrate that we all have different perceptions of vulnerable adults.

2.　Divide the group of course participants into sub-groups consisting of approximately six per group. Give each group copies of the scenarios. Ask group members to consider the situations outlined in the scenarios and to explore factors that they consider may make adults vulnerable.

3.　Using the material generated by the groups ask each sub-group to produce a group definition of the term 'vulnerable adult'.

4. Put all the definitions on the wall and suggest the group as a whole compare and contrast the different definitions.

5. Compare the groups' definitions of vulnerability with definitions from the literature or local guidance and procedures. Highlight commonalities and differences.

6. Ask the group to consider whether differences in perceptions varied depending on participants' specialist areas of practice. Finish the exercise by asking them to consider the implications of these differences for work across specialisms.

   Adaptation: This exercise can be adapted using material from this book to enable group participants to produce other working definitions of terms such as: 'domestic violence' or 'drug and alcohol misuse'.

   Acknowledgement: Bridget Penhale and Jonathan Parker.

Exercise 5   **Walking the Walk Talking the Talk**

Aims: The purpose of this exercise is to provide an opportunity for course participants to begin to consider needs from the perspective of a service user, and explore the extent to which specialist practice influences our perceptions.

Target group: Practitioners.

Time required: 45 minutes.

Preparation: You may wish to use the scenario below that relates to learning disability. Alternatively, you may wish to devise a scenario to reflect the service users whose needs are being considered on the course. Ensure that there are sufficient scenarios for each course participant.

The facilitator should read the relevant chapters in this book.

Scenario One

John is twenty-seven years of age, the eldest child of a family of seven, brought up by maternal grandparents. John's mother had an alcohol problem and left home when John was a baby. John never had any contact with his father. John, from an early age had a 'borderline IQ' and was seen as exhibiting antisocial behaviour at home and at school. He was very solitary and often played on his own. He was viewed by his local community as the 'village idiot' and was taunted and teased frequently by his peers. He attended mainstream school but was unable to cope very well and was transferred to a special school because of his particular needs at thirteen years of age. Prior to his transfer he began to keep company with local youths who were involved in petty crime in the neighbourhood. He began to abuse alcohol and solvents and continued to use them heavily throughout his adolescence. During one such occasion when he was nineteen he attacked and sexually assaulted an older woman and was admitted to a specialist learning disability hospital on a hospital order for a period of assessment and treatment.

Method:

As the facilitator:

1. Divide the group of participants into small specialist sub-groups and give each participant a copy of the scenario. Ask the groups to explore the following questions:

- What impact do you think John's childhood experiences have had on his sense of identity and self-worth?
- How do you think John perceives himself?
- What do you think he would want from involvement with social workers?

2. Then invite participants to reform as a large group, each group should share their assessment with the main group. Draw out commonalities and differences. If there are different opinions expressed by group members, ask the group why they think there are different perceptions regarding John? What does this mean for working together?

3. Based on the answers to the questions above, what would practitioners need to consider when working with John?

4. Once the group have completed this task, ask them to write down key messages for social work specialists working together with John. These can either be for the sub-group alone or shared, for example by typing them up subsequently.

Acknowledgment: Roy McConkey and Theresa Nixon.

Exercise 6　**Perspectives on Care Planning**

Aim: The purpose of this exercise is to enable course participants to consider different ways in which social workers view care planning and the impact these views may have on working together across specialisms.

Target group: Practitioners from different community care services who are, or will be working together.

Time required: 60-90 minutes.

Preparation: Using the material from Chapter 2 by French, Gillman and Swain and any other additional local material that is relevant, prepare practitioner quotes (i.e. something that a practitioner may have said – some may be 'fairly conventional' a few might be quite outrageous!) on pieces of card about working in a community care team.

Try and select quotes that reflect:

- the care management process
- the task
- staffing issues
- impact on service users

Ensure there are enough sets of quotes so that there is one complete set for each of the anticipated number of sub-groups.

Method:
As the facilitator:

1. Briefly introduce the exercise by acknowledging that there are differences in workers' experiences of care planning. You may wish to use local examples of differences in practice as illustrations.

2. Divide participants into sub-groups and ask them to read each quote in turn and discuss whether they agree or disagree with the quote.

3. Once they have completed the exercise ask participants in their small groups to consider:

- What were the commonalities and differences in perception?
- What would need to be resolved in terms of difference for effective working together?

4. Invite the participants to reform as a large group. Then ask the group members to identify the key issues related to both policy and practice that need to be resolved in order to promote effective working together. Ask the group who needs to know about these issues and suggest that you, as the facilitator, would be willing to pass this information to the relevant operational managers.

Acknowledgement: Sally French, Maureen Gillman and John Swain.

Exercise 7   **Completing Assessments across Specialisms, Roles and Responsibilities**

Aim: The purpose of this exercise is to explore the issues and tensions in terms of working together across specialisms when completing an assessment.

Target group: Practitioners and front line managers.

Time required: 60-90 minutes.

Preparation: Have case studies prepared, using the case below or a case related to the particular specialist areas. If working with experienced staff, you make wish to prepare a case study that is controversial and raises current issues regarding roles and responsibilities.

Case Study
Michael Moore is subject to a three-year probation order with a requirement that he receives psychiatric treatment as an outpatient at the local psychiatric hospital. He received the orders for two offences of actual bodily harm against his partner Elaine. He expresses remorse about the offences but claims to remember very little about the actual attacks that took place when he had been drinking heavily. He has a previous conviction twelve months ago for an assault on a woman in a chip shop who had refused to serve him because he was drunk. He was fined for this offence. Michael is unemployed and lives with his partner Elaine, and her ten-year-old daughter Sally, from a previous relationship. Elaine calls at your office (social service access team, community mental health team, probation office, family support team, school office…) to tell you that she is frightened because Michael has started to drink again, having remained sober for some six weeks since the court case. They had had a row about her ten year old daughter's behaviour within the home: Michael thinks she should help out more with household tasks, and Elaine is 'too soft' with her. Michael does not know that Elaine has come to the office to see you, and she does not want you to tell him.

Method:
As the facilitator

1. Introduce the session by reminding course participants that working across specialisms can raise issues in terms of roles and responsibilities.

2. Divide the group into their specialist areas and ask them to read the case study and then answer the questions listed below:

- What are the key issues you would need to take into account in undertaking an assessment of this situation from your perspective or job role?

- What, if any, differences might there be if you were in another role?
- How might a multi-agency assessment take place? Who would be the key workers involved? How would the risks and needs in this situation be assessed and what plan of action might be proposed?
- Who would be the key worker in this case?

3. Based on their answers to these questions, ask each group to prepare an assessment plan highlighting:

- aims of the assessment
- personnel involved and their roles, including key worker
- work to be done with family and by whom

4. Once the groups have completed these tasks, ask each group to share their assessment plans. Compare and contrast and highlight issues regarding different perceptions of roles. Bring the discussion to a conclusion by considering the consequences for the service users and staff involved in the assessment. Refer to local policy and practice to clarify actual roles and responsibilities.

Acknowledgement: Charlotte Knight.

Exercise 8   So Change is Easy?

(In two parts and linked to Exercise 10.)

Aims: The purpose of this exercise is to explore the complex nature of lifestyle choices, and to reflect on what change of behaviour really demands of individuals.

Target group: Practitioners.

Time required: 45-60 minutes.

Preparation: Be familiar with the model of change as outlined in Chapter 3.

Part 1 Contemplating Change

Method:
As the facilitator:

1. Ask course participants to imagine an activity that they do every day, or perhaps once or twice a week. Perhaps this is an activity that they hardly ever think about or it may be an activity for which they plan and to which they look forward with enthusiasm. This activity could be similar to smoking; seeing close friends; a regular sporting or leisure activity.

   (NB Remind participants they will be asked to share their thoughts with one other person in the group).

2. Now ask the participants to imagine giving up this activity in terms of what it actually involves and what the activity means to them. Suggest they draw up a list of what they might lose if they give up the activity and a list of the things they might gain.

3. Once they have completed this task, ask participants to form pairs and invite each pair to compare and contrast their feelings about what would change if they gave up the activity.

4. Collect verbal feedback from the group as a whole.

    As a facilitator you may want to try and elicit the following comments:

    ● The loss of any 'thrill' or 'feelings of well-being' that you obtain from the activity.

    ● The loss of any psychological well-being associated with the ritualistic or routine aspects of your activity.

    ● The loss of friends who continue with the activity.

    ● Losing an identity and a sense of belonging to a community.

    ● More money to spend on other activities.

    ● More time to spend on other activities.

    ● Better physical and mental health.

    ● Reunion and reconciliation with people who matter to you.

    ● New friends from new activities.

    Acknowledgement: Philip Guy and Larry Harrison.

Part 2 The Change Process

Method:
As the facilitator:

1. Ask participants to think about a time they tried to make a significant change in their life. Inform them they will not need to share the actual experience but share the experience of the process of change. Ask them to consider what happened. For example, did change occur easily or was the change slow with one move forward and two back?

2. Take group feedback regarding their experiences of process of change.

3. Present the model of change developed by Protchaska and Diclementi (see Chapter 3) linking the group experience to the different stages of the model. For example, did course participants find they could manage change, if it was sustaining a change that proved difficult?

4. Ask participants to consider the implications of the model for work with service users.

5. Draw up a list of ten points for practice when working with change. This can be done in large or small groups.

    Acknowledgement: Adapted from an exercise in The Child's World: Assessing Children in Need. Education and Development Pack, NSPCC and University of Sheffield, 2000.

Exercise 9   Issues That Impact on Parenting Capacity

Aim: The purpose of this exercise is to provide opportunities for participants to consider:

● Ways in which parents' issues impact on parenting capacity.

● The impact of these issues on children.

● The importance of specialists working together as part of the assessment process.

Target group: Practitioners from adult and children's services.

Time required: 90 minutes.

Preparation: Be familiar with Chapter 8. It would also be useful to read *Children's Needs – Parenting Capacity. The Impact of Parental Mental Illness, Problem Alcohol and Drug Use and Domestic Violence on Children's Development* by Cleaver, Unell and Aldgate and prepare a handout on the key issues.

Prepare sufficient copies of the scenarios described below for all course participants. Alternatively, make up relevant scenarios yourself providing a copy for each participant.

Scenario One

Jane is a single parent with two children, a boy Adrian who is two years old and a girl Stacey who is six months old. Jane has been using heroin for the last four years. She managed to maintain her habit and provide a reasonable standard of care for her children until her partner and father of her children John left her three months ago. Since then, professionals involved with the family have been concerned that Jane is neglecting the children. Both children have lost weight. In addition, neighbours have rung social services stating that Jane leaves the children unattended at night. A social worker discussed these concerns with Jane. She acknowledged that she had left the children but stated it was necessary, as she needed to collect her drug supplies. An initial child protection conference was held to consider the concerns. At the conference the police noted that Jane was allowing known drug dealers to live in her house. As part of the child protection plan Jane has agreed to work with a social worker and other professionals from a drug rehabilitation programme in an attempt to give up heroin. She stated at the conference that she knows if she does not give up she will lose her children and she is determined that this will not happen.

Scenario Two

Siobhan and Neil have had a very volatile relationship. Siobhan has been hit by Neil on a number of occasions. The injuries have been so severe she has required inpatient hospitalisation on a number of occasions. The couple have one child Gail aged six. Gail has witnessed this violence and was placed on the child protection register following an incident when she tried to protect her mother from her father and was consequently injured. The injuries to Gail included a fractured wrist and bruising. Siobhan and Gail are now living in a refuge with a view to being re-housed. Neil is being charged with actual bodily harm and as part of his bail conditions is not allowed contact with Siobhan or Gail. The child protection plan is designed to assist Siobhan and Gail to establish a new life without Neil. Initially, Siobhan was highly motivated to achieve this goal. However, in the past two weeks, she has begun to talk about wanting to see Neil again, with a view to reconciliation. She has spoken to him on the telephone on a number of occasions and states that he is so devastated at losing his family he will change his behaviour.

Method:
As the facilitator:

1. Introduce the exercise with a brief presentation regarding the impact of parenting issues on parenting capacity using the material in Chapter 8 and recommended reading.

2. Divide participants into small groups consisting of six to seven participants ensuring a mix of participants from adult and children's services. Give each group the same scenario. Alternatively, vary the scenarios dependent on the parental issues to ensuring that participants are addressing issues relevant to their specialist area of practice.

3. Ask each group to read the scenario and consider the following:

- What is it about the parents' issues that could potentially impact on their parenting capacity?
- What would seem to be the current impact of the parents' issues on the child's development?
- What does your group consider needs to change in terms of the parents' behaviour?
- Who should be involved in working with each family?

Collect brief feedback from each group, highlighting any differences in perceptions.

4. Ask the groups to comment on the commonalities and differences in their approach to the issues raised. Explore with the group what this might mean for working together?

Acknowledgement: Jan Horwath.

Exercise 10   Working With Service Users to Bring About Change

(This exercise is closely linked to Exercises 8 and 9. Together, these three exercises might be used to form the basis for a day of education on motivation and change.)

Aim: The purpose of this exercise is to explore the meaning of change for particular service users and the role of social workers in supporting them through this process.

Target group: Practitioners and front line managers.

Time required: 45 minutes.

Preparation: Complete Exercise 6 and if relevant Exercise 7, ensuring participants understand the model of change and the importance of motivation to change. Use the scenarios from Exercise 7 or develop scenarios related to the particular specialisms. Prepare a sheet of flipchart for each group divided up as follows in Figure 13.2

Method:

As the facilitator:

1. Introduce the exercise, highlighting that the focus is up on ways in which social workers can support service users through the change process.

2. Divide the group into sub-groups, ensuring that each group is mixed in respect of specialist areas of practice. Give each participant a case scenario and each group a sheet of flipchart as described above.

- Using the flipchart, the groups should record the potential losses and gains for the parent/s of changing their behaviour as suggested in the case scenarios.
- How could social workers take these losses and gains into account and work together with the service user to support them through the change process?
- What supports would the service user need at different stages of the change process?

Acknowledgement: Jan Horwath.

Bibliography

Abrahams, C. (1994). *Hidden Victims*. London: NCH Action for Children.

Adcock, M. (2001). The Core Assessment – How to Synthesis Information and Make Judgements. In Horwath, J. (Ed.) *The Child's World Assessing Children in Need*, pp75-97. London: Jessica Kingsley.

Adcock, M. and White, R. (Eds.) (1998). *Significant Harm: Its Management and Outcome*. Croydon: Significant Publications.

Africare (1998). *Report of Listening to Children: A National Conference on HIV, Children and Young People*. London: Africare.

Ahmed, W.I.U. and Atkin, K. (1996). *Race and Community Care*. Buckingham: Open University Press.

Aldberg, C., Hatfield, B. and Huxley, P. (1996). *Learning Materials on Mental Health. Risk Assessment*. Manchester: University of Manchester.

Alderidge, J. and Becker, S. (1993). *Children Who Care: Inside the World of Young Carers*. Loughborough: Loughborough University Young Carers Research Group.

All-Party Parliamentary Group on AIDS (1998). *Parliamentary Hearings for National HIV/AIDS Strategies: Summary and Recommendations*. London: APPGA.

Allsop, J. (1984). *Health Policy and the National Health Service*. London: Longman.

Andrews, D.A. and Bonta, J.L. (1995). *The Level of Service Inventory: Revised Manual*. New York and Toronto: Multi-Health Systems Inc.

Arber, S. and Ginn, J. (1995). *Connecting Gender and Ageing: A Sociological Approach*. Buckingham: Open University Press.

ARC/NAPSAC (1993). *It could never happen here*. Bradford: Thornton and Pearson.

Aubrey, R. and Hough, M. (1997). *Assessing Offenders' Need: Assessment Scales for the Probation Service*. London: Home Office.

Audit Commission. (1992). *The Community Revolution: Personal Social Services and Community Care*. London: HMSO.

Azrin, N.H. (1976). Improvements in the Community-Reinforcement Approach to Alcoholism. *Behavioral Research and Therapy*, 14(3): pp 339-348.

Bamford, T. (1990). *The Future of Social Work*. Houndmills, Basingstoke: Macmillan.

Banks, P., Cheeseman, C. and Maggs, S. (1998). *The Carers Compass: Directions for Improving Support to Carers*. London: Kings Fund.

Barclay, P.M. (1982). *Social Workers: Their Role and Tasks (The Barclay Report)*. London: Bedford Square Press.

Barker, P. (1998). *Suicide Risk Security Plan Guidance Notes*. London: UKCC.

Baron, S., Phillips, R. and Stalker, K. (1996). Barriers to Training for Disabled Social Work Students. *Disability and Society*, 11(3): pp361-377.

Barr, H. and Waterton, S. (1996). *Interprofessional Education in Health and Social Care in the United Kingdom*. Report of a CAIPE Survey. London: CAIPE.

Barr, H., Freeth, D., Hammick, M., Koppel, L. and Reeves, S. (1999). *Evaluating Interprofessional Education: A United Kingdom Review for Health and Social Care*. London: BERA CAIPE.

Bayley, M., Parker, P., Seyd, R. and Tennant, A. (1987). *Practising Community Care. Sheffield: Joint Unit for Social Services Research*. University of Sheffield.

Beaumont, W. and Mistry, T. (1996). Doing a Good Job under Duress. *Probation Journal*, 43(4): pp200-204.

Beck, U. (1992). *Risk Society: Towards a New Modernity*. London: Sage.

Becker, S., Aldridge, J. and Dearden, C. (1998). *Young Carers and their Families*. Oxford: Blackwell.

Beecham, J., Hallam, A., Kapp, et al. (1997). Costing Care in Hospital and the Community. In Lell, J. (Eds.) *Care in the Community: Illusion or Reality?* London: John Wiley Press.

Bennett, G.C., Kingston, P.A. and Penhale, B. (1997). *The Dimensions of Elder Abuse: Perspectives for Practitioners*. Houndmills, Basingstoke: Macmillan.

Berridge, V. (1989). History and Addiction Control: The Case of Alcohol. In Robinson, D. Maynard, A. and Chester, R. (Eds.) *Controlling Legal Addictions*, pp24-42. Houndmills, Basingstoke: Macmillan.

Best Value in Social Care. London: HMSO.

BHAN (1995). *Assessment and Case Management: HIV and Minority Communities*. London: Black HIV/AIDS Network.

Bhatti-Sinclair, K. (1994). Asian Women and Violence from Male Partners. In Lupton, C. and Gillespie, T. (Eds.) *Working with Violence.* Houndmills, Basingstoke: Macmillan.

Biestek (1961). *The Casework Relationship.* London: Allen and Unwin.

Biggs, S., Phillipson, C. and Kingston, P. (1995). *Elder Abuse in Perspective.* Buckingham: Open University Press.

Blakemore, K. and Boneham, M. (1995). *Age, Race and Ethnicity: A Comparative Approach.* Buckingham: Open University Press.

BMA (1998). *Domestic Violence: A Health Care Issue?* London: British Medical Association.

Booth, T. and Booth, W. (1994). *Parenting Under Pressure: Mothers and Fathers With Learning Difficulties.* Buckingham: Open University Press.

Bowker, L., Arbitell, M. and Mcferron, J. (1988). The Relationship Between Wife Beating and Child Abuse. In Yllo, K. and Bograd, M. (Eds.) *Feminist Perspectives in Wife Abuse.* Newbury Park, CA: Sage.

Brain, K., Parker, H. and Bottomley, T. (1998). *Evolving Crack Cocaine Careers: Home Office Research Findings No 85.* London: HMSO.

Brandon, M. and Lewis, A. (1996). Significant Harm and Children's Experiences of Domestic Violence. *Child and Family Social Work,* 1(1): pp33-42.

Brechin, A., Brown, H. and Eby, M.A. (Eds.) (2000). *Critical Practice in Health and Social Care.* London: The Open University and Sage Publications.

Breckman, R. S. and Adelman, R.D. (1988). *Strategies for Helping Victims of Elder Mistreatment.* Newbury Park and London: Sage.

Bridges, B.S. and Steen, S. (1998). Racial Disparities in Official Assessments of Juvenile Offenders: Attributional Stereotypes as Mediating Mechanisms. *American Sociological Review,* 63(4): pp554-570.

Bright, L. (1997). *Care Betrayed.* London: Counsel and Care.

Bronfenbrenner, U. (1979). *The Ecology of Human Development.* Cambridge: Harvard University Press.

Brookfield, S.D. (1996). *Understanding and Facilitating Adult Learning.* Milton Keynes: Open University Press.

Brown, G. and Harris, T. (1979). *The Social Origins of Depression.* London: Tavistock.

Brown, H. and Turk, V. (1992). Defining sexual abuse as it affects adults with learning disabilities. *Mental Handicap,* 20(2): pp44-55.

Brown, H., Kingston, P. and Wilson, B. (1999). Adult Protection: An Overview. *Journal of Adult Protection,* 1 (1): pp6-15.

Browne, D. (1997). *Black People and Sectioning: The Black Experience of Detention under the Civil Sections of The Mental Health Act.* London: Little Rock Publishing.

Browne, K. and Herbert, M. (1997). *Preventing Family Violence.* Chichester: John Wiley and Sons.

Brownlee, I. (1998). *Community Punishment: A Critical Introduction.* Harlow: Longman.

Bruce, I., Mckennell, A. and Walker, E. (1991). *Blind and Partially Sighted Adults in Britain. The RNIB Survey.* London: HMSO Publications.

Brummer, N. and Simmonds, J. (1992). Race and Culture: The Management of 'Difference' in the Learning Group. *Social Work Education,* 11(1): pp54-64.

Buckley, R. and Caple, J. (1995). *The Theory and Practice of Training.* London: Kogan Page.

Burchardt, T. (2000). *Disabled People, Income and Work.* York: Joseph Rowntree Foundation.

Burke, J., Chandy, J., Dannerbeck, A. and Watt, J.W. (1998). The Parental Environment Cluster Model of Child Neglect: An Integrative Conceptual Model. *Child Welfare,* IXXVII(4): pp389–405.

Burke, P. (1990). The Fieldwork Team Response: An Investigation Into The Relationship Between Client Categories, Referred Problems and Outcomes. *British Journal of Social Work,* 20: pp469-482.

Butler, R.N. (1987). *Ageism in the Encyclopaedia of Aging.* New York: Springer.

Calder, M.C. and Horwath, J. (Eds.) (1999). *Working for Children on The Child Protection Register: An Inter-Agency Guide.* Aldershot: Arena.

Calderdale Metropolitan Council (1995). *Guidelines for Assessment of Mistreatment of Vulnerable Adults.* Calderdale: Calderdale Social Services.

Cambridge, P. (1998). The Physical Abuse of People with Learning Disabilities and Challenging Behaviours: Lessons for Commissioners and Providers. *Tizard Learning Disability Review,* 3 (1): pp18-27.

Carers National Association (1997). *Still Battling? The Carers Act One Year on.* London: CNA.

Cassell, D. and Coleman, R. (1995). Parents with Psychiatric Problems. In Reder, P. and Lucey, C. (Eds.) *Assessment of Parenting Psychiatric and Psychological Contributions,* pp169-181. London: Routledge.

Cavadino, M. (1997). Pre-sentence Reports: The Effects of Legislation and National Standards.

British Journal of Criminology, 37(4): pp529-548.

Cavadino, M. and Dignan, J. (1997). *The Penal System: An Introduction* (2nd edn.) London: Sage.

CCETSW (1989). *Requirements and Regulations for the Diploma in Social Work (Paper 30).* London: CCETSW.

CCETSW (1995). *Assuring Quality in the Diploma in Social Work: Rules and Requirements for the DipSW.* London: CCETSW.

CCETSW (1996). *Assuring Quality: Rules and Requirements for the Diploma in Social Work.* London: CCETSW.

CCETSW (2000). *Assuring Quality for Mental Health Work Requirements for the Training of Approved Social Workers in England, Wales and Northern and of Mental Health Officers in Scotland.* London: CCETSW.

Chapman, T. and Hough, M. (1998). *Evidence Based Practice. A Guide to Effective Practice.* London: Home Office Publications Unit.

Chinouya-Mudari, M. and O'Brien, M. (1999). African Refugee Children and HIV/AIDS in London. In Aggleton, P. Hart, G. and Davies, P. (Eds.) *Families and Communities Responding to AIDS,* pp21-34. London: UCL Press.

Cleaver, H. (2001). When Parents' Issues Influence Their ability to Respond to Children's Needs. In Horwath, J. (Ed.) *The Child's World Assessing Children in Need,* pp273-286. London: Jessica Kingsley.

Cleaver, H. and Freeman, P. (1995). *Parental Perspectives in Cases of Suspected Child Abuse.* London: HMSO.

Cleaver, H., Unell, I. and Aldgate, J. (1999). *Children's Needs – Parenting Capacity. The Impact of Parental Mental Illness, Problem Alcohol and Drug Use, and Domestic Violence on Children's Development.* London: The Stationery Office.

Clegg, J. (1998). *Critical Issues in Clinical Practice.* London: Sage Publications.

Clifford, D. and Williams, G. (2002). Important Yet Ignored: Problems of 'Expertise' in Emergency Duty Social Work. *British Journal of Social Work,* 32(2): pp201–15.

Cohen, J. and Fisher, M. (1988). Recognition of Mental Health Problems by Doctors and Social Workers. *Practice,* 1(3): pp225-240.

Colombo, A. and Neary, M. (1998). Square Roots and Algebra: Understanding Perceptions of Combined Risk/Needs Assessment Measures. *Probation Journal,* 45(4): pp231-219.

Community Care Development Centre (1999). *Services for People with Learning Disabilities in the Modernised Social Services.* London: King's College.

Cook, D. and Hudson, B. (1993). *Racism and Criminology.* London: Sage.

Cope, R. (1989). The Compulsory Detention of Afro-Caribbeans Under The Mental Health Act. *New Community,* 15(3): pp343-356.

Cotson, D., Friend, J., Hollins, S. and James, H. (2001). Implementing The Framework for The Assessment of Children in Need and Their Families When the Parent Has a Learning Disability. In Horwath, J. (Ed.) *The Child's World: Assessing Children in Need,* pp287-302. London: Jessica Kingsley.

Coulshed, V. and Orme, J. (1998). *Social Work Practice: An Introduction.* Houndmills, Basingstoke: Macmillan.

Cowling, V. (1999). In Weir, A. and Douglas, A. (Eds.) *Child Protection and Adult Mental Health Conflict of Interest?* Oxford: Butterworth Heinemann.

Crawford, L., Devaux, M., Ferris, R. and Hayward, P. (1997). *The Report Into the Care and Treatment of Martin Mursell.* London: Camden and Islington Health Authority.

Criminal Justice Conference: Towards The Seamless Sentence 27-28 February 2001, Highgate House, Northampton (Website: www.Homeoffice.Gov.Uk/Pfd/Scu/Ttsscontents.Htm).

Crittenden, P., Partridge, M. and Claussen, A. (1991). Family Patterns of Relationships in Normative and Dysfunctional Families. *Development and Psychopathology,* 3: pp491-512.

Cross, M. (1994). Side by Side. *Community Care,* 20th Jan, pp20-21.

Cross, M. (1999). *Review of Domestic Violence and Child Abuse: Policy and Practice Issues for Local Authorities and Other Agencies.* Boadicea, London: Greater London Action on Disability (GLAD).

Dale, P. and Fellows, R. (1999). Independent Child Protection Assessments: Incorporating a Therapeutic Focus From an Integrated Service Context. *Child Abuse Review,* 8(1): pp4-14.

Davies, B. and Challis, D. (1986). *Matching Resources to Needs in Community Care: An Evaluated Demonstration of a Long-Term Care Model.* Aldershot: Gower.

Davies, M. (1985). *The Essential Social Worker.* Aldershot: Arena.

Davies, M. (Ed.) (2000). *The Blackwell Encyclopaedia of Social Work.* Oxford: Blackwell.

Denney, D. *Racism and Anti-racism in Probation.* London: Routledge.

Department of Health (1988). *Protecting Children: A Guide for Social Workers Undertaking A Comprehensive Assessment.* London: HMSO.

Department of Health (1989). *Caring for People: Care in the Community in the Next Decade and Beyond.* London: HMSO.

Department of Health (1992a). *Children and HIV: Guidance for Local Authorities.* London: HMSO.

Department of Health (1993). *No Longer Afraid: The Safeguard of Older People in Domestic Settings.* London: HMSO.

Department of Health (1993). *No Longer Afraid: The Safeguard of Older People in Domestic Settings.* London: HMSO.

Department of Health (1995). *Child Protection Messages From Research Studies in Child Protection.* London: HMSO.

Department of Health (1996). *Building Bridges.* London: HMSO.

Department of Health (1996a). *Carers (Recognition and Services) Act 1995 Policy Guidance.* London: HMSO.

Department of Health (1996b). *Carers (Recognition and Services) Act 1995 Practice Guidance.* London: HMSO.

Department of Health (1997). *The New NHS: Modern, Dependable* (Cm. 3807). London: HMSO.

Department of Health (1998). *Crossing Bridges.* London: HMSO.

Department of Health (1998). *Modernising Social Services. Promoting Independence, Improving Protection, Raising Standards* (Cm. 4169). London: HMSO.

Department of Health (1998). *Our Healthier Nation: A Contract for Health* (Cm. 3852). London: HMSO.

Department of Health (1998). *Partnership in Action.* London: HMSO.

Department of Health (1998). *Review of The Mental Health Act Report of The Expert Committee.* London: Department of Health.

Department of Health (1998). *Working Together to Safeguard Children Consultation Paper.* London: Department of Health.

Department of Health (1998a). *Tackling Drugs to Build A Better Britain.* London: Stationery Office.

Department of Health (1998a.) *National Priorities for Health and Social Services 1999-2002.* London: HMSO.

Department of Health (1998b). *Modernising Social Services. Promoting Independence, Improving Protection, Raising Standards* (Cm. 4169). London: HMSO.

Department of Health (1998b). *Quality Protects Programme: Transforming Children's Services.* LAC, 98: p28. London: Stationery Office.

Department of Health (1999). *A Systematic Review of Research Relating to The Mental Health Act (1983).* London: HMSO.

Department of Health (1999). *Caring About Carers. A National Strategy for Carers.* London: HMSO.

Department of Health (1999). *Drug Misuse and Dependence: Guidelines on Clinical Management.* London: HMSO.

Department of Health (1999). *Modernising Mental Health Services.* London: HMSO.

Department of Health (1999). *National Service Framework for Mental Health.* London: HMSO.

Department of Health (1999). *No Secrets: The Protection of Vulnerable Adults – Guidance on the Development and Implementation of Multi-agency Policies and Procedures.* London: HMSO.

Department of Health (1999). *'Open All Hours' Inspection of Local Authority Social Services Emergency Out of Hours Arrangements.* http://www.doh.gov.uk/ pub/docs/ doh/oahrep.pdf

Department of Health (1999). *A New Approach to Social Services Performance.* Department of Health.

Department of Health (1999). *Quality Protects.* London: HMSO.

Department of Health (1999). *Reform of The Mental Health Act 1983.* London: HMSO.

Department of Health (1999). *Saving Lives: Our Healthier Nation.* London: Stationery Office.

Department of Health (1999). *Still Building Bridges.* London: HMSO.

Department of Health (1999). *The Government's Objectives for Children's Social Services.* London: Department of Health.

Department of Health (1999a.) *National Priorities for Health and Social Services 1999-2002.* London: Department of Health.

Department of Health (2000). *National Priorities for Health and Social Services 2000-2003.* London: Department of Health.

Department of Health (2000). *No Secrets: Guidance on Developing and Implementing Multi-agency Policies and Procedure to Protect Vulnerable Adults from Abuse.* London: Department of Health.

Department of Health (2000). *Shifting the Balance of Power.* London: HMSO.

Department of Health (2001). *A Practitioners Guide to Carers Assessments under The Carers and Disabled Children Act 2000.* London: Department of Health.

Department of Health (2001). *Carers and Disabled Children Act 2000: Carers and People With Parental Responsibility for Disabled Children. Policy and Practice Guidance.* London: Department of Health.

Department of Health (2001). *National Service Framework for Older People*. London: Stationery Office.

Department of Health (2001). *Valuing People: A New Strategy for Learning Disability for the 21st Century*. London: HMSO.

Department of Health (2001a). *The National Strategy for Sexual Health and HIV*. London: Stationery Office.

Department of Health (2001b). *HIV and Infant Feeding: Guidance from the UK Chief Medical Officer's Expert Advisory Group on AIDS*. London: Department of Health.

Department of Health (2001). *Care Homes for Older People: National Minimum Standards*. London: The Stationery Office.

Department of Health (2002). *Reform of Social Work Education*. Department of Health. http://www.doh.gov.uk/swqualification/

Department of Health (2002). *Women's Mental Health: Into the Mainstream*. London: The Stationery Office.

Department of Health (2002). *White Reform of the Mental Health Act*. London: HMSO.

Department of Health and Home Office (1992). *Review of Health and Social Services for Mentally Disordered Offenders and Others Requiring Similar Services*. Final summary report (Cm. 2088). London: HMSO.

Department of Health and Home Office (1999). *Managing Dangerous People with Severe Personality Disorder*. London: HMSO.

DfEE (2000). *Sex and Relationship Education Guidance*. London: DfEE.

DHCI (2002). *Getting the Best From Best Value: Sharing The Experience of Applying Best Value in Social Care*. London: HMSO.

Diggins, M. and Mazey, K. (1998). *Crossing Bridges: The Impact of Parental Mental Ill Health on Child Welfare: A Training Pack*. London: Department of Health.

Department of Health and Home Office (1992). *Review of Health and Social Services for Mentally Disordered Offenders and Others Requiring Similar Services*. Final summary report (Cm. 2088). London: HMSO.

Department of Health and Home Office (1999). *Managing Dangerous People with Severe Personality Disorder*. London: HMSO.

Department of Health, Home Office and Department for Education (1991). *Working Together Under The Children Act 1989: A Guide to Arrangements for Inter-Agency Cooperation for The Protection of Children From Abuse*. London: HMSO.

Department of Health, Home Office and DfEE (2000). *Framework for the Assessment of Children in Need and Their Families*. London: The Stationery Office.

DoHSS (1977). *Prevention and Health* (Cm. 7047). London: HMSO.

DoHSS (1981). *Prevention and Health: Drinking Sensibly*. London: HMSO.

DoHSS and The Welsh Office (1977). *Prevention: Report of The Advisory Committee on Alcoholism*. London: HMSO.

DoHSS and The Welsh Office (1978). *The Pattern and Range of Services for Problem Drinkers: Report of The Advisory Committee on Alcoholism*. London: HMSO.

DoHSS Northern Ireland (1995). *Review of Policy for People with a Learning Disability*. Belfast: HMSO.

Dominelli, L. (1996). Deprofessionalising Social Work: Anti-Oppressive Practice, Competencies and Postmodernism. *British Journal of Social Work*, 26(2): pp153-p75.

Dominelli, L., Jeffers, L., Jones, G., Sibanda, S. and Williams, B. (1995). *Anti-Racist Probation Practice*. Aldershot: Arena.

Douch, C. and Ross, M. (1998). *Response to Children Living With Domestic Violence*. Michael Sieff Foundation Report No. 13 Violence Between Parents: Children as Victims.

Draucker, C.B. (1992). *Counselling the Victims of Childhood Sexual Abuse*. Newbury Park: Sage.

Drew, L. (1968). Alcoholism as A Self-Limiting Disease. *Quarterly Journal of Studies on Alcohol*, 29(4): pp956-967.

DTLR (2002). *Best Value Performance Indicator Index*. London: The Stationery Office.

Dubowitz, H. (Ed.) (1999). *Neglected Children. Research, Practice and Policy*. London: Sage.

Edwards, G., Anderson, P., Babor, T.F., Casswell, S., Ferrence, R., Giesbrecht, N., Godfrey, C., Holder, H.D., Lemmens, P.H.M.M., Makela, K., et al. (1994). *Alcohol Policy and the Public Good*. Oxford: Oxford University Press.

Eguland, T. (1996). Bureaucracy or Professionalism? The Work Tools of Child Protection Services. *Scandinavian Journal of Social Work*, 5: pp165-174.

Evason, E. and Whittington, D. (1995). *The Cost of Caring*. Belfast: Equal Opportunities Commission for N. Ireland.

Fadden, G. (1998). Family Intervention in Psychosis. *Journal of Mental Health*, 7: pp115-122.

Fagin, L. and Chapman, S. (1986). Interdisciplinary Association of Mental Health Workers, Report of the Policy Group. *IAMHW Bulletin*, 4: pp14-18.

Falkov, A. (1995). *Study of Working Together Part 8: Reports DH ACPC Series 1996, Report No.1.* London: Department of Health.

Falkov, A. (1996). *Study of Working Together Part 8 Reports. Fatal Child Abuse and Parental Psychiatric Disorder: An Analysis of 100 Area Child Protection Committee Case Reviews Conducted Under the Terms of Part 8 of Working Together Under The Children Act 1989.* London: Department of Health.

Fallon, P. (1999). *The Report of The Committee of Inquiry into the Personality Disorder Unit, Ashworth Special Hospital (Fallon Report).* London: HMSO.

Falloon, I.R.H., Boyd, J. and Mcgill, C.W. (1984). *Family Care of Schizophrenia.* New York: Guilford.

Farmer, E. and Owen, M. (1995). *Child Protection Practice Private Risks and Public Remedies.* London: HMSO.

Feeley, M. and Simon, J. (1992). The New Penology: Notes on the Emerging Strategy of Corrections. *Criminology*, 30(4): pp449-45.

Feldman, M.A., Leger, M. and Walton-Allen, N. (1997). Stress in Mothers with Intellectual Disabilities. *Journal of Child and Family Studies*, 6(4): pp471-485.

Fernando, S. (1988). *Race and Culture in Society.* London: Croom Helm.

Fernando, S. (1995). *Mental Health in a Multi-Ethnic Society.* London: Routledge.

Finkelstein, V. (1981). To Deny or Not to Deny Disability. In Brechin, A., Liddiard, P. and Swain, J. (Eds.) *Handicap in a Social World*, pp33-36. Sevenoaks: Hodder and Stoughton.

Finkelstein, V. (1993). Disability: A Social Challenge or an Administrative Responsibility? In Swain, J., Finklestein, V., French, S. and Oliver, M. (Eds.) *Disabling Barriers – Enabling Environments*, pp34-43. London: Sage.

Finkelstein, V. and Stuart, O. (1996). Developing New Services. In Hales, G. (Ed.) *Beyond Disability: Towards an Enabling Society*, pp170-187. London: Sage.

Forman, J. (1995). *Is There a Correlation Between Child Sexual Abuse and Domestic Violence? An Exploratory Study of The Links between Child Sexual Abuse and Domestic Violence in a Sample of Interfamilial Child Sexual Abuse Cases.* Glasgow: Women's Support Project.

Forrester, D. (2000). Parental Substance Misuse and Child Protection in a British Sample: A Survey of Children on the Child Protection Register in an Inner London District Office. *Child Abuse Review*, 9(4): pp235-246.

Fratter, J. (1993). Positive Options Planning Scheme. In Batty, D. (Ed.) *HIV Infection and Children in Need*, pp71-83. London: BAAF.

French, S. (1988). *Experiences of Disabled Health and Welfare Professionals. Sociology of Health and Illness*, 10(2): pp170-188.

French, S. (1994). Disabled People and Professional Practice. In French, S. (Ed.) *On Equal Terms: Working with Disabled People*, pp103-118. Oxford: Butterworth-Heinemann.

French, S. (1996). Simulation Exercises in Disability Awareness Training: A Critique. In Hales, G. (Ed.) *Beyond Disability: Towards an Enabling Society*, pp114-123. London: Sage.

French, S. (1998). Surviving the Institution: Working as a Visually Disabled Lecturer in Higher Education. In Malina, D. and Maslin-Prothero, S. (Eds.) *Surviving the Academy: Feminist Perspectives*, pp31-41. London: Falmer Press.

French, S. and Vernon, A. (1997). Health Care for People from Ethnic Minority Groups. In French, S. (Ed.) *Physiotherapy: A Psychosocial Approach* (2nd edn.) pp59-72. Oxford: Butterworth-Heinemann.

French, S., Gillman, M. and Swain, J. (1997). *Working with Visually Disabled People: Bridging Theory and Practice.* Birmingham: Venture Press.

Fuller, R. and Tulle-Winton, E. (1996). Specialism, Genericism and Others: Does it Make a Difference? A Study of Social Work Services to Elderly People. *British Journal of Social Work*, 26(5): pp679-698.

Fulmer, T. and O'Malley, T. (1987). *Inadequate Care of the Elderly: A Health Care Perspective on Abuse and Neglect.* New York: Springer.

Gates, B. (1997). *Learning Disabilities,* (3rd edn). Edinburgh: Churchill-Livingstone.

Gearing, B., Johnson, M. and Heller, T. (Eds.) (1988). *Mental Health Problems in Old Age: A Reader.* Chichester: Wiley Medical Publication and The Open University.

Gibbons, J., Conroy, S. and Bell, C. (1995). *Operating the Child Protection System.* London: HMSO.

Gilders, I. (1997). Round Pegs in Round Holes: A Social Work Care Management Service for Vulnerable Adults in West Oxfordshire. *Practice*, 9(3): pp45-58.

Gill, A. and Marshall, T. (1993). Working With Racist Offenders. An Anti-Racist Response. *Probation Journal*, 40(2): pp54-59.

Gillie Report (1963). *The Field of Work of the Family Doctor. Report of the Sub-Committee of the Standing Advisory Medical Committee of the Central Health Services Council.* London: HMSO.

Glendenning, F. (1999). The Abuse of Older People in Institutional Settings: An Overview. In Stanley, N., Manthorpe, J. and Penhale, B. (1999). *Institutional Abuse: Perspectives across the lifecourse*, pp173-190. London: Routledge.

Glennie, S. and Norman, J. (2000). Delivering Inter-Agency Training: The development of alternative structures. In Charles, M. and Hendry, E. (Eds.) *Training Together to Safeguard Children*. London: NSPCC.

Gold, S. (1997). The Civil Way. *New Law Journal*, October: pp1424-1431.

Goldberg, D. and Huxley, P. (1992). *Common Mental Disorders: A Biosocial Model*. London: Routledge.

Gondolf, E.W., Mulvey, E.P. and Lidz, C.W. (1990). Characteristics of Perpetrators of Family and Non-Family Assaults. *Hospital and Community Psychiatry*, 41(2).

Gooding, C. (1996). *Blackstone's Guide to the Disability Discrimination Act 1995*. London: Blackstone Press.

Grafstrom, M., Norberg, A. and Wimblad, B. (1992). Abuse is in the Eye of the Beholder. Reports by Family Members about Abuse of Demented Persons in Home Care. A Total Population Based Study. *Scandinavian Journal of Social Medicine*, 24(4): pp247-55.

Gravestock, S. (1999). Adults with Learning Disabilities and Mental Health Needs: Conceptual and Service Issues. *Tizard Learning Disability Review*, 4(6): p13.

Griffiths, S.R. (1988). *Community Care: Agenda for Action*. London: HMSO.

Grounds, A. (1995). Risk Assessment and Management in a Clinical Context. In Crichton, J. (Ed.) *Psychiatric Patient Violence: Risk and Response*. London: Duckworth.

GSCC (2002). *Social Work Education and Training – Annual Quality Assurance Report 2001–02*. London: General Social Care Council.

Guillebaud, J. (1956). *Report of the Committee of Enquiry into the Cost of The National Health Service*. London: HMSO.

Hadley, R. and Mcgrath, M. (1981). *Going Local: Neighbourhood Social Services*. London: Bedford Square Press.

Hagell, A. and Newburn, T. (1994). *Persistent Young Offenders*. London: Policy Studies Institute.

Hague, G., Malos, E. and Dear, W. (1996). *Multi-Agency Working and Domestic Violence*. Bristol: Policy Press.

Haines, K. and Drakeford, M. (1998). *Young People and Youth Justice*. Houndmills, Basingstoke: Macmillan.

Hallett, C. (1995). *Interagency Coordination in Child Protection*. London: HMSO.

Hammersmith and Fulham Domestic Violence Forum (Undated). *Domestic Violence: A Health Issue*. London: Hammersmith and Fulham Domestic Violence Forum.

Harbour, A. and Bailey, S. (2000). Reforming The Mental Health Act: What are the Implications for Children? *Young Minds Magazine*, 45: p3.

Harrison, L., Guy, P. and Sivyer, W. (1996). Community Care Policy and the Future of Alcohol Services. In Harrison, L. (1996). *Alcohol Problems in the Community*, pp241-265. London: Routledge.

Hayes, S. (1998). Justice for All? Advocacy, People with Learning Difficulties, Crime and the Law. In Ward, L. (Ed.) *Innovations in Advocacy and Empowerment for People with Intellectual Disabilities*, pp245-264. Chorley: Lisieux Hall Publications.

Heidensohn, F. (1985). *Women and Crime*. Houndmills, Basingstoke: Macmillan.

Henderson, S. (1997). *Service Provision to Women Experiencing Domestic Violence in Scotland*. Edinburgh: The Scottish Office.

Hendessai, M. (1999). *A Space for Us: The Needs of Asian Women and Children Experiencing Domestic Violence in Milton Keynes*. Milton Keynes: Milton Keynes Women's Aid.

Hendry, E. (2000). The Content of Inter-Agency Training to Safeguard Children. In Charles, M. and Hendry, E. (Eds.) *Training Together to Safeguard Children. Guidance on Inter-Agency Training*. London: NSPCC.

Hendry, E. and Horwath, J. (2000). Can We Talk? *Community Care*, 2-8 Nov: pp26-27.

Henwood, M. (1998). *Ignored and Invisible? Carers Experience of the NHS*. London: Carers National Association.

Herbert Report (1960). *Royal Commission on Local Government in Greater London 1957-60* (Cm.1164). London: HMSO.

Heron, C. (1998). *Working With Carers*. London: Jessica Kingsley.

Hester, M. and Pearson, C. (1998). *From Periphery to Centre: Domestic Violence in Work with Abused Children*. Bristol: Policy Press.

Hester, M. and Radford, L. (1996). *Domestic Violence and Child Contact Arrangements in England and Denmark*. Bristol: Policy Press.

Hester, M., Pearson, C. and Harwin, N. (1999). *Making an Impact: Children and Domestic Violence – A Reader*. London: Jessica Kingsley.

HMIP (1995). *Dealing With Dangerous People: The Probation Service and Public Protection*. London: HMSO.

HMSO (1978). *Social Services Team: The Practitioners View*. London: HMSO.

Hodgins, S. (1992). Mental Disorder, Intellectual Disability and Crime. Evidence from A Birth Cohort. *Archives of General Psychiatry*, 49(6): pp476–83.

Hogan, D.M. (1998). The Psychological Development and Welfare of Children of Opiate and Cocaine Users: Review and Research Needs. *Journal of Child Psychology and Psychiatry*, 39(5): pp609–20.

Hollin, C. (1990). *Cognitive-behavioural Interventions with Young Offenders*. Oxford: Pergamon.

Hollin, C. and Howells, K. (1992). *Clinical Approaches to Sex Offenders and their Victims*. Chichester: Wiley.

Hollin, C.R. (Ed.) (2000). *Handbook of Offender Assessment and Treatment*. Chichester: Wiley.

Holman, A. and Collins, J. (1998). Choice and Control: Making Direct Payments Work for People With Learning Difficulties. In Ward, L. (Ed.) *Innovations in Advocacy and Empowerment for People with Intellectual Disabilities*, pp215-232. Chorley: Lisieux Hall Publications.

Holzhausen, E. (1997). *Still Battling? The Carers Act One Year On*. London: Carers National Association.

Home Office (1983). *Mental Health Act*. London: HMSO.

Home Office (1988a). *Home Office Letter to Chief Probation Officers July 1988: The Registration and Review of Serious Offenders*. London: Home Office.

Home Office (1988b). *Punishment, Custody and the Community*. London: HMSO.

Home Office (1990). *The Victims Charter*. London: HMSO.

Home Office (1991). *Criminal Justice Act*. London: HMSO.

Home Office (1995). *National Standards for the Supervision of Offenders in the Community*. London: Home Office.

Home Office (1996). *Protecting the Public: The Government's Strategy on Crime in England and Wales*. London: HMSO.

Home Office (1996). *The Victim's Charter: A Statement of the Rights of Victims of Crime*. London: HMSO.

Home Office (1997a). *The Crime (Sentences) Act*. London: HMSO.

Home Office (1997b). *Pre-Sentence Report Learning Programme*. London: Home Office.

Home Office (1998). *The Crime and Disorder Act*. London: HMSO.

Home Office (1999). *A Learning and Development Programme for Work With Mentally Disordered Offenders*. London: Home Office.

Home Office (2000a). *Criminal Justice and Courts Services Act 2000*. London: HMSO.

Home Office (2000b). *National Standards for the Supervision of Offenders in the Community*. London: Home Office.

Home Office (2000c). *The Victim Perspective: Ensuring the Victim Matters*. London: HMIP (Website: Http://Homeoffice.Gov.Uk/Hmiprob/Thenvict.Htm).

Home Office/Department of Health (1999). *Managing Dangerous People with Severe Personality Disorder Proposals for Policy Development*. London: HMSO.

Homer, A. and Gilleard, C. (1990). Abuse of Elderly People by their Carers. *British Medical Journal*, 301: pp1359-1362.

Horwath, J. and Morrison, T. (1999). *Effective Staff Training in Social Care: From Theory to Practice*. London: Routledge.

Hughes, B. (1995). *Older People and Community Care: Critical Theory and Practice*. Buckingham: Open University Press.

Hughes, H. (1988). Psychological and Behavioural Correlates of Family Violence in Child Witnesses and Victims. *American Journal of Orthopsychiatry*, 58(1): pp75-79.

Hugman, R. (1991). *Power in Caring Professions*. Houndmills, Basingstoke: Macmillan.

Hugman, R. and Phillips, N. (1993). Like Bees Round the Honey Pot, Social Work Responses to Parents with Mental Health Needs. *Practice*, 6(3): pp193-205.

Hull-York Research Team (1993). *Social Care and HIV-AIDS*. London: HMSO.

Humphreys, C. (1999a). Avoidance and Confrontation: Social Work Practice in Relation to Domestic Violence and Child Abuse. *Child and Family Social Work*, 4(1): pp77-88.

Humphreys, C. (1999b). The Judicial Alienation Syndrome – Failures to respond to Post-Separation Violence. *Family Law Journal*, June: pp1-4.

Humphreys, C. and Kaye, M. (1997). Third Party Applications for Protection Orders: Opportunities, Ambiguities and Traps. *Journal of Social Welfare and Family Law*, 19(4): pp403-41.

Humphreys, C., Hester, M., Hague, G., Mullender, A., Abrahams, H. and Lowe, P. (2000). *From Good Intentions to Good Practice*. Bristol: Policy Press.

Hunter, (1999). Possible Child Abuse Cases Being Ignored. *Community Care*, 18-24 March: p3.

Hurst, J. (1996). Moral Crusaders. *Community Care*, 7(13): p12.

Imam, U. (1994). Asian Children and Domestic Violence. In Mullender, A. and Morley, R. (Eds.) *Children Living With Domestic Violence*. London: Whiting and Birch.

Improving Protection, Raising Standards. London: The Stationery Office.

Intercollegiate Working Party for Enhancing Voluntary Confidential HIV Testing in Pregnancy (1998). *Reducing Mother to Child Transmission of HIV Infection in The United Kingdom*. London: Royal College of Paediatrics and Child Health.

Jack, G. (1997). Discourses of Child Protection and Child Welfare. *British Journal of Social Work*, 27: pp659-678.

Jack, G. (2000). Ecological Influences on Parenting and Child Development. *British Journal of Social Work*, 30: pp703-720.

Jack, G. (2001). Ecological Perspectives in Assessing Children and Families. In Horwath, J. (Ed.) *The Child's World Assessing Children in Need*. London: Jessica Kingsley.

Jackson, C. (1998). Listen to Mother. *Mental Health Care*, 1(7): pp217-219.

Jacobs, B. (1990). Ageing and Politics. In Binstock, R.H. and George, L. K.(Eds.) *Handbook of Ageing and the Social Sciences*. London: Academic Press.

Jacobson, A. and Richardson, B. (1987). Assault Experiences of 100 Psychiatric Inpatients: Evidence of Need for Routine Inquiry. *American Journal of Psychiatry*, 144: pp908-913.

Jaffe, P., Wolfe, D. and Wilson, S. (1990). *Children of Battered Women*. London: Sage.

James, P. and Thomas, M. (1996). Deconstructing a Disabling Environment in Social Work Education. *Social Work Education*, 15(1): pp34-45.

Jenkins, A. (1989). *Invitations to Responsibility*. Adelaide, Australia: Dulwich Centre Publications.

Jenner, H. (1998). *Pygmalion in Treatment of Addictions: The Role of Expectations in Therapeutic Transaction*. Stockholm: Stockholm Institute of Education Press.

Johnson, M. (1976). That Was Your Life: A Biographical Approach to Later Life. In Munnichs, J.M.A. and Van Den Heuval, W.J.A. (Eds.) *Dependency and Interdependency in Old Age*. Martinus Nijoff: The Hague.

Johnson, M. (1988). Biographical Influences on Mental Health in Old Age. In Gearing, B., Johnson, M. and Heller, T. (Eds.) *Mental Health Problems in Old Age: A Reader*. Chichester: Wiley Medical Publication and The Open University.

Jones, L. (2002). *Nursing the Person: The Role of the Biographical Approach in the Nursing Care of Older People*. Unpublished Dissertation Submitted for A MA in Gerontology. University of Salford.

Jordan, B. and Jordan, C. (2000). *Social Work and the Third Way*. London: Sage.

Jouriles, E., Stephens, R., Norwood, W., Collazos, L., Spiller, W. and Shinn Ware, H. (1998). Breaking the Cycle of Violence: Helping Families Departing from Battered Women's Shelters. In Jouriles, E. (Ed.) *Children Exposed to Marital Violence. Theory, Research and Applied Issues*. Washington DC: American Psychological Association.

Karr-Morse, R. and Wiley, M.S. (2000). *Ghosts from the Nursery. Tracing the Roots of Violence*. New York: The Atlantic Monthly Press.

Kemshall, H. (1995). Risk in Probation Practice: The Hazards and Dangers of Supervision. *Probation Journal*, 42(2): pp67-72.

Kemshall, H. (1996). Offender Risk and Probation Practice. In Kemshall, H. and Pritchard, J. (Eds.) *Good Practice in Risk Assessment and Management (Vol. 1)*. London: Jessica Kingsley.

Kemshall, H. (1996). *Reviewing Risk. A Review of Research on the Assessment and Management of Risk and Dangerousness: Implications for Policy and Practice in the Probation Service: A Report for the Home Office Research and Statistics Directorate*. London: Home Office.

Kemshall, H. (1997a). *Training Materials for Risk Assessment and Risk Management. In Management and Assessment of Risk in the Probation Service, Part 3*. London: Home Office/Association of Chief Officers of Probation.

Kemshall, H. (1998). *Risk in Probation Practice*. Aldershot: Ashgate.

Kemshall, H. and Pritchard, J. (1999). *Good Practice in Working With Violence*. London: Jessica Kingsley.

Kemshall, H., Parton, N., Walsh, M. and Waterson, J. (1997b). Concepts of Risk in Relation to Organisational Structure and Functioning within the Personal Social Services and Probation. *Social Policy and Administration*, 31(3): pp213-232.

Kershaw, C. (1997). *Reconviction of those Commencing Community Penalties in 1993*. London: Home Office Statistical Bulletins Issue 6/97.

Kingdom, D.G. and Turkington, D. (1995). *Cognitive: Behavioural Therapy of Schizophrenia*. Hove, Sussex: Psychology Press.

Kochman, A. (1997). Gay and Lesbian Elderly: Historical Overview and Implications for Social Work Practice. *Journal of Gay and Lesbian Social Services*, 6(1): pp29-39.

Kuipers, L., Leff, J. and Lam, D. (1992). *Family Work for Schizophrenia. A Practical Guide*. London: Gaskel/Royal College of Psychiatrists.

Law Commission (1995). *Mental Incapacity, Report No. 231*. London: HMSO.

Leathard, A. (1994). *Going Interprofessional-Working Together for Health and Welfare*. London: Routledge.

Lee, J.A. (1989). Invisible Men: Canada's Ageing Homosexuals. Can they be Assimilated into Canada's 'Liberated' Gay Communities? *Canadian Journal on Ageing*, 8 (1): pp79-97.

Liberty (National Council for Civil Liberties) (1994). *Access Denied: Human Rights and Disabled People*. London: Liberty.

Littlewood, R. and Lipsedge, M. (1997). *Aliens and Alienists* (3rd edn.) London: Routledge.

Lloyd, M. and Taylor, C. (1995). From Hollis to the Orange Book: Developing a Holistic Model of Social Work Assessment in the 1990s. *British Journal of Social Work*, 25(6): pp691-710.

Local Authority Associations' Officer Working Group on AIDS (1995). *Learning from African Families*. London: The Local Government Management Board.

London Borough of Hounslow (1994). *Domestic Violence: Help, Advice and Information for Disabled Women*. London: London Borough of Hounslow.

Lord Chancellor's Department (1998). *Who Decides?* London: HMSO.

Lord Chancellor's Department (1999). *Making Decisions*. London: HMSO.

Lord President of The Council (1995). *Tackling Drugs Together* (Cm. 2846). London: HMSO.

Lord President of The Council (1998). *Tackling Drugs to Build a Better Britain* (Cm. 3945). London: HMSO.

Loxley, A. (1997). *Collaboration in Health and Welfare*. London: Jessica Kingsley.

Macdonald, G. (2001). *Effective Interventions for Child Abuse and Neglect*. Chichester: Wiley.

Mahon, A. and Higgins, J. (1995). *A Life of our Own Young Carers: An Evaluation of 3 RHA Funded Projects in Merseyside*. Manchester: Health Services Management Unit.

Mair, G. and May, C. (1997). *Offenders on Probation. Home Office Research Study 167*. London: Home Office Research and Statistics Directorate.

Marsh, P. and Triseliotis, J. (1996). *Ready to Practice? Social Workers and Probation Officers: Their training and First Year at Work*. Aldershot: Avebury.

Martinson, R. (1974). What Works? Questions and Answers about Prison Reform. *Public Interest*, 10 Mar: pp22-54.

Matovu, L., Mwatsama, M. and Ndagire, B. (1998). Family Patterns in East African Communities: Implications for Children Affected by HIV/AIDS. *Adoption and Fostering*, 22(1): pp17-22.

Mayhew, P., Maung, N.A. and Mirrless-Black, C. (1993). *The 1992 British Crime Survey. Home Office Research Study No. 132*. London: HMSO.

Maynard, A. (1989). The Costs of Addiction and the Costs of Control. In Robinson, D., Maynard, A. and Chester, R. (Eds.) *Controlling Legal Addictions*. Houndmills, Basingstoke: Macmillan.

McCarthy, M. (1999). *Sexuality and Women with Learning Disabilities*. London: Jessica Kingsley.

McGibbon, A., Cooper, L. and Kelly, L. (1989). *What Support? An exploratory study of Council Policy and Practice and Local Support Services in the area of domestic violence within Hammersmith and Fulham, Final Report*. London: Polytechnic of North London, Child Abuse Studies Unit.

McGuire, J. (2000). *Cognitive Behavioural Approaches: An Introduction to Theory and Research*. HM Inspectorate of Probation: Home Office.

McGuire, J. (Ed.) (1995). *What Works: Effective Methods to Reduce Re-offending*. Chichester: Wiley.

McHale, J.V. (1991). Harm Reduction and the Needle Exchange Scheme: Some Legal Problems. *Journal of Social Welfare and Family Law*, 13(1): pp27-36.

McIvor, G. (1990). *Sanctions for Serious or Persistent Offenders*. Stirling: Social Work Research Centre.

McKellar, S. and Coggans, N. (1997). Responding to Family Problems, Alcohol and Substance Misuse. *Children and Society*, 11(1): pp53-59.

McLaughlin, E. and Muncie, J. (Eds.) (2001). *Controlling Crime*. London: Sage.

McLeod, J. (1999). What can be Done to Make Sure that Counselling Does Not Harm People? *Journal of Adult Protection*, 1 (1): pp17-22.

McWilliams, M. and McKiernan, J. (1993). *Bringing It Out in the Open*. Belfast: HMSO.

Means, R. and Smith, R. (1998). *From Poor Law to Community Care*. Bristol: Policy Press.

Meichenbaum, H. (1977). *Cognitive Behaviour Modification: An Integrative Approach*. New York: Plenum Press.

Mental Health Foundation (1993). *Fundamental Facts about Learning Disability*. London: Mental Health Foundation.

Mercer, C., Mueser, K. and Drake, R. (1998). Organizational Guidelines for Dual Disorders

Programmes. *Psychiatric Quarterly*, 69(3): pp145-167.

Mertin, P. (1995). A Follow-up Study of Children From Domestic Violence. *Australian Journal of Family Law*, 9: pp76-85.

Meuser, K., Bond, G., Drake, R. and Resnick, G. (1998). Models of Community Care for Severe Mental Illness: A Review of Research on Case Management. *Schizophrenia Bulletin*, 24: pp37-73.

Mezey, G. (1997). Domestic Violence and Pregnancy. *British Journal of Obstetrics and Gynaecology*, 104: pp528-523.

Middleton, L. (1999). *Disabled Children: Challenging Social Exclusion*. Oxford: Blackwell Science.

Miller, W. and Rollnick, S. (1991). *Motivational Interviewing*. New York: Guilford Press.

Miller, W.R. (1983). Controlled Drinking: A History and a Critical Review. *Journal of Studies on Alcohol*, 44(1): pp68-83.

Miller, W.R. and Rollnick, S. (Eds.) (1991). *Motivational Interviewing: Preparing People for Change*. New York: Guildford Press.

Milner, J. (1993). A Disappearing Act: The Differing Career Paths of Fathers and Mothers in Child Protection Investigations. *Critical Social Policy*, 13: pp48-61.

Milner, J. and O'Byrne, P. (1998). *Assessment in Social Work*. Houndmills, Basingstoke: Macmillan.

Ministry of Health (1962). *Hospital Treatment of Alcoholism. Memorandum HM 62, 43*. London: Ministry of Health.

Modood, T. and Berthoud, R. (1997). *Ethnic Minorities in Britain*. London: Policy Studies Institute.

Monahan, J. (1981). *The Clinical Prediction of Violence*. Beverley Hills, CA: Sage.

Mooney, J. (1994). *The Hidden Figure: Domestic Violence in North London*. London: London Borough of Islington, Police and Crime Prevention Unit.

Morgan, L. and Kunkel, S. (1998). *Aging: The Social Context*. California: Pine Forge.

Morris J. (1993). *Independent Lives: Community Care and Disabled People*. London: Macmillan.

Morris, J. (1989). *Able Lives: Women's Experiences of Paralysis*. London: The Women's Press.

Morris, J. (1991). *Community Care of Independent Living?* York: Joseph Rowntree Foundation.

Morrison, T. (1996). Partnership and Collaboration: Rhetoric and Reality. *Child Abuse and Neglect*, 20(2): pp127-140.

Mounteney, J. and Shapiro, H. (1997). *Drugs, Children and Families*. Birmingham: Venture Press.

Mullender, A. (1996). *Rethinking Domestic Violence. The Social Work and Probation Response*. London: Routledge.

Mullender, A. (1996). *Rethinking Domestic Violence: The Social Work and Probation Response*. London: Routledge.

Mullender, A. and Morley, R. (1994). *Children Living with Domestic Violence*. London: Whiting and Birch.

Mullender, A., Debbonaire, T., Hague, G., Kelly, L. and Malos, E. (1998). Working with Children in Women's Refuges. *Child and Family Social Work*, 3(1): pp87-98.

NACRO (1994). *Working with Mentally Disordered Offenders. A Training Pack for Social Services Staff and Others Dealing With Mentally Disordered Offenders*. London: Department of Health.

Nathan, P.E. (1988). The Addictive Personality is The Behaviour of The Addict. *Journal of Consulting and Clinical Psychology*, 56(2): pp183-188.

National AIDS Trust (1999). *Are Health Authorities Failing Gay Men?* London: NAT.

National Probation Service for England and Wales, and The Home Office Communication Directorate (2001). *A New Choreography. An Integrated Strategy for the National Probation Service for England and Wales: Strategic Framework 200-2004*. London: National Probation Service for England and Wales and the Home Office Communication Directorate.

National Schizophrenia Fellowship (1999). *Caring and Coping*. Kingston upon Thames: NSF.

Nettleton, H., Walklate, S. and Williams, B. (1997). *Probation Training With The Victim in Mind*. Keele: Keele University Press.

NHS Executive (1998). *Commissioning in the New NHS (HSC 1998/198)*. NHS Executive.

NHS Executive (1999). *Reducing Mother to Baby Transmission of HIV (HSC 1999/183)*. NHS Executive.

Norman, A. (1985). *Triple Jeopardy: Growing Old in a Second Homeland*. London: Centre for Policy on Ageing.

Nosek, M., Howland, C. and Young, M. (1998). Abuse of Women with Disabilities: Policy Implications. *Journal of Disability Policy Studies*, 8: pp158-175.

Nutley, S.M. and Davies, H.T.O. (1999). The Fall and Rise of Evidence in Criminal Justice. *Public Money and Management*, 19(1): pp47-54.

O'Hara, M. (1994). Child Deaths in the Context of Domestic Violence: Implications for Professional Practice. In Mullender, A. and Morley, R. (Eds.) *Children Living with Domestic Violence*. London: Whiting and Birch.

O'Hare, P.A., Newcombe, R., Matthews, A., Buning, E.C. and Drucker, E. (Eds.) (1992). *The Reduction of Drug Related Harm*. London: Routledge.

Oliver, M. (1990). *The Politics of Disablement*. Houndmills, Basingstoke: Macmillan.

Oliver, M. (1991). Disability and Participation in the Labour Market. In Brown, P. and Scase, R. (Eds.) *Poor Work*, pp132–145. Milton Keynes: Open University Press.

Oliver, M. (1996). *Understanding Disability: From Theory to Practice*. London: Macmillan.

Oliver, M. and Barnes, C. (1998). *Disabled People and Social Policy*. London: Longman.

Oliver, M. and Sapey, B. (1999). *Social Work with Disabled People* (2nd edn.) Houndmills, Basingstoke: Macmillan.

Oliver, M. and Zarb, G. (1992). *Personal Assistance Schemes: Greenwich Association of Disabled People*. London: Greenwich Association of Disabled People Ltd.

Parker, J. (2001). Seeking Effective Approaches to Elder Abuse in Institutional Settings. *Journal of Adult Protection*, 3: pp21-29.

Parker, J. and Eaton, D. (1994). Opposing Contact. *Family Law Journal*, Nov: pp636-641.

Parker, J. and Penhale, B. (1998). *Forgotten People? Positive Approaches to Dementia Care*. Aldershot: Ashgate Arena.

Parker, R., Ward, H., Jackson, S., Aldgate, J. and Wedge, P. (1991). *Looking after Children: Assessing Outcomes in Child Care*. London: HMSO.

Parkinson, P. and Humphreys, C. (1998). Children Who Witness Domestic Violence: The Implications for Child Protection. *Child and Family Law Quarterly*, 10(2): pp147–159.

Parton, N. (1996). Child Protection, Family Support and Social Work: A Critical Appraisal of the Department of Health Research Studies in Child Protection. *Child and Family Social Work*, 1(1): pp3–11.

Patel, M. (1997). *Domestic Violence and Deportation*. London: Southall Black Sisters.

Patmore, C. (Ed.) (1987). *Living After Mental Illness*. London: Croom Helm.

Payne, M. (1995). *Social Work and Community Care*. Houndmills, Basingstoke: Macmillan.

Payne, M. (1996). *What Is Professional Social Work?* Birmingham: Venture Press.

Payne, M. and Shardlow, S.M. (Eds.) (2002). *Social Work in the British Isles*. London: Jessica Kingsley.

Penhale, B. and Kingston, P. (1997). Elder Abuse, Mental Health and Later Life: Steps Towards an Understanding. *Ageing and Mental Health*, 1(4): pp296-304.

Penhale, B., Parker, J. with Kingston, P. (2000). *Elder Abuse: Approaches to Working with Violence*. Birmingham: Venture Press.

Pense, E. and Paymar, M. (1988). *Education Groups for Men Who Batter. An Educational Curriculum: The Duluth Model*. New York: Springer.

Performance Indicators Index. London: The Stationery Office.

Philips, R. and Hugman, N. (1993). Like bees round the honeypot. *Practice*, 6(3): pp193-205.

Philpot, T. (Ed.) (1999). *Political Correctness and Social Work*. London: IEA.

PHLS AIDS Centre and The Scottish Centre for Infection and Environmental Health (2001). *AIDS/HIV Quarterly Surveillance Tables: Cumulative UK Data to End September 2001 No. 55. 02/02.*

Pillemer, K.A. (1986). Risk Factors in Elder Abuse: Results From a Case Control Study. In Pillemer, K.A. and Wolf, R.S. (Eds.) *Elder Abuse: Conflict in the Family*, pp 239-263. Dover, MA: Auburn House.

Pillemer, K.A. and Finkelhor, D. (1988). The Prevalence of Elder Abuse: A Random Sample Survey. *The Gerontologist*, 28(1): pp51-7.

Pilling, S. (1991). *Rehabilitation and Community Care*. London: Routledge.

Pithouse, A., and Scourfield, J. (2002). Ready for Practice? The DipSW in Wales: Views from the Workplace on Social Work Training. *Journal of Social Work*, 2(1): pp7-27.

Pitts, S. (1998). What Works in Probation Service Practice and Management? The Contribution of Quality Standards. *Vista*, 4(1): pp57-72.

Polansky, N.A., Gaudin, J.M., Ammons, P.W. and David, K.B. (1985). The Psychological Ecology of the Neglectful Mother. *Child Abuse and Neglect*, 9: pp265-75.

Powell, M. (Ed.) (1999). *New Labour, New Welfare State? The Third Way in British Politics in British Social Policy*. Bristol: The Policy Press.

Power, R., Jones, S., Kearns, G., Ward, J., Gibson, N., Perera, J. and Smith, J. (1995). *Coping With Illicit Drug Use*. London: Tufnell.

Prins, H. (1997). Risk Assessment and Management. The *Journal of Forensic Psychiatry*, 7(1): pp42-62.

Pritchard, J. (1999). *Elder Abuse Work: Best Practice in Britain and Canada*. London: Jessica Kingsley.

Prochaska, J.O. and Di Clemente, C.C. (1984). *The Transtheoretical Approach: Crossing Traditional Boundaries of Therapy*. Homewood, Ill: Dow-Jones-Erwin.

Prochaska, J.O. and Di Clemente, C.C. (1986). Toward a Comprehensive Model of Change. In Miller, W.R. and Heather, N. (Eds.) *Treating Addictive Behaviours. (Processes of Change* 3-26). New York: Plenum Press.

Pryke, J. and Thomas, T. (1998). *Domestic Violence and Social Work.* Aldershot: Ashgate.

Pugh, S. (1996). Abuse Directed Towards Older People. In Matthew, L. *Professional Care for the Elderly Mentally Ill.* London: Chapman and Hall.

Pugh, S. (2002). The Forgotten: A Community Without a Generation – Older Lesbians and Gay Men. In Richardson, D. and Seidman, S. (2002). *Handbook of Lesbian and Gay Studies.* London: Sage.

QAA (2000). *Social Policy and Administration and Social Work. Quality Assurance Agency for Higher Education.* http://www.qaa.ac.uk/crntwork/benchmark/benchmarking.htm

QAA (2001). *Code of Practice for the Assurance of Academic Quality and Standards in Higher Education: Placement Learning.* http://www.qaa.ac.uk/public/cop/copplacementfinal/precepts.htm

Rai, D. and Thiara, R. (1997). *Re-Defining Spaces: The Needs of Black Women and Children in Refuge Support Services and Black Workers in Women's Aid.* Bristol: Women's Aid Federation of England.

Raistrick, D., Hodgson, R. and Ritson, B. (Eds.) (1999). *Tackling Alcohol Together.* London: Free Association Books.

Ramsay, M. and Percy, A. (1996). *Drug Misuse Declared: Results of the 1994 British Crime Survey.* London: Home Office RSD.

Ramsay, M. and Spiller, J. (1997). *Drug Misuse Declared: Results of the 1996 British Crime Survey.* London: Home Office RSD.

Raynor, P. (1988). *Probation as an Alternative to Custody.* Aldershot: Avebury.

Raynor, P., Smith, D. and Vanstone, M. (1994). *Effective Probation Practice.* Houndmills, Basingstoke: Macmillan.

Reder, P., Duncan, S. and Gray, M. (1993). *Beyond Blame – Child Abuse Tragedies Revisited.* Routledge.

Renn, P. (2000). The Link Between Childhood Trauma and Later Violent Offending: A Case Study. In Boswell, G. *Violent Children and Adolescents: Asking the Question Why.* London and Philadelphia: Whurr Publishers Ltd.

Ritchie, J.H., Dick, D. and Lingham, R. (1994). *The Report of the Inquiry Into the Care and Treatment of Christopher Clunis.* London: HMSO.

Roberts, A.R. and Camasso, M.J. (1991). The Effect of Juvenile Offender Treatment Programs on Recidivism: A Meta-Analysis of 46 Studies. *Notre Dame Journal of Law, Ethics and Public Policy,* 5: pp421-441.

Roberts, C. (1991). *Towards Effective Probation Policy and Practice.* Paper Given at Mid Glamorgan Staff Conference, 5.9.91.

Rogers, A. and Pilgrim, D. (2001). *Mental Health Policy in Britain.* London: Palgrave.

Rogers, A. and Pilgrim, D. (1996). *Mental Health Policy in Britain: A Critical Introduction.* London: Macmillan.

Rose, W. (2001). Assessing Children in Need and their Families: An Overview of the Framework. In Horwath, J. (Ed.) *The Child's World: Assessing Children in Need.* London: Jessica Kingsley.

Ross, R.R. and Fabiano, E.A. (1985). *Time to Think: A Cognitive Behavioural Model of Delinquency Prevention and Offender Rehabilitation.* Johnson City, Tennessee: Institute of Social Sciences and Arts.

Ross, R.R., Fabiano, E.A. and Ewles, C.D. (1988). Reasoning and Rehabilitation. *International Journal of Offender Therapy and Comparative Criminology,* 32: pp29-35.

Ross, S. (1996). Risk of Physical Abuse to Children of Spouse Abusing Parents. *Child Abuse and Neglect,* 20(7): pp589-598.

Royal College of Obstetricians and Gynaecologists (2001). *Newsletter 46: National Study of HIV in Pregnancy.* London: Royal College of Obstetricians and Gynaecologists.

Ryan, J. and Thomas, F. (1987). *The Politics of Mental Handicap.* London: Free Association Books.

Ryder, N.B. (1965). The Cohort as a Concept in The Study of Social Change. *Sociological Review,* 30: pp843–61.

Sage Statham, R. and Whitehead, P. (1992). *Managing the Probation Service.* London: Longman.

Sainsbury Centre for Mental Health (1998). *Keys to Engagement: A Review of Care for People with Severe Mental Illness who are Hard to Engage with Services.* London: Sainsbury Centre for Mental Health.

Sainsbury Centre for Mental Health (2000). *Taking Your Partners. Using Opportunities for Inter-Agency Partnership in Mental Health.* London: The Sainsbury Centre for Mental Health.

Sainsbury, E. (1977). *The Personal Social Services.* London: Pitman.

Sanderson, H., Kennedy, J., Ritchie, P. and Goodwin, G. (1997). *People, Plans and Possibilities: Exploring Person-centred Planning.* Edinburgh: Scottish Human Services.

Sashidaran, S. (1989). Schizophrenia or Just Black. *Community Care*, 783: pp14-16.

Schneider, A.L., Ervin, L. and Snyder, J.Z. (1996). Further Exploration of the Flight from Discretion: The Role of Risk Need Instruments in Probation Supervision Decisions. *Journal of Criminal Justice*, 24(2): pp109-121.

Scott, J. (1993). Homelessness and Mental Illness. *British Journal of Psychiatry*, 162: pp314-324.

Scottish Executive (2000). *The Same as You? A Review of Services for People with Learning Disabilities*. Edinburgh: Scottish Executive.

Seebohm Report (1968). *Report of the Committee on Local Authority and Allied Personal*. London: HMSO.

Shakespeare, T. (2000). *Help*. Birmingham: Venture Press.

Sheppard, M. (1993). The External Context for Social Support: Towards a Theoretical Formulation of Social Support, Child Care and Maternal Depression. *Social Work and Social Sciences Review*, 4(1): pp27-58.

Sheppard, M. (1994). Maternal Depression, Child Care and the Social Work Role. *British Journal of Social Work*, 24(1): pp33-51.

Singh Bhui, H. (1996). Cognitive-Behavioural Methods in Probation Practice. *Probation Journal*, 43(3): pp127-131.

Skyner, D.R. and Waters, J. (1999). Working with Perpetrators of Domestic Violence to Protect Women and Children: A Partnership Between Cheshire Probation Service and the NSPCC. *Child Abuse Review*, 8(1): pp46-54.

Smart, C. (1989). *Feminism and The Power of Law*. London: Routledge.

Smith, G. (1997). Risk Assessment and Management at the Interface Between the Probation Service and Psychiatric Practice. *International Review of Psychiatry*, 9(2-3): pp283-288.

Scottish Needs Assessment Programme Women's Health Network (1997). *Domestic Violence*. Glasgow: SNAP.

Social Services Inspectorate (1995). *A Way Ahead for Carers. Priorities for Managers and Practitioners*. Wetherby: Department of Health.

Social Services Inspectorate (1998). *A Matter of Chance for Carers? Inspection of Local Authority Support for Carers*. London: Department of Health.

Social Work Practice. *Journal of Gay and Lesbian Social Services*, 6(1): pp29-39.

Stanko, E., Crisp, D., Hale, C. and Lucraft, H. (1998). *Counting the Costs: Estimating the Impact of Domestic Violence in the London Borough of Hackney*. London: Crime Concern.

Stanley, J. and Goddard, C. (1997). Failures in Child Protection: A Case Study. *Child Abuse Review*, 6(1): pp46-54.

Stanley, N. and Manthorpe, J. (2001). Reading Mental Health Inquiries: Messages for Social Work. *Journal of Social Work*, 1(1): 77-99.

Stanley, N. and Penhale, B. (1999). The Mental Health Problems of Mothers Experiencing the Child Protection System: Identifying Needs and Appropriate Responses. *Child Abuse Review*, 8(1): pp34-45.

Stark, E. (1984). *The Battering Syndrome: Social Knowledge, Social Therapy and Abuse of Women*. Binghamton, NY: State University of New York-Binghamton.

Stark, E. and Flitcraft, A. (1988). Women and Children at Risk: A Feminist Perspective on Child Abuse. *International Journal of Health Services*, 18(1): pp97-118.

Stark, E. and Flitcraft, A. (1996). *Women at Risk: Domestic Violence and Women's Health*. London: Sage .

Statham, R. and Whitehead, P. (1992). *Managing the Probation Service*. London: Longman.

Steadman, H.J. and Morrisey, J.P. (1982). Predicting Violent Behaviour: A Note on a Cross Validation Study. *Social Forces*, 61: pp475–83.

Stevens, A. (1992). *Disability Issues: Developing Anti-Discriminatory Practice*. London: CCETSW.

Stevenson, O. (1981). *Specialisation in Social Service Teams*. London: George Allen and Unwin.

Stevenson, O. (Ed.) (1998). *Child Welfare in the UK*. Oxford: Blackwell Science.

Stevenson, O. and Parsloe, P. (1993). *Community Care and Empowerment*. York: Joseph Rowntree Foundation.

Stickland, G. (1992). Positioning Training and Development Departments for Organisational Change. *Management Education and Development*, 23(1): pp307-316.

Stone, N. (1995). *A Companion Guide to Mentally Disordered Offenders*. Ilkley, West Yorkshire: Owen Wells.

Sutherland Report (1999). *With Respect to Age: A Report by the Royal Commission on Long Term Care* (Cm. 4192-1). London: HMSO.

Swain, J. and French, S. (1998). Normality and Disabling Care. In Brechin, A., Walmsley, J., Katz, J. and Peace, S. (Eds.) *Care Matters: Concepts, Practice and Research in Health and Social Care*, pp81-95. London: Sage.

Swain, J. and French, S. (2000). Towards An Affirmative Model of Disability. *Disability and Society*, 15(4): pp569-582.

Swain, J. and Lawrence, P. (1994). Learning about

Disability: Changing Attitudes or Challenging Understandings. In French, S. (Ed.) *On Equal Terms: Working with Disabled People*, pp87-102. Oxford: Butterworth-Heinemann.

Swain, J., Finkelstein, V., French, S. and Oliver, M. (Eds.) (1993). *Disabling Barriers: Enabling Environments*. London: Sage.

Swain, J., Gillman, M. and French, S. (1998). *Confronting Disabling Barriers: Towards Making Organisations Accessible*. Birmingham: Venture Press.

Tan, H. (1993). Issues for Black Families Affected by HIV Infection and AIDS. In Batty, D. (Ed.) *HIV Infection and Children in Need*, pp84-96. London: BAAF.

Temple, M.T. and Leino, V. (1989). Long-term Outcomes of Drinking: A 20 Year Longitudinal Study of Men. *British Journal of Addiction*, 84(8): pp889-899.

Tham, S., Ford, T. and Wilkinson, D. (1995). A Survey of Domestic Violence and Other Forms of Abuse. *Journal of Mental Health*, 4: pp317-321.

Thoburn, J., Lewis, A. and Shemmings, D. (1995). *Paternalism or Partnership? Family Involvement in the Child Protection Process*. HMSO.

Thomas, M. and Pierson, J. (1995). *Dictionary of Social Work*. London: Collins Educational.

Thompson, N. (1997). *Anti-Discriminatory Practice* (2nd edn.) Houndmills, Basingstoke: Macmillan.

Tidmarsh, D. (1997). Risk Assessment Among Prisoners: A View from a Parole Board Member. *International Review of Psychiatry*, 9(2-3): pp273-281.

Tolson, E.R., Reid, W.J. and Garvin, C.D. (1994). *Generalist Practice: A Task Centred Approach*. New York: Columbia University Press.

TOPSS (2002). *National Occupational Standards for Social Work. Training Organisation for the Personal Social Services: England*. http://www.topss.org.uk/uk_eng/framesets/engindex.htm

Towell, D. (1988). *An Ordinary Life in Practice*. London: King's Fund Centre.

Townsend, P. (1962). *The Last Refuge*. London: Routledge and Kegan Paul.

Townsend, P. (1973). *The Social Minority*. London: Allen Lane.

Trade Union Disability Alliance (1997). *Why the Disability Discrimination Act must be Repealed and Replaced with Civil Rights for Disabled People*. London: TUDA.

Tunstill, J. (1997). Implementing The Family Support Clauses of The 1989 Children Act: Legislative, Professional and Organisational Obstacles. In Parton, N. (Ed.) *Child Protection and Family Support: Tensions, Contradictions and Possibilities*. London: Routledge.

Twigg, J. and Atkin, K. (1994). *Carers Perceived: Policy and Practice in Informal Care*. Buckingham: Open University Press.

Underdown, A. (1995). Community Supervision: A Policy Which can Deliver. *Vista*, Sept: pp43-50.

Underdown, A. (1998). *Strategies for Effective Offender Supervision: Report of The HMIP What Works Project*. London: Home Office Publications Unit.

Union of the Physically Impaired Against Segregation (1976). *Disability Challenge*, Number 1 (May).

University of Oxford (Probation Studies Unit) and Warwickshire Probation Service (1977). *Assessment, Case Recording and Evaluation System*. University of Oxford.

Unlinked Anonymous Surveys Steering Group (2001). *Prevalence of HIV and Hepatitis Infections in the United Kingdom 2000*. London: Department of Health.

Vaillant, G. (1988). What Can Long-Term Follow-Up Tell Us About Relapse and Relapse Prevention? *British Journal of Addiction*, 83(10): pp1147-1157.

Vaillant, G. (1995). *Natural History of Alcoholism Revisited*. London: Harvard University Press.

Vass, A.A. (Ed.) (1996). *Social Work Competencies: Core Knowledge, Value and Skills*. London: Sage.

Vaughan, P.J. (1995). *Suicide Prevention*. Birmingham: Pepar.

Walker, A. (1982). *Community Care: The Family, the State and Social Policy*. Oxford: Blackwell.

Ward, L. (1998). *Innovations in Advocacy and Empowerment for People With Intellectual Disabilities*. Chorley: Lisieux Hall Publications.

Warr, P. (1987). *Work Unemployment and Mental Health*. Oxford: Oxford University Press.

Weightman, G. (1999). *A Real Break. A Guidebook for Good Practice in the Provision of Short-Term Breaks as a Support for Care in the Community*. London: Department of Health.

Wendell, S. (1996). *The Rejected Body: Feminist Philosophical Reflections on Disability*. London: Routledge.

Westcott, H. (1993). *Abuse of Children and Adults with Disabilities*. London: NSPCC.

White, S. (1996). Regulating Mental Health and Motherhood in Contemporary Welfare Services. *Critical Social Policy*, 46(16): pp67-94.

White, T. (1999) Tiger, Tiger Burning Bright. *Positive Nation*, March: pp32-34.

Williams, A.F. (1976). The Alcoholic Personality. In Kissin, B. and Begleiter, H. (Eds.) *The Biology of Alcoholism, Vol. 4, Social Aspects of Alcoholism*. New York, NY: Plenum Press.

Williams, J. (2002). Public Law Protection of Adults: The Debate Continues So Does the Abuse. *Journal of Social Work*, 2(3): pp293–316.

Williams, J. and Keating, F. (1999). The Abuse of Adults in Mental Health Settings. In Stanley, N., Manthorpe, J. and Penhale, B. (1999). *Institutional Abuse: Perspectives Across the Lifecourse,* pp130-151. London: Routledge.

Williams, R. (1996). *The Substance of Young People's Needs*. London: HMSO.

Wolfe, D., Sak, L., Wilson, S. and Jaffe, P. (1986). Child Witnesses to Violence between Parents: Critical Issues in Behavioural and Social Adjustment. *Journal of Abnormal Child Psychology*, 14(1): pp95-104.

Wolfensberger, W. (1972). *The Principle of Normalization in Human Services*. Toronto: National Institute of Mental Retardation.

Worrall, A. (1990). *Offending Women: Female Lawbreakers and the Criminal Justice System*. London: Routledge.

Worrall, A. (1998). *Punishment in the Community*. London: Longman.

Wykes, T., Tarrier, N. and Lewis, S. (1998). *Outcome and Innovation in Psychological Treatment of Schizophrenia*. Chichester: Wiley.

Index

abstinence 33–35, 37, 45, 95–96

abuse
- *emotional* 63, 80
- *physical* 72, 78, 177, 188
- *racial* 93
- *sexual* 36, 64, 69, 8, 83–84, 89, 92, 177, 180–181

accountability 12–13, 18, 68, 82–83, 115

accreditation 104

acutely distressed families 94

adolescents 95, 130, 188

adult
- *protection* 78, 83–85, 88–89, 143, 152, 177, 185, 187
- *services* 14, 61–62, 68, 73, 91, 93, 97–100, 102, 126, 144

Advanced Award in Social Work (AASW) 3, 5, 16

advocacy 29, 31, 50, 55, 67, 74, 124, 126, 145, 151, 182, 190

African 41–42, 44, 47–50, 178, 184–185

ageism 19, 32, 147–149, 151, 153, 155–156, 177

aggression 95–96, 108

alcohol misuse 70, 96, 117, 169

anger management programme 101

anti-psychotic medication 121

anti-racism 120, 178

anti-social 35, 106, 140

appropriate adult 19, 143

approved social worker (ASW) 5, 11, 45, 130, 140

area child protection committee (ACPC) 71, 83, 180

area team 3

Ashworth Hospital 127

Asian 60, 67, 69, 73, 177, 182–183

assault 63, 66, 68, 82, 171, 184

assertive outreach 122, 124, 130

assessment
- *comprehensive* 43, 75, 91, 124, 141, 179
- *needs-led* 147
- *process* 19, 68–69, 73–74, 81, 84, 88, 103–105, 107, 109, 111–113, 115, 117, 173
- *psychiatric* 107, 124
- *tool* 104, 109–110, 115

asylum seekers 42, 50, 65

asylums 119, 132

Barclay Report 4, 176

benzodiazepines 95

Best Value 122, 153–154, 159, 176, 179–180

Beveridge 7, 121

biographical approach 147, 150–151, 184

cannabis 33

care
- *flexible* 50
- *in-patient* 123
- *intimate* 97
- *management* 19, 27–28, 59, 61, 80, 84, 88, 123–124, 142, 152, 170, 181
- *managers* 9, 43, 60, 68, 152
- *packages* 137
- *person-centred* 19, 138, 142, 145
- *plan* 10, 27–28, 59, 99–100, 123, 127, 165
- *programme approach* 19, 121, 123
- *reception into* 7, 90
- *residential* 20, 115, 138, 147, 151–153, 155
- *shared* 34, 44
- *trusts* 44, 121, 128–129, 153

Care Standards Act 82, 88, 154–155

carers 11, 15, 18, 22, 30, 42, 48–49, 53–62, 72, 74, 80, 91, 93, 95–101, 118–123, 125–126, 128–129, 135–138, 141–143, 145–146, 152, 176–177, 179–180, 182–183, 185, 189–190
- *young* 48, 53, 56–58, 60–61, 96–97, 101, 125–126, 176, 185

Carers (Recognition and Services) Act 1996 42, 54, 143, 152

Carers and Disabled Children

Act 2000   42, 55, 62, 180

Central Council for Education and Training in Social Work (CCETSW)   14–15, 26, 30–32, 79, 82, 124, 130, 178, 189

Certificate of Qualification in Social Work (CQSW)   14

challenging behaviours   137, 177

child
 – *care*   3–5, 16, 28, 70, 74, 76, 84, 92, 102, 187, 189
 – *in need*   10, 49, 93
 – *protection*   19–20, 30, 32, 36, 39–40, 47, 49–51, 63–65, 67, 69–72, 74–75, 83–84, 88–92, 95, 97, 99–100, 102, 106, 114–116, 126, 130, 139, 142, 145, 163, 174, 177–183, 186–187, 189–190
 – *protection case conference*   100
 – *protection inquiry*   92
 – *protection register*   64, 75, 95, 100, 106, 174, 177, 181
 – *safety*   90, 93

Children Act 1989   10, 36, 42, 57, 65–67, 82, 91–93, 99, 135, 139, 151, 180
 – *s47 investigations*

Children and Family Court Advisory Service   109

children's department   7

Children's Panel   6

Chronically Sick and Disabled Persons Act 1970   42, 134

clinical assessment   105, 112

cognitive functioning   96

cognitive behavioral approaches   25, 38–39

cohort effects   149–151

collective movements   120

Commission for Mental Health   126

Community Care Act 1990   9, 26, 42, 57, 81, 151–153

community
 – *care team*   27, 29–30, 170
 – *resources*   2, 94, 100, 111, 128

community mental health teams (CMTs)   5, 12, 107, 124, 130

community psychiatric nurse (CPN) 107

complex disabilities   61, 135, 137

compulsorily
 – *detained*   123
 – *admitted*   11, 87, 123, 168

compulsory
 – *powers*   126–127
 – *treatments*

confidentiality   2, 37, 42, 45, 49–51, 61, 68, 71, 79, 98, 102, 124

consent   19, 42, 47, 66, 98, 110–111, 114, 127, 151, 156

Conservative Government   9, 149

contact arrangements   65, 67, 182

contract culture   20, 155

core
 – *assessment*   10, 98–100, 176
 – *group*   100

counselling   30, 37, 44, 55, 57, 61, 70, 72, 80, 128, 135, 137–138, 144, 180, 185

Crime and Disorder Act 1998   36, 103

Criminal Justice Act 1991   103, 110, 112

Criminal Justice and Court Services Act 2000   108–109, 111

crisis
 – *services*   122, 128
 – *situations*   125
 – *teams*   122, 124, 128

cultural values   90

curriculum   14–15, 30–31, 45, 136, 187

custody   111, 113, 125, 150, 183, 188

Data Protection Act 1998   42, 98

dementia   42, 53, 56, 59, 87, 89, 138, 156, 168, 187

delusion   95, 121

Department of Health   5, 9, 11, 14–16, 21, 34–36, 42, 47, 51–59, 61–62, 66, 70–71, 80–85, 88–93, 97–102, 108, 115, 120–121, 123–126, 130, 134, 146, 152, 157, 178–179, 187

depression   33, 46, 69–70, 74, 96–97, 125–126, 148, 177, 189

detention in hospital   123

detoxification   37, 39, 45

Diploma in Social Work (DipSW)   14–16, 30–31, 26–27, 104, 130, 178, 187

direct payments   28–29, 55, 138, 142, 182

Disability Discrimination Act 1995   135, 181

Disabled People's Movement   22–23, 32

disabled women   64, 68, 73,
    185

disturbance of mental
    functioning   126

Domestic Violence Units   84

domestic violence
    – *women*   63–72, 74, 101
    – *black*   64, 73
    – *old*   77–78, 81, 83–84,
      86–88
    – *gay*   63

double jeopardy   148

Drug Action Teams   35

drug misuse   35, 92, 94–95,
    113, 179, 188

drug users   36–37, 41, 43, 45,
    47, 52

dual diagnosis   124

duty of care   78

ecological approach   90

educational
    – *potential*   93
    – *programmes*   125, 157

emergency   5, 56–57, 63, 66,
    68, 123–124

emotional needs   64, 95–97

employment   2–3, 7, 12,
    23–25, 27, 29–30, 37, 52,
    54, 62, 94, 102, 106, 112,
    128, 133–134, 136–137,
    149, 154

England   5–6, 8, 14–16, 21,
    35, 71, 75, 103, 134, 136,
    153, 155, 178, 182–183,
    186, 188

ethnic minority   59, 64, 181

evidence-based practice   19,
    37, 145

exclusion order   66

exosystems   90

family
    – *allowances*   7
    – *care*   137, 180
    – *centre*   10–11
    – *focus*   18, 51
    – *group conference*   100
    – *history*   49, 94, 124
    – *protection units*   84
    – *responsibility*   90
    – *support*   11, 36, 61, 66,
      70, 72, 75, 136, 138, 171,
      187, 190
    – *violence*   89, 177, 183

Family Law Act 1996   64, 81

feminism   120, 189

foetal alcohol syndrome   95

forcible treatment   123

fostering and adoption   8, 49

Framework for the
    Assessment of Children
    in Need and Their
    Families   11, 19, 51–52,
    93, 97, 102, 178,
    180

General Social Care Council
    (GSCC)   5, 16, 21, 82

government guidance   91,
    102

groupwork   4

guardianship   81, 123,
    140–141, 143

harm minimisation   35, 37

Health and Social Services
    Boards   6

health
    – *authorities*   36, 43–44, 46,
      61, 121, 186
    – *children*   43, 136, 183
    – *education*   35, 45, 94, 159

    – *professionals*   68, 125,
      127, 130, 154
    – *services*   12, 44, 55, 61,
      67, 70, 121–122, 124, 126,
      128–130, 135, 139, 156,
      159, 179, 181, 185,
      189

heroin   33–34, 51, 96, 174

higher education institute
    (HEI)   15

HIV/AIDS   17–18, 24, 34,
    41–52, 176, 178–181, 183,
    184–188, 190

holistic   41, 43, 45, 47, 49, 51,
    88, 92, 100–101, 105, 112,
    115, 184

Home Start   100

home support   155

hospital admission rates   122

hospital orders   123, 143

Housing Act 1996   65

housing problems   122

Human Rights Act 1998   135,
    156

impaired intellectual
    development   97

inclusion   120, 132–134, 145

independent tribunal   126,
    136

information sharing   71, 98,
    109

initial assessment   10, 59, 72,
    98, 128

institutional
    – *discrimination*   17,
      22–25, 27, 32
    – *settings*   78, 181, 187

intake-teams   4

inter-agency
    – *child protection*   99–100
    – *collaboration*   119

– *training*   18, 75, 161, 181–182
– *work*   107, 119
interpreters   29, 50, 73
inter-professional   12, 118, 121, 162
intra-agency   126, 159–161

joint working   13, 18, 50, 52, 69–71, 74, 130, 144, 153, 195

legislative framework   18, 42, 65, 67, 91, 152, 155–156
locality based education   162
locally based social work   9
lone parents   93
long term incapacity   126
long-term teams   4

macrosystem   90
maintenance prescribing   34
management of change   129
mental
– *disorder*   95, 107, 112, 117, 123, 125–127, 139, 182
– *illness*   7, 42, 81, 95, 102, 107, 121, 123, 125, 156, 174, 178, 185, 187–188
– *impairment*   123
mental health
– *crisis teams*   122
– *issues*   60, 92, 97, 99, 124
– *needs*   74, 123, 125, 182–183

– *policy*   118, 131, 188
– *problems*   53–54, 56, 61, 66, 69–70, 95, 121, 123, 125–126, 134, 139, 151, 156, 178, 181, 184, 189
– *promotion*   121
– *tribunal*   126–127
Mental Health Act 1983   5, 11, 42, 66, 80–81, 99, 107, 113, 121, 123–124, 127, 135, 179
methadone   34, 39
microsystems   90
MIND   9, 23–24, 40, 57, 63, 77, 85, 87, 126, 128, 139, 186
minority groups   42–43, 59, 111, 181
model of change   17, 172–173, 175, 187
modernising social services   54, 121, 155, 179
motivational interviewing   17, 38–39, 113–114, 185
multi-agency   18, 51–52, 75, 85, 89, 103, 108–109, 115, 172, 178–179, 182
multi-disciplinary   19, 48, 83–84, 88, 106, 130, 141
multiple disabilities
multi-problem families   94

National Care Standards Commission   82
National Commission for Care Standards   154
National Health Service and Community Care Act 1991   91
National Schizophrenic Fellowship   125
National Service Framework

for Older People   81, 149, 153, 155, 179–180
neglect   40, 69, 74–75, 77–79, 88, 93, 95–96, 123–124, 177, 181, 185–188
neonatal abstinence syndrome   95
NHS (Venereal Diseases) Regulations 1974   42
NHS and Community Care Act 1990   26, 42, 57
non-molestation orders   64–65
Northern Ireland   6–8, 14–15, 35, 71, 75, 136, 139, 143–144, 155, 180
NSPCC   73, 97–98, 101, 173, 181–182, 189–190

occupational therapists   27, 130
operational managers   13, 157–160, 162, 171
organisational
– *forms*   6
– *management*   119
– *specialisation*   4
– *structure*   3, 5, 184
outreach   11, 37, 74, 122, 124, 128, 130

parental needs   92
parenting
– *ability*   96
– *capacity*   91–94, 96–97, 99–102, 173–175, 178
– *issues*   90–94, 97, 99, 101–102, 174
parents with learning disabilities   96–97

partnership 4, 6, 9, 15, 17, 20, 26, 31–32, 36, 51, 57, 66–67, 71, 74, 88, 91, 101, 106, 116, 120, 128–131, 139, 144–145, 156, 158, 160, 179, 186, 188–190

patch based social work 4, 8

performance management 118, 121, 129

peri-natal difficulties 95

personality disorder 122, 127, 179–180, 183

physical disability 30, 78, 85, 94

post professional qualification 4

potentially dangerous offenders 103

practice teaching 3, 5

pregnancy 46, 64, 68, 96, 132, 183, 185, 188

pre-sentence reports 109, 117, 177

preventative work 126

primary care 12, 44, 54–56, 121, 125, 128–129, 140, 142, 144

primary care groups 12, 128

professional
– *assessment* 6, 9, 15–20, 22, 26–32, 40, 42–43, 49–51, 53, 55, 57–59, 61–62, 66, 68-75, 80–84, 88, 91, 93, 96–101, 103–117, 119, 122–128, 130, 135–136, 138, 140–144, 147, 150–154, 156, 164–165, 167–168, 170–173
– *competence* 5, 15
– *co-operation* 119
– *education* 13–16, 18, 20, 32, 157
– *identity* 4, 128
– *judgement* 20, 30, 105

– *qualification* 3, 7, 14–16

Protection from Harassment Act 1997 65, 81

Protection of Vulnerable Adults List 82

protocol 13, 36, 98, 101, 124, 141

psychologist 130, 139

psychopathic disorder 123

psychosocial approaches 121

psychotic illness 122

public
– *inquiries* 84, 92, 98, 113, 127
– *protection* 12, 104, 108, 114, 117, 182
– *protection panels* 108

purchaser/provider split 152

Quality Assurance Agency (QAA) 15–16, 21

quality assurance mechanisms 13

Quality Protects 42, 121, 136, 179

reception teams 3–4

risk
– *factors* 67, 89, 96, 104, 106–108, 124–125, 187
– *management* 21, 109, 113, 141, 184
– *needs* 178
– *taking* 86, 116

schizophrenia 61, 95, 121, 125, 180, 184–186, 188, 191

Scotland 6, 8, 14–15, 35, 41, 44, 47, 71, 75, 103, 139, 153, 155, 178, 182

sectioning orders 126

Seebohm Report 8, 188

self-harm 105, 122–124, 126

service level agreements 102, 167

Sexual Offences Act 1957 81

sexual offenders 97

significant
– *harm* 10–11, 47, 66, 69, 96–97, 99–101, 176–177
– *risk* 72, 107, 123

social
– *disadvantage* 33
– *exclusion* 42, 54, 128, 185

Social Services Inspectorate 57–58, 67, 84–85, 189

special needs 27, 137–138, 140

specialisation by
– *community* 4
– *expertise* 4
– *method* 4
– *organisation* 4
– *setting* 5

specialist
– *posts* 1
– *practice* 1–2, 4–9, 11, 16–17, 19–21, 163–164, 169

statutory agencies 73, 125, 128

stigma 37, 42, 48, 147

strategic health authorities 121

suicide 53, 63, 107, 121, 123–126, 176, 190

supervision register 123